MEMORIES OF THE OPEN SEA

MEMORIES OF THE OPEN SEA

Eric Tabarly

Translated by Robert Pralle

Published by SportsBooks Ltd
February 2013

Copyright: Editions Fallois 2011

SportsBooks Limited
1 Evelyn Court
Malvern Road
Cheltenham
GL50 2JR
United Kingdom
Tel: 01242 256755
Fax: 0560 3108126
e-mail   randall@sportsbooks.ltd.uk
Website www.sportsbooks.ltd.uk

All rights reserved. No part of this publication may be produced or transmitted in any form or by any means, including photocopying and recording, without written permission of the publishers. Such written permission must also be obtained before any part of the publication is stored in any retrieval system of any nature.

Cover designed by Alan Hunns

A CIP catalogue record for this book is available from the British Library.

ISBN 9781907524363

Print and production managed by Jellyfish Solutions.

Contents

	Acknowledgements	vii
	Note	viii
	Photo credits	viii
Chapter 1	My old gentleman	1
Chapter 2	Owner of a wreck	13
Chapter 3	My nose does not fit	17
Chapter 4	Your Boat has had it	24
Chapter 5	Last by a distance	32
Chapter 6	'Pay when you can...'	43
Chapter 7	Sailing single-handed	55
Chapter 8	Valentine is not a girl; Chichester is the favourite	59
Chapter 9	The undermining influence of a drop of water	69
Chapter 10	My self-steering packs up and I feel like doing the same	79
Chapter 11	Winner without knowing it	96
Chapter 12	In New York's grey-blue waters	106
Chapter 13	Fame is not the spur when I race	113
Chapter 14	Free to incur new debts, having paid old debts	122
Chapter 15	Somewhat bruised, I win	130

Chapter 16	Kersauson, Colas, Guégan, English, plus the cyclone	139
Chapter 17	I have a dream: a flying boat	145
Chapter 18	The Japanese speak only Japanese	155
Chapter 19	Every cloud has a silver lining	165
Chapter 20	Of *Pen Duick VI*'s misfortunes and Gérard Petipas' tribulations	174
Chapter 21	The shredding of the sails	185
Chapter 22	Of *Pen Duick VI*'s misfortunes (cont...)	196
Chapter 23	Peddler – navigator	204
Chapter 24	Five storms and a second single-handed victory	211
Chapter 25	That was clever!	230
Chapter 26	Why I slung my duffel bag ashore...	239
Chapter 27	And why I slung it back on board	242
	Index	243

ACKNOWLEDGMENTS

Publisher's thanks for permissions

The publisher wishes to thank Mme Jacqueline Tabarly for giving her consent to this English language version of *Mémoires du Large* and for her kind permission that photographs from her private collection be used in its illustration. We are also grateful for the use of photos belonging to 'Éditions de Fallois' that appeared in the French publisher's original version of the book.

Translator's thanks for assistance

In organising this translation of Éric Tabarly's Memoirs, I have received the co-operation of 'Éditions de Fallois'. Thanks are due to M Bernard de Fallois for his original encouragement and to Mme Anne Maksud for her involvement in the project.

I have also received assistance from my friend, Fabienne Rieser and from Mlle Sophie Caignault. James Palmer kindly checked the translation for nautical terms. Any errors that remain are my own.

Robert Pralle

Note re: boats being called 'He'

The French naming of boats as 'He' will obviously be novel to English language readers. However, because it is not possible to substitute 'she/her' for 'he/him' without frequently affecting the original version's meaning, this translation continues to use the French description.

Photo credits

Tabarly collection, 1, 2, 3a, 3b, 4a, 5a, 5b
Éditions de Fallois, 4b, 5c, 6, 7a, 7b, 8, 9a, 9b, 10a
Bettman/Corbis, 10b
J-P. Laffont, Sygma/Corbis 11
Gilles Martin-Raget 12a
Jean Guichard, Sygma/Corbis 12b

CHAPTER 1

MY OLD GENTLEMAN

For me, in his black suit, with full-breasted sails, he brings to mind an old, dignified gentleman. Between us – he with his old fashioned lines, me a naval pensioner – has developed an affection that has influenced both our lives. Without me he would have remained a wreck; without him my life would not have been as it is.

His name is *Pen Duick* – 'Black Headed Tit' in Breton. Unlike his successors he does not have a number. I could just about have baptised him Pen Duick the First ... like one speaks of first love, because the story of this one hundred-year-old cutter is a sentimental one.

Although it may disappoint tender souls, my attachment to this black vessel is not based on his belonging to my father. It would be wrong to think that I was infatuated with him, that I went into debt on his account and that I was obsessed with salvaging him out of filial love. I salvaged *Pen Duick*, rotting in a marsh, because I had always recognised his beauty. Time had not lessened his nobility. Man requires some form of passion: so, some struggle to keep Venice afloat and others spend their lives restoring the ruins of a château. *Pen Duick* was a classic from a bygone age of marine design. He couldn't be allowed to die. I always wanted him to be salvaged and then to sail.

This then is the story of me and my boat and the emotions involved in such a long relationship – that will no doubt come as a surprise to those who have given me the false reputation of gruffness, taciturnity and a media-disaster. It is not actually the way I am. I may not be an effusive talker; nor am I the silent type. Au contraire. I like to talk and, given a topic that interests me, I can become unstoppable. But when the conversation turns to subjects about which I feel indifferent then mentally I absent myself, fall silent and sometimes even fall asleep. In spite of trying not to appear impolite, my head will droop and eyelids close. It happens to me. I particularly remember falling asleep after a regatta, at a reception at the Hôtel de Ville in Marseille. The then Mayor, Gaston Deferre, discoursed at length. His idiosyncratic delivery of an interminable speech tested my patience. I was in the front row, directly in front of him. I slipped into a gentle sleep. My friend Gérard Petipas, with an elbow in the ribs, brought me out of it.

I get this monosyllabic character from my mother, a strong and discreet woman who hated talk for the sake of talk.

A final word on my silences. I freely admit that I have difficulty answering banal, if not idiotic, questions. A typical example is being asked at the finish of a race: 'So, are you happy to have won?' What is there to say other than 'Yes'? I don't know of a victor who was left feeling down, having won. And when, regarding *Pen Duick* , I'm asked if I'm happy that he's still sailing at his age, I am unable to make the effort to respond. Clearly, to feel this wooden deck beneath my feet makes me happy, and to hear his familiar sounds – his way of talking to me – brings me pleasure. Otherwise, why would I have slaved and saved but been in debt for nearly forty years in order that *Pen Duick* should once again make his way on the sea? I remember all that we have been through together.

Going back ... it is coming up to Easter 1938 and I am almost seven years old. Often vague and imprecise, there is something curious about childhood memories, which can also be troublingly fresh. My father, Guy Tabarly, was driving my mother, my sister Annick – younger by eighteen months – and myself to Basse-Indre, a part of the Loire downstream from Nantes. I remember nothing of the

Memories of the Open Sea

journey from Préfailles, where we were spending our holidays, to this part of the river. By contrast, the sudden apparition of the yacht from amongst the reeds where he had been left over winter, is etched in my memory. With a child's logic I thought: 'This isn't the place for a boat.'

My father in front, we went on board. I was impressed and astonished by the immensity of the fifteen-metre deck. Because I was a wild child my mother held me firmly by the hand. I wanted to crawl all over it. It is hard to judge what my next naughtiness will be. I am given to impetuous ideas. So one afternoon mother comes looking for my sister and me. She goes from one room to another, worried because she cannot hear us playing or squabbling. Finally she goes out into the garden which is covered in snow. She had scarcely put her nose outside when a wooden ladder, leaning against the front of the house, caught her attention. She looks up and remains as if rooted to the spot, not daring to shout from fear of causing a catastrophe. She watches us in mute terror: Annick snuggled up against me, leaning back on the tiles with our feet wedged in the gutter – blissfully happy. I am four and my sister just two and a half. It was me who had positioned the ladder and then lifted Annick to the top. My intention is praiseworthy. The garden snow is walked on and dirty; I want to show my little sister a white, unsullied stretch. My mother does not approve of this initiative. My return to earth merited punishment. One of many.

Mother held onto me firmly on deck, at the same time following my father during his inspection of the boat. *Pen Duick* is already old. Conceived by a talented Scottish nautical engineer, William Fife III at Fairlie in 1898, originally named *Yum*, he is well past forty – and in urgent need of repair, particularly the deck which is splitting throughout ... costly repairs which the Lebec brothers of Nantes do not wish to take on. Hence their decision to sell.

My mother later told me that, seduced by the beauty of his lines, my father had already resolved to buy the boat – in spite of its appalling condition. This he did, becoming owner number twelve. *Pen Duick* had already suffered a lot, under a lot of names, according to the taste of his masters: *Yum, Magda, Griselidis, Cora V, Astarté, Panurge, Butterfly*. After having raced in Great Britain and having known various ports of registry – Le Havre, Brest, Douarnez, La Trinité-sur-Mer – it seemed as if he must finish his days amongst the reeds.

Soon after the purchase, my father and crew brought the boat to Bénodet, which became his new base. My parents, who had lived at Quimper before I was born, liked this region very much. It is not a bad time at all for the family. Father is the sales representative of a textile business. His area covers the west of France: Brittany, Normandy, la Vendée.

He leaves in his car on Monday and doesn't get back home before Friday or Saturday. So my mother rules the house. Every weekend, weather permitting, and during the holidays from July 1 to August 31, we go sailing. Our first cruises take place on a little nine-metre cutter *Annie*, based at Préfailles, where my paternal grandparents have a holiday home. It is on this boat that I learn to crawl.

I recall our jaunts which led us principally along the Breton coastline; navigating to Concarneau, La Trinité, Belle-Île and l'Île d'Yeu. Papa is a genuine sailor – unflappable. It is while watching him and his crew steer, read the sky, run the currents, manoeuvre, change and set sails that I learn to sail. A professional sailor is needed because *Pen Duick*, with his old, heavy rigging, cannot be handled by one man, however strong. This sailor not only has to cook and clean but also to act the part of nanny to Annick and me when our parents go ashore to dine and meet their friends.

I liked sailing instantly. Above all on *Pen Duick*, because, all the way back to my childhood memories, I always considered him better than the others. I have never felt such pleasure as when my father allowed me to steer for the first time and it remains a constant pleasure. A passion cannot be explained.

Memories of the Open Sea

I liked boats from when I was in short trousers. I liked best to read yachting magazines and accounts of voyages. My favourite toys were boats. Apart from the odd tin soldier, it was a waste of time giving me anything else. I could spend hours in my bedroom in the house in Blois where we lived, playing with boats. They were from the general store, cheap and not particularly well made. So, consulting my magazines, I rearranged the rigging and adjusted the miniature sails.

School I did not like. It really did not interest me. I studied, in spite of myself, because my parents made me. But I was stifled in the classroom. It was a physically painful sensation, like being in prison. My mother (particularly) and father dreamed of my going to naval college, followed by a glittering career in the Navy. I caused them a great deal of worry. When I was five my ambition was to be an admiral, an ambition on the grand scale that was quickly jettisoned once I understood the academic hurdles standing in my way. Above all I liked to sail but, later, when I helped my father during the war cutting down trees and chopping logs, I decided to become a lumberjack. These were intense, muscular activities which took place in the great outdoors. At that time the wretched chainsaw did not exist and I pictured myself in the Great Forest, alone, with axe in hand. And for this career your studies did not need to be brilliant.

Just over a year had passed since my father became the new owner of *Pen Duick*. Just as every other summer, we set off cruising on July 1. But this is summer 1939. In Europe war is in the air. I myself am eight and almost oblivious to the situation. When we are at Port-Louis my father goes ashore to buy some bread. In the foreground I look at the sailing boats on the beach, their masts pointing up into the sky and in the distance the chimneys of the fortifications at Lorient. Helped by my mother, the crew is in the middle of preparing a meal when Papa arrives back. He looks calm but I sense, from the set of his jaw, that something has happened. He puts down the cob loaves and then announces in his clear voice:

Eric Tabarly

'I have been mobilised. The recall of my corps is posted at the bakers.'

'What will you do?' my mother asked.

'We will return to the house straightaway. I must rejoin my regiment.'

The cruise ended somewhat prematurely. Within an hour we left. With the help of a friend, our crew brought *Pen Duick* back to his customary mooring at Bénodet and laid him up in the basin at Pen Foul where he wintered each year. This time it was to be for several winters.

My father's mobilisation to Lorraine took place via the transport of military equipment. His reassuring letters reached us at Blois and we listened to TSF (the wireless) for news from the Front. I remember the adults talking optimistically of how the French army was going to 'give the Boches a hiding.' There was rationing and preparation on the Home Front, with windows camouflaged against light which would attract the Luftwaffe like moths. Confidence lasted as long as the 'phony war' and crumbled at the German offensive. The debacle of the smashed Front placed soldiers and civilians on the road to exodus.

Maman naively placed her trust in the strongly stated conviction of our leaders that 'the Germans will not cross the Loire.'

'We are going to go away to Préfailles,' she announced to us. 'There we will be safe with Grandfather and Grandmother.'

So we crammed into Papa's car with a load of bags and packages. Since my mother did not know how to drive, a cousin drives us there. The weather is magnificent, but not our morale. The army's rout together with the country's invasion plunged my grandparents and mother into a sadness that is hard to describe. Three days after we reach our 'safe haven' the first German columns entered Préfailles. The Loire had not detained them for long!

'Where is Guy?' We haven't received any news of my father. Annick and I may have only been children but we sensed that significant events had overtaken us and the country.

Memories of the Open Sea

One morning, shortly after the armistice, my father arrived back at the house. He is dressed in civvies which don't really fit and which he found God knows where. Amidst the general chaos and having to retreat, he found himself with the bedraggled remnants of his regiment in the Lot, where he was demobilised. From Lorraine to Quercy is quite a tack.

For the Tabarly family Préfailles had been a holiday spot. The lower Loire, as it used to be known, invited us to sample her good natured tranquillity, her white sand beaches and fruits de mer and bike rides and a lasting sense of freedom. That liberty has gone. The occupier occupied. Everything. If the country consoles itself with the memory of the battleship *Jean-Bart*, an imposing war machine which was able, though still unfinished, to descend the Loire straight from the naval boatyard, slaloming between the sandbanks to just escape the Germans, an infinite sadness and the humiliation of captivity was written on every face. People resented the enemy's presence in the manner of a personal offence. As a child I felt the shame myself. 'We can't just accept this submission, arms crossed,' my father sighed.

I later learnt that he was part of an intelligence network and that he spied on the strategic defences of St-Gildas Point. This refrain of his taught me never to give in. An attitude towards life which has always characterised Bretons and which I have inherited seventy-five percent, as my maternal grandparents and paternal grandmother were born in the Armor region; my paternal grandfather alone was a 'foreigner', having been born in Poitiers.

There was a primary school at Préfailles but that was all. My sister and I had to go to Tharon, a little village seven kilometres away, where the priest had started a small class for children at secondary level. That was where I attended fourth, fifth and sixth form. The first year I went by myself. The second, Annick came with me. Our parents had bought us a tandem. We left in the morning, came back home for lunch, left again after lunch and came back again in the evening: in total, twenty-eight kilometres of legwork. Each time I came back I raged that, while Annick, beatific, rested her feet on the frame, I was left to do all the pedalling. We argued. Often. Make that very often. Annick is a bit of a vixen. She was well aware that, being older and stronger, I was not allowed to take advantage of and hit her. She knew that she was safe. And that she could take advantage. The eldest is always wrong.

It is wartime with its privations. Allied planes bombard the German base at St-Nazaire. In spite of all that, I, like many the same age, had a happy childhood. I could amuse myself, as I have already explained. I could play with my companions. The thing to do at that time was to make a little windmill with the wheel frame which we took from abandoned bicycles. We use wood for heating and I help my father to cut down wood on my grandfather's land. As I have already mentioned, I wield the axe vigorously. A tree which falls with a crash fills me with pleasure.

The coast is watched by the Germans. To go out to sea in a boat is forbidden. On the beach we amuse ourselves making rafts with minesweeper floats, retrieved from the coast, types of catamaran whose equilibrium was unpredictable. Sometimes we go into forbidden waters. This provokes the Germans to shoot. Into the air, for certain, but it is enough to make us step ashore.

At St-Gildas Point, just below the mouth of the Loire, there is a semaphore by which a small garrison of French sailors sheltered. The Germans, when they arrived, took them prisoner. They then stacked all their captured equipment in a field signposted 'military area'. This is a true El Dorado for me and my pals. We rampage through it, taking what we can: belts and cartridges, gas masks and flasks. All that one could dream of in order to play soldiers. Obviously the German guards can see us but let it go, up until the day the local commandant of the Wehrmacht warns our parents that there will be reprisals if we don't stop thieving.

My schooling does not go smoothly. It doesn't interest me at all. My parents are desperate. But they are also persevering and do not capitulate, using both hard and soft means to make me study,

Memories of the Open Sea

including tying me to my desk with a chain and padlock. But locking me in my room is not enough. I slip out by the window. They don't allow me to swim, taking my trunks. I swim fully dressed and when I return, soaked to the skin, I lie brazenly, not stopping to consider whether I am believable or not: 'I fell into the sea ... ' Préfailles' temptations – fields, sea, rocks and creeks – are irresistible. As a boy and a teenager it spells independence. School, on the other hand, is synonymous with captivity.

I have forgotten how old I was when I received my last slaps but there had been many. I was obdurate, making it very difficult for my parents. For example, my father would administer a beating. No problem. I would look him directly in the eye and say: 'That's all right. That didn't hurt.' My provocative manner was bound to exasperate him and he would slap me again. His finger marks were clear on my face – his hands were not soft. I repeated, 'That's all right, you are not hurting me.' He could have beaten me unconscious and I would continue the incantation: 'That's all right,' etc, etc.

Nevertheless my father loved me. I understood and admired him. But things were different back then: children were expected to be obedient and to work. In those days no one worried about the possible trauma being hit might cause naughty children. Really, it was quite the opposite. Neither me nor my pals, who underwent the same treatment, were ever traumatised. It was the rule: each naughty or disobedient act was met with a slap. It was a simple equation.

I will not linger over the war years, so well chronicled. I will simply say that for us children and adolescents, too young to have experienced peace and its good times, the low hum of allied bombers sometimes passing high up in the black sky and sometimes dropping their cargo on nearby St-Nazaire, or on Nantes, not so far away, was part of the fabric of our everyday lives – we hadn't known anything else. Food shortages induced nostalgia for the adults. They affected us too. We had to eat stuff that we did not like. I remember the corn bread, truly disgusting. If we suffered less than those who lived in town, nevertheless poor nutrition led to me having significant and painful boils for a long time. That and the fact that neither home nor school had any heating was also responsible for chilblains.

But the most serious concerns belonged to our parents. My mother, in particular, was stressed and fretted if my father was late coming home in the evening. In front of the wood fire in winter, or in the garden when it was warm, she anxiously awaited his return. I was unaware then that Papa was part of a resistance network and that, as the Allies gained the upper hand in the war, the occupier mercilessly hunted down those they called terrorists. My father was a strong and reliable man. At the time of his military service he came second in the Combined Services 'complete athlete' championship. I feared him but admired him too. He was a courageous man who faced up to adversities without ever complaining. He could rant but he never whined.

Following the unconditional surrender of the Third Reich, the Tabarlys, minus myself, returned to Blois. I was nearly fifteen so they put me into St-Charles College in St-Brieuc. 'There he will be brought into line,' was my parents' hope. Annick was thirteen. My sister Armelle was five. Patrick, the youngest, was barely two.

During the occupation my father's business continued, but it was very slow. The textile factories worked at reduced capacity and people could only buy clothes or fabric with a coupon. Everything was rationed. In spite of these difficulties, my father succeeded, via letter writing, in maintaining his intermediary role between the factories and the wholesalers, except during the final months of the war during which we were cut off from the world. Préfailles formed part of the 'St-Nazaire pocket' which the Allies had bypassed in order to continue their advance. The German garrison they left behind them no longer represented a danger and they hadn't wanted to lose time bringing it to the point of surrender. So whilst everywhere around us the country was liberated, in Préfailles we were still occupied. An occupation in tatters more or less. The uniforms of the soldiers of the Wehrmacht were worn, mended, threadbare and, their boots having given up the ghost, they went around in clogs. The population was short of everything. I remember that there were no more flints for lighting the fire. So my father, using a magneto and some ingenuity, succeeded in producing sparks to ignite the lighter wick and then light the fire. Neighbours came to us with garden pots which my father filled with smoking charcoal. With a windmill powered dynamo he sorted out our electricity. Préfailles was not rid of Germans until the moment the Third Reich capitulated.

As for myself, I continue to get good tickings off on account of my studies but, in spite of doing the minimum, I do not have to retake any class, so why force me to work harder? The two little ones spice up everyday life with their episodes of infant illness. On Sunday all of us, except Papa, go to mass. In brief, we are one more provincial family, like so many others, with the difference that our main pastime is sailing. Now and again, throughout the occupation, Papa would ponder to himself: 'I don't know what state we will find *Pen Duick* in.'

During these sorrowful years he had many preoccupations other than his boat. But in spite of everything he did not forget him.

We receive the answer to this question in 1945, going to Bénodet. Brittany had suffered from the occupation and the fighting. Reconstruction started and one began to hope. Those nightmarish years over, each person is persuaded there will be no more conflicts in this land. Rationing remains in force; everyone looks forward to the moment of really letting go. The first fishing boats put out to sea again, having been forbidden from doing so for years. Life picked up from where it had left off before.

'He looks shabby,' remarked my father. The yacht is in a truly pathetic condition. He has been sheltering in the swamp for six years.

Letting your boat winter in the swamp was normal at the time as at high tide the hull floated and at low tide it gently settled. This was excellent for it since mud helped preserve the wood. The problem with the system was that the deck and topsides remained exposed to the elements. It was not significant so long as the boat was refitted and painted and varnished each year. But now, six years of neglect had aggravated the ageing of an already old boat.

'He looks shabby,' repeated my father.

We stand in a line, not saying anything and looking at *Pen Duick* in a state of shock, having gone round him and inspected the topsides. Looking at the boat one cannot help but feel sorry for him. There is nothing of the dashing yacht who, in his garlanded youth, lorded it on the seas. We know that he took part in the Royal Corinthian Yacht Club regattas held in 1899, finishing fourth out of fourteen entries. He had won the Handicap Match in Ramsgate Week, organised by the Royal Temple Yacht Club. In 1900 he finished second in the Port Victoria to Harwich race and then first from Harwich to Burnham-on-Crouch. At the Trouville regattas of 1902 he bagged places of honour. A year later he won at Duclair and achieved second at Trouville, St-Malo and Meulan. Later, in 1911 and 1912, two more seconds and from 1919 to 1921, prizes at Morgat and Douarenez. Having become the property of a French yachtsman, he raced on the Atlantic with a similar brio and was admired not just for his maritime qualities but for his good looks, too. A record which says much about this real greyhound of the waves. There, hunched in the basin, he put one in mind of a melancholy old dog, sick and abandoned. Confronted by our own sad expressions the sailor who, come what may, had kept an eye on him during the war, inspecting his mooring, bailing out water, told us by way of consolation: 'Don't complain. You've had some luck still having him in one piece. During the occupation, Germans were requisitioning keel lead. When they asked me if *Pen Duick*'s keel was of lead or cast iron, I said: "It seems pretty sure that it is cast iron". That was enough for them and they turned on their heel.'

CHAPTER 2

OWNER OF A WRECK

Not without difficulty, my father, assisted by me and the sailor, refits *Pen Duick*. Finally he makes him just about fit for navigation. And so the Tabarly family – Papa and Mum and their four children – resume cruising along the Breton coast. Sometimes there are soakings because the deck is like a sieve in spite of its caulking. As soon as it rains or there is sea-spray you get doused below decks. In the cabin, you live with the damp. This yacht is in pressing need of major repairs.

We have a new port of registry: La Trinité-sur-Mer. The skipper chose it for a simple reason: the sailor from Bénodet having retired, my father finds another handyman based at La Trinité to take care of *Pen Duick* during winter. La Trinité, built on a hillock by the mouth of the Auray river, enjoys at that time a high reputation in the little world of yachting. Already, before the war, Nantais, Rennais, Lyonnais and even some wealthy Parisian yacht owners have their mooring buoys in the renowned harbour, well sheltered from westerly winds. English yachtsmen, invariably dressed in blazer and Royal Yacht Club tie, liked to drop anchor here.

So it is a corner of Brittany full of life and charm. The quay is still of well-worn earth and is enlivened by a few fishing boats that come alongside, from Séné and Bono or Étel. The industrial freezer constructed shortly after the war to stimulate fishing proves a failure. The town's main livelihood is oyster farming.

On the other side of the river is a single boatyard, specialising in racing and cruising yachts – or a combination of the two. It is run by Gino Costantini, father of Gilles and Marc, twins who I will become close friends with and who will play an important part in my life. I look. I listen. I feel at home in this world of work and friendship where 'my word is my bond'. I like La Trinité-sur-Mer.

My father is concerned. He and Joseph, the crew, have come to the same conclusion: the cutter can no longer be sailed without risking serious problems. 'He's old,' grumbles Joseph. 'If we do not repair the deck, one of these days he'll split in two.'

'I know only too well!' my father responded with irritation. The urgency of doing it stares one in the face. 'But it's too costly,' he adds morosely.

The tone of family life is depressive. My father, on returning home at the end of the week, is sombre and announces that such and such a wholesaler – an old and faithful client – has just shut up shop. Modernism in the post-war period commences its first ravages; financial difficulties suddenly loom over our household. That is not to say that we lack for anything or that our meals are not abundant, but economies have to be made until better days arrive.

It was during this period, towards the end of 1947, that my father for the first time envisaged selling the boat. There are a range of jobs that should be attended to on *Pen Duick*: a running stay cleat has lifted off the deck; screws are no longer holding in the worm-eaten wood; the fashion piece is gone as are all the topsides. One can no longer sail him without running stupid risks. Hoping that business will soon pick up, my father winters *Pen Duick* in the basin at La Trinité. He does not know that this will be the last time. The following summer my godfather let my father use his international eight metre. We spend the whole summer sailing this superb, high performance white boat. The succeeding season, as crew, we take part with boats entered in English races organised by the RORC (Royal Ocean Racing Club). In the small world of racing I begin to be known.

I have suggested, somewhat hypocritically perhaps, that my schooling was some kind of Calvary. In most subjects my teachers simply noted: 'Does not contribute at all.' One evening, having undergone the ritual recriminations of my parents, I ingratiatingly proposed a solution to satisfy all.

'You could make some economies, Papa ... '

'Aha ... and how?'

'Well, you stop paying for my schooling and then you will be able to pay some of the repair costs.'

My father glared at me. I did not press the point. *Pen Duick* was put on sale. I was desolate. But time goes by and I am left believing in divine mercy by the marked absence of a buyer. I live for this boat, even in his current state. Thunderstruck, you might say. Both my parents are also very attached. I am young and still unaware that in life one has to know when to accept sacrifices, however hard they may be.

There came a day when a fellow, intending to buy him, came to visit *Pen Duick*. It was just before laying up. I accompanied my father. I listened as he paraded the yacht's qualities. He praised his handling in all conditions and his speed and robustness. Clinically, I interrupted this eulogy:

'Still, you should be careful ... '

'Ah?'

'It is only by a miracle that the cleats are still in place, as the wood is disintegrating like sawdust.'

My father gave me a sulphurous look, before recommencing his spiel, evoking the old boat's glorious victories. Ignoring the vivid look of anger in my father's eyes, I tearfully added that: 'If refurbishment didn't cost a fortune, we would have definitely kept him.'

'It will be very expensive?' the potential buyer asked me, suddenly interested in what I had to say.

'About the same as buying a new boat.'

The guy replied with: 'I will think about it.' But one could tell from his tone that we were not about to see him again. Following his departure I receive a hell of a tirade, but danger had been momentarily averted.

Pen Duick is no longer spoken of on the quay at La Trinité-sur-Mer. He belongs to the past.

Eric Tabarly

I am alone in refusing to accept his loss. 1952: the boat, in his fifty-fourth year, is festering in a sorry state of decomposition. Each time I happen to be in La Trinité I make sure that I go to see him. I stroke his flanks, scrutinising the accumulated wounds which infect him like gangrene. 'What a shame,' sigh those who love boats and regard them as living objects, almost human.

That year my father took a decision which would affect the course of my life. It is early September and we are just finishing dinner at La Chalouère. Without warning, he interrupts the little ones' yapping to announce: 'Seeing as *Pen Duick*'s decline makes him impossible to sell, I am going to take the lead from his keel and sell it. That would amount to a tidy sum.'

We all fall silent, feeling shocked. The whole family is attached to the cutter. We think of him rather like a family home. Evidently, father's decision sounds the death knell for *Pen Duick*. I am twenty-one, with all the fervour and insouciance that goes with it. With help from above I have my baccalauréat in my pocket. I clear my throat and, looking my father straight in the eye, commence:

'Papa, next year I start in the Navy. I will be getting a wage. With that money I can save the boat – or at least try to. I will scrape and save for as long as I need to, just so long as he can sail again.' My father looks at me long and hard. He can be tough and gruff but he is a man with a heart, true to his word, whom I take after. He is a man who loves his family, capable of devotion and of making sacrifices for the clan. He is a proper father. His look softened as he said to me:

'It is agreed Éric. I give you *Pen Duick*. We will go to the notary tomorrow to sort out the formalities.'

Then, with a little smile, he added:

'You will be *Pen Duick*'s thirteenth owner; maybe that will bring you luck ... '

It was a generous present he had given me, seeing as the keel's six tonnes of lead represented a fair sum of money then.

It was in this manner that, aged twenty-one, I became skipper of a wreck, laid up in a basin for the past five years.

CHAPTER 3

MY NOSE DOES NOT FIT

I thought that I would enjoy flying, although I had never set foot in a plane. The idea of being a sailor pleased me. The Fleet Air Arm was the service which suited me. In heavy November rain, I was summoned to Versailles to undergo a medical at the 'Little Stables'. There is nothing wrong with me, except for one small detail: my nose. The military doctor says to me: 'We will take you on the condition that you should get your nasal passage fixed.'

'What's the matter with my nasal passage?' I say, taken aback.

'It is askew and could cause you respiratory problems while flying.'

My nose, to be true, had been a little skew-whiff since birth; it had not given me any trouble, not that I had been paying attention. But one doesn't argue in the Armed Forces. I undergo corrective surgery to provide me with a nice straight nose which conforms to regulations. At my own – or, more precisely, my parents' – expense, of course. In February 1953 I am finally allowed in.

After two months of training I am assigned to St-Mandrier, near Toulon where the selection of trainee pilots takes place. There are three possibilities: Marrakech for those training with Air Force pupils; Pensacola in the United States; or Kourigba, at the naval college. Barely able to mumble a handful of words in English, Pensacola is out of the question. I thus found myself at Kourigba, one hundred kilometres to the east of Casablanca.

Kourigba is a village of narrow streets which wind their way between whitewashed houses on ground that is hard and dry, like a desert. In its outreaches are some farms and emaciated flocks that graze on the unusual looking tufts of hard grass. The Fleet Air Arm training base is further afield, in the middle of nowhere. The only amusement for us is a swimming pool at the nearby phosphate mines.

We are divided into groups of twenty; there is one group per term. Each group occupies a small barrack and is subdivided into bunk-bed dormitories for four. By the end of the day these little pads are like steam rooms, so we go to bed and fall asleep undressed. But during the night the temperature plummets, we wake up and get under some blankets.

We're stressed – me particularly – knowing from past statistics that, at the end of rigorous and continuous training, only ten of us will remain.

I, who had disliked studying with such intensity, find myself back at school with courses to follow, tests, homework, and time spent in front of the blackboard like a school kid. One must learn, note and inwardly digest. Our initiation is perfunctory: we start to fly straightaway. The initial flight, consisting of various acrobatics is memorable: loops, four-point hesitation rolls, flying upside down ... I can't make out what is happening with the horizon constantly moving about. Supported solely by safety straps, with one's head upside down in the air, is a strange sensation.

Our first flights are made in a biplane, a Stampe. Following several flying hours with a teacher comes the dreaded moment in the company of an unapproachable examiner, who – with reason – is merciless. You take off, fly, then land with him. If the performance was good, he simply says: 'Over to you.' He gets out and you take off alone. The critical moment, known as the 'unleashing', has arrived, when one finds oneself alone at the controls. To be honest, when my turn comes I am not truly relaxed. I am aware that my future depends on this trial and that with a single error or omission it would be over. I can't stand these tests which knot my stomach and dry out my throat. Moreover, my

Memories of the Open Sea

various examiners realise this and in the margin of my notes they write: 'Did much better solo.'

The night of this first solo flight in the Stampe, two of our band are already handed their cards. The survivors are exultant and beaming, as one tends to be having experienced a drawn out, purgatorial nervous tension. My comrades swap their sensations, occasionally with a certain amount of exaggeration. I remain contained. I do not share the general exuberance. I am satisfied and that is all. The main thing is to have cleared the first hurdle. But I am conscious of those that remain and that, as yet, nothing concrete has been achieved. Plus my nature is not exactly extrovert. I turn instead to future difficulties. I am going to have to get to grips with the SNJ, a naval version of the T6, an American monoplane like a small fighter which can go 250kph, whereas the Stampe's flat out maximum speed is 150kph.

Lectures, training, studying take up all our time. The student-soldier existence leaves us with little time to turn our thoughts to pleasure, girls and parties. Besides, we are all hard up. Although commissioned, throughout the period comparable to obligatory national service, we get the same wage as those 'called to the colours'. That is to say a pittance. Within the base perimeter we live like recluses, except at the weekend which follows the monthly hand-out of our meagre wage. On Saturdays, with this modest sum in our pocket, we hitch-hike. Our inevitable destination: Casablanca.

The moment I get to the swarming Moroccan metropolis, I head straight to the army residence to reserve a bed for the night. Then I go for a saunter in town. For one who before knew only Brittany and Anjou – and have come out of my hole, as they say – this great commercial city-port, with its heavy traffic and cosmopolitan inhabitants, gives me the impression of being at the cinema. Amongst my favourite strolls is the fishing port. Under an indigo sky, the returning fishermen pull up their motorised dinghies and in enormous pots, blackened by burning wood, cook fish soup, or fry in pans as big as bicycle wheels. The scene and the smells are mouth-watering. I bite into the only meal my finances will permit – a ham and butter sandwich. After a visit to the cinema I am early to bed. The following day some pals and I go and pass the day at the municipal swimming pool where another sandwich serves as dinner. We eye up the girls but there is no chance of getting acquainted or of buying them an ice-cream. All we have left is the price of the train ticket to take us back to Kourigba. The Spartan jamboree is over – until next month. The military takes us back to her comforting bosom.

As foreseen, at the end of the Kourigba course there are ten of us left to continue with our training. The top four – the cracks – are assigned to fighter planes. The remaining six, counting myself, are destined for land based operations which in the Fleet Air Arm comprises anti-submarine activities, sea searches and reconnaissance of shipping lanes, together known as Sea Patrol. There are also transport convoy flights and a variety of other jobs.

My new training centre was at Agadir. Meanwhile, a year having passed since I joined up, I am due a long leave. So I am back at my room at La Chalouère, to my family and evenings with them, being looked at and questioned affectionately. My father and mother, above all, are overjoyed. Following all the worries I had caused them regarding my future, they can now relax. The Fleet Air Arm may not be naval college but at least I have found a career.

Naturally, I return to La Trinité-sur-Mer to check the state my boat is in. *Pen Duick*'s condition has deteriorated further. Soon, I tell myself, I will be able to start taking care of him. Not a day passes without my thinking of him.

We return from leave to an environment fertile in comparison to Kourigba, ringed by barracks and hangars. Mechanics work on the big grounded planes which cook in the sun.

We are here for six months special training on multi-engine aircraft. This is going to be a little bit different to the old crates in which we made our first flights. First we familiarise ourselves with the twin engine Beechcraft. At this point one is awarded the

Memories of the Open Sea

pilot's badge and is commissioned. At the same time one is made second master. Next I pilot the four-engine Lancaster, 1250 CV per propeller. During the last war this British aircraft distinguished itself in the Ruhr: the dambuster. It was the only airplane which could carry a ten-ton bomb – a special bomb which had to be released horizontally and at a certain altitude and speed in order to ricochet along the water, catapult over the anti-torpedo nets and find its target: the dam. For the Lancaster, this was mission accomplished.

I like the Lancaster a lot. Obviously it is different to anything I have previously flown. In contrast to a cabin built close to the ground, here I am five metres above the runway with a panoramic view of the world.

They instruct us to land on 'three points'. This means touching down on all three wheels – there is one at the rear on this aircraft – at the same time. The trick consists in pulling the plane up at the exact moment it is adjacent to the ground, its wheels almost touching the runway. Initially this is not easy! If, as pilots put it, one levels out too late, only the front two wheels will hit the ground first time and, immediately, one is airborne again. If one reacts well a clean landing can be made within a few metres. Or one can continue bouncing along the greater part of the runway. If, on the other hand, you level out too early and pull the plane up too high it will hit the ground with all the grace of a brick: boom! Unsurprisingly, one gets bawled out, but, after all, one is there to learn – which, finally, I did.

With my commission secured, I receive my first wages. Not exactly a gold mine but enough to let me start saving for *Pen Duick* at last. Practically everything I earn goes into my bank account. This hoarding earns me a reputation for being tight but I am not bothered, having only one goal in mind: my boat.

In Indochina the forces have fallen. Amidst them there reigns a profound feeling of sadness and humiliation. All the expeditionary force's sacrifices, suffering and heroism have been in vain and have ended in defeat. A lot of our countrymen back home were happy, if not rejoicing, when we gave up fighting. But those of us in uniform are heavy hearted. Our troops had fought with all the Vietnamese who had not wanted to live under a communist regime. Regrettably, the communists had won. Within a few years, terrible hardships would come to the Vietnamese and Cambodian peoples.

France proceeded to bring home her officials, citizens and the last of the military. To offset this, the Navy proposed that two of us should join 28F – 'F' for fleet – at the end of our training. For sure, the double time I would receive was an incentive in volunteering for these final missions to this most distant country where we fought and served. But it isn't the principal reason in prompting me to go for one of these two posts in Indochina. I want to see the country. Peace was signed on July 21 1954. The following year I flew to Saigon on board an Armagnac, a powerful four-engine French design intended to compete with the predominant long distance American planes of the time. In spite of its qualities it had not broken into the commercial routes and was used instead as a troop carrier to Indochina.

The South Vietnamese capital, Saigon, carried on as normal as if compensating for the misfortune experienced by the northern half of the peninsula: chaotic traffic, shops, louche goings-on, soldiers on leave, nightclub girls and bars …

For the first six months I fly the four-engine Privateer, the Fleet Air Arm version of the American Liberator bomber which had pounded Germany and been involved in the D-day landings. Then, at our morning briefing session, we are informed that, as a matter of urgency, these planes are headed for North Africa where the situation is deteriorating.

'Tabarly, you will go to Special Liaisons.' Nothing special. Some Cessnas and Morane 500s, light aircraft that an aero club would not get excited about.

At Special Liaisons our principal missions involve taking officer parachutists in our biplanes, so that they can carry out their duties checking out the drop and landing zones, or releasing the parachutists' equipment to keep them in working order.

Memories of the Open Sea

Because of the weather we make an early start. A post-lunch siesta is obligatory. Following which there is a 2-1 chance of leave. I go and play tennis at the army courts in Saigon. Then on to the swimming pool with my playing partners and finally, before returning, a fine chocolate ice cream in the rue Catinat. Dinner in the Junior Ratings' Mess leads to a film at the base's open air cinema. And so to bed. These are frugal days. Besides, I carry very little money on me, the greater part of my salary going into my bank account where it is earmarked for *Pen Duick*.

Originally I should have stayed in Indochina for two years, but this was shortened to just one. I had made the decision to prepare for an exam for the Navy's introductory course, a stepping stone to the naval college entry competition. In Saigon, while my companions napped after lunch, I had crammed ... and negotiated the written exam successfully. As for the oral, that is held at the CPEOM – the preparatory course for trainee naval officers – situated in a barrack in the naval college precinct at Poulmic, near Brest. It is why I am returning early to France.

I passed the exam. May 1 1956 I enter the CPEOM for fifteen months.

CHAPTER 4

YOUR BOAT HAS HAD IT

A good year and a half's savings – rigorously garnered – are waiting for me, stashed away in my bank account. While it is not a king's ransom – nobody got rich in the Navy – my stash will permit me to make a start on the boat's resurrection.

Feeling confident, I arrive at the Costantini brothers' boatyard in Kerisper. Following the death of their father Gino, who had set it up, the twins, barely twenty-four, took over. Between them there was a division of labour: Marc, a recognised helmsman, overlooks the administration and accounts; Gilles, the artist, is responsible for the conception and execution of the yacht designs he gets commissioned.

When I pitch up at his office, Gilles is leant over the drawing board, sketching a hull. Hearing my approach, he raises his head and, seeing me, smiles. 'Back at last!' he proclaims. 'It feels like forever since you left ... '

'A year, that's all ... '

'And?'

'We can get going with *Pen Duick*.'

We set the frame in place which will cradle the vessel at low tide. Mounted on a trolley it is guided down rails to the water's edge. Then at high tide the boat is manoeuvred onto the cradle. Then, slowly – gently even – we winch out my boat, creaking like an old man as we lift his sad carcass. Finally, *Pen Duick* is out of the water, his flanks oozing damp and mud. Gilles gets on board and inspects the goods with his customary thoroughness. Following which he returns to me, downcast, to pronounce: 'Your boat has had it.'

This hits me hard. 'Had it!' That I cannot accept.

'All the same it can be repaired, can't it?' I suggest, in spite of this evidence to the contrary.

'Too much work, Éric. All the frame ends are rotten. To set that right will break the bank.'

That morning, intrigued, Paul Gentet, who is an oyster farming friend of my father's, arrives at the yard. From the deck of *Pen Duick* we see him coming towards us and Gilles, happy to have an ally, says to me: 'Look, here's Paul. He's sure to tell you the same as me. Hey Paul!' He turns towards him, 'Do you agree that *Pen Duick*'s had it?' To which Paul replies in his sing song Auray voice:

'Lord yes, *Pen Duick*'s had it for sure!'

I could have killed him. Why was he interfering? He hadn't even looked. Not that the two of them weren't right.

In the boathouse was *Cuty*, a pretty boat classified as an eight metre, which had been on sale for years. When I approached his owner, he told me: 'I am really sorry but I am in the process of selling him.'

There was no other boat that attracted me.

At the CPEOM I settle down to my studies with rare application. My only absences are the odd weekend spent at La Trinité-sur-Mer, where Gilles puts me up.

We have known each other since adolescence. At the time, La Trinité was a haven for the best cruising and racing yachts. Everybody – adults and children – knew one another from regular holidays there. We used to be in the same dinghy races. Afterwards, we would discuss them and, even then, analyse ways to better our performances. Later, with Gilles, his father and brother and other friends, we set off to crew in British regatta races.

Our parents were very close. The final cruise Gilles' father made was with my father. They had set off for England to look for – what was then hard to find in France – Dacron sails for future races. Alas, soon after, Gilles' father was dead.

We loved our fathers without reservation. They weren't doters or new men before the fact. Equally strong and stocky men, they loved racing and hated losing. On board, you couldn't get in a muddle with manoeuvres, or hesitate, without some reproach. My father was intrigued by Gino's artistic side; he was a calm and painstaking Italian, friendly and completely straight. 'My word is my bond,' Gino would say, an attitude my father shared. Gilles and I inherited this moral code. When we take on a project, neither signed papers nor a notary are necessary: one's word is enough.

The Costantinis' flat-roofed house is not hard to find. It was built in the Italian style, according to Gino's wishes. Its windows give a view of all the channel's traffic, La Trinité quay, clouds gathering in the south and, in the distance, the ocean.

On Saturday we are drinking a whisky in the living room. My nerves are on edge with the question of *Pen Duick*'s salvage. As often happens on these occasions we delved a little into the past. Doing so, I put to him that night a solution that I had been nurturing since the purchase of *Cuty* had fallen through – 'You build small hulls in polyester ... why not do the same with a bigger hull?'

'Go on ... '

'Well, one could use my boat as a mould: straightaway I would have a new hull'.

'We can try,' said Costantini, tempted by my idea. 'Your boat is fine; salvaging him is worth the effort.' *Pen Duick* – and Gilles agrees – is a cutter from a bygone age, a piece of history representing the difference between then and now.

The work was started during my August 1956 leave. It would last three years.

I take up all the deck, apart from its beams, removing all the fittings. Then we disengage the bolts from the keel. The boat can

Memories of the Open Sea

now go back into the water. Its ballast will remain on the cradle. The hull sits at an angle, letting in water via the bolt – and other – holes. A metal cable has been fixed onto the keel. We connect it to the hook of a crane; this allows us to capsize the keel and lift it up, upside down. It is then laid on a barge that has been beached as high as possible. We did it all at spring tide. My leave ended, the job is put on hold for a year.

'Life teaches patience,' was my mother's refrain when, like all children, I jumped up and down to get what I wanted. Patience ... I needed it in spades to bring my projects to fruition.

In September I returned to CPEOM – until June '57, when I failed the exam. I then had leave before rejoining my command at Lann-Bihoué 2S. I return to *Pen Duick*. First of all I sandpaper the hull, a lot of sanding. It needs to be absolutely smooth to serve as a mould for the new hull.

I do this rather monotonous work by myself. Curious passers-by stop, look at me and then leave with a doubting or astonished look. Some ask me what I am doing. I reply: 'I'm on holiday. I'm just keeping myself busy.' It is typically Breton to ask somebody what they are up to, even if this is plain to see. For example, if a fellow is repainting his house he will be asked: 'You are painting?' 'I'm painting,' he replies. In Brittany it is a form of greeting, a way of showing one's interest in others.

Bit by bit, at weekends and on leave, I finished the sanding and wiped the whole hull free of dust so that the polyester resin will not stick to the hull and the mould can be removed smoothly. The next, most important, stage is applying the fibreglass webbing. Gilles has shown me the appropriate amount of resin that needs to be used to bind these sections together.

It was not until Easter 1958 that I was able to undertake this operation.

'You need to get some manual labour,' he told me.

'I know.'

'I'll see what I can find on the oyster farms.'

Eric Tabarly

According to my schedule, I need six helpers. Gilles provides them. In those days life was very tough for some women, particularly those who worked on the oyster farms in the wind and the rain. Once this seasonal work came to an end they sought employment in restaurants or hotels. They are not clock watchers. These are difficult times just to secure one's daily bread. Helping me to coat my hull is a painstaking process but, nevertheless, not so tiring as scrubbing tiles at their workplace and helps my female team to augment their wage. From a distance our work must resemble a well synchronised ballet. Three girls hold onto one side and three to the other. First we apply a covering of resin. Then we spread sections of fibreglass over the upturned hull. After this, another coat of resin, worked well into the gauze. When putting it on it is important not to trap any air, which will later develop into bubbles. If, after taking all this trouble, they still appear I sand down any blisters before proceeding to the next coat.

Gilles, who is sure of the method, had calculated that we require seven coats to produce a solid hull. We do one a day. The girls do not work on Sundays so it is an eight day job.

The thickness of the new hull is about fifteen millimetres. To reassure myself of its strength, I drop a load onto it: it does not break.

'Incredible, huh?' remarks Gilles, as he casts an eye over the final result.

'It's solid. Now we just need to do the finishing coat.' The worst part of the job. The sections of fibre overlap and the cast is inevitably uneven. My hull has some of the appearance of corrugated iron. It needs to be ironed out with the finishing coat. But the clock is ticking. I have to prepare once more for the spring entrance exam to the naval college. I must put the job on hold. Fortunately, luck was on my side. During the whole of this outdoor job, not a single drop of rain fell in Brittany.

The Navy's rules are clear: once a candidate has failed the CPEOM exam, he has a second opportunity the following year, rejoining the course in the final revision term, having sat out the time in between.

Memories of the Open Sea

As I started once again as a student at the CPEOM, I buckled down hard for the test which could prove to be a turning point in my career. I am tense and nervous before the exam. I am tense and nervous the day of the results.

'Papa, I've been accepted by the naval college!'

'Brilliant, Éric!' cried my father down the telephone line. 'I'll pass you over to your mother.'

'I've got in, Mummy!'

'Bravo, my boy. You gave us a hard time, but today is the happiest day of my life: my son a naval officer. It has always been my dream.'

I am twenty-seven. In October I will find myself amongst fellows six or seven years younger than me. Out of a field of one hundred candidates, the class of '58, six of us have made it. In naval slang we are known as zebras – on account of our sailors' blue and white striped jersey.

I discover an old US army Harley-Davidson in a garage in Jossclin. A 'golden opportunity,' the vendor assured me, specifically because 'she was part of the landing,' suggesting that this was a cast-iron guarantee. On the strength of it, I arrive at La Chalouère by motorcycle, my engine growling. I am on leave. I celebrate my upcoming entry into the Navy at my parents'. I am happy – after my own, calm, manner. I have no need of extravagant displays of emotion. For me it is enough to say, 'I am happy'. That suffices. My parents and brother and sisters are overjoyed. My mother pulled out all the stops and put on a first rate meal. As supper ends, my father asks me:

'And what are you going to do now?'

'I'll go back to La Trinité to coat the hull. I'd like to get the job done before going back.'

'So the boat will be sailing again?'

'Yes.'

My father's eyes lit up – a sure enough sign that he was satisfied. My mother, brother and sisters all smiled. In my family we had always expressed high emotion with understatement.

Eric Tabarly

At the weekend I go back on the Harley to La Trinité-sur-Mer, where *Pen Duick* is waiting.

Several months have elapsed between the final layer of fibreglass and the time to apply the finishing coat, during which the resin has hardened. Once again, I have to sand the hull in order to get rid of a thin, but hard, film which has formed and which could hamper the adhesion of the finish. Gilles has lent me a big disc sander. It is an awful job. Nowadays, yards have ventilators which automatically suck up the glass-wool dust produced by sanding. I didn't have one.

Unprotected, I go around enveloped in a cloud of fine dust like itching powder. My eyes are red and puffy. My forearms have doubled in size, thanks to a thousand glass-wool pinpricks. Just wearing my shirt becomes unbearable. First sand down. Apply a coat. Second sand down. Second coat. Re-re-sanding. Re-re-coating. At the fifth sanding I finally get a smooth surface. The longer the job takes, the more I appreciate the expanse of the boat's surface.

With a sense of relief I sand it for the last time. Before re-launching the hull, I position two hundred-litre barrels, one at the bows and one at the stern of the boat. At the first spring tide the barge goes back into the water. Once it is far enough away from shore, I raise the barge's bows so that it fills up with water. It bows beneath *Pen Duick*'s weight, to the point where he turns over and is afloat, albeit full of water, the decking – thanks to the ballast – apart. We get rid of the water with an electric pump, before bringing the boat back to dry land on the cradle. He then goes back into the boathouse.

Costantini takes over in the yard, cutting away any polyester excess above the gunwale, getting rid of the old planking above a certain height, in order to insert a temporary frame which will permit the demolition of the remainder of the old hull without damaging the new one. He then constructs a deck with hatches, openwork, bulwarks and cockpit. In short, a new boat.

Memories of the Open Sea

My finances are low, but Gilles is not concerned. 'Let's concentrate on the boat. We will sort out the rest later, when you're able ... ' The hull is done. The yard will work throughout autumn and winter 1958, making the boat look like a boat again. *'Pen Duick* will be ready next year, in time for Easter. The Navy awaits; don't worry about anything else.'

CHAPTER 5

LAST BY A DISTANCE

In my time the naval college did not have the imposing aura of the current establishment, built at the end of Brest harbour at Poulmic.

It is a collection of temporary barracks where the intake's one hundred pupils, together with the previous year, are housed and study. Spartan quarters, not conducive, for example, to pillow fighting – and anyhow, we didn't have pillows, just hammocks. We are grouped together in 'stations' of five Officer Cadets, the traditional term for naval students. We get kitted out: one change for work and a single set of clothes for outside the barracks are adjusted by the resident tailor. We sleep fifty to a dormitory. My comrades are young people for whom I feel friendship and respect. I often say that in any group of individuals you always get some jerks. But I reckon that in the Navy they are less common than elsewhere. So, from my own year, I still have ten close friends, eighty whom it is always a pleasure to encounter and ten ... with whom it is best we go our own separate ways. Not jerks, just people with whom I have nothing in common. Nevertheless, they are sound and liveable with.

I made a mark in my time at naval college. I am aware that I am still spoken of there, long after leaving, thanks to sailing – in the days before I had a reputation – and sport.

In most sports I am top of the class. I overwhelm all the other fellows, finishing first with an average eighteen out of twenty, compared to their sixteen-and-a-half out of twenty. We compete in the one hundred and eight hundred metres, the shot put, rope

Memories of the Open Sea

climbing, weightlifting and the long and high-jump. The last two are not exactly my forte. On the other hand, I consistently get twenty out of twenty rope climbing and weightlifting, and, running, nineteen out of twenty. Without remembering the exact times, I recall breaking the college records in the four hundred, eight hundred and one thousand metres. Any such success granted us a few days leave. So, when I needed forty-eight hours leave I accordingly upped my efforts, to improve on my performances.

Sailing, my chosen sport, earns me regular visits to the cooler, or naval college prison. These occur nearly every Thursday night.

That afternoon there is 'free sport', allowing everyone to pursue his chosen activity. I compete in harbour races between the college's dinghies. This does not entirely please the college's sports administration which, on account of my nice running style, enters me for – however small – all the regional cross countries, representing the college. Seeing that everyone has the right to choose his preferred sport, I opt for a sailing race. And so each Thursday night, the director of studies, a frigate captain known, in the language of the officer cadet, as the 'widow' calls me into his office and prescribes four or five days in the cooler. During the day I follow the course in the normal manner. At night I am back in my little cell with its plank bed and single blanket. There is an armed guard, of course, and so I organised myself. In the ceiling is a hatch where I stash a sheet. No sooner has the door closed behind me than I dispense with the wooden planks of my bed and install the sheet in their place, like a hammock. I sleep soundly.

Gilles Costantini is a man of his word. He had promised me that *Pen Duick* would be ready for Easter 1959. He fulfilled his promise. *Pen Duick* looks magnificent with his new hull. Naturally he has been repainted in black. The paint glistens. I had re-done all the rigging because the original spars, left to one side in the yard twelve years before, had vanished. Maybe someone, thinking that they would never be used again, had turned them into a log cabin. I had to have a new mast and gaff and bowsprit. I had found a boom at Anatole le Rouzic's, who had stored the boat and whose little boathouse was a veritable Aladdin's cave. He tells me: 'This boom will be suitable for *Astarté*.'

He had known *Pen Duick* under this name at La Trinité in the mid '20s, and for him *Pen Duick* has always remained *Astarté*. This superb boom in pitch pine had one drawback: it was a little bit short. He had to add on a small end section to achieve the correct length.

As for the sails, which dated from our purchase of the boat, with the exception of the jib, they were too battered. I had them repaired. Using second-hand parachutes, I made a spinnaker. Luckily, all the old shrouds are in good condition.

When the boat's refitting began I had a regrettable flash of inspiration. To improve *Pen Duick*'s performance, I added an extra fifty centimetres to the new mast; consequently the shrouds were too short. Rather than getting replacements – for which I did not have the means – I lengthened the originals with little oak footings which, to me, seemed solid ...

Pen Duick had not been to sea for twelve years. Fitting out took me all the Easter holidays. There remains just enough time for a trial; the voyage to Brest will be made later. We were my father, my brother Patrick and the Costantini twins, Gilles and Marc. No grand gestures, just smiles all around. At such moments words tend to sound a false note or to be tiresomely trite. True happiness is accompanied by silence. I have a look at my father. He had not thought *Pen Duick*'s salvage was possible and is moved by it. When the sails are raised and the hull reverberates to the sound of the ocean ... these are magical moments for us. The longstanding dream has become a reality.

Under a lavender blue sky, typical of La Trinité and worthy of a tourist brochure, we wind our way between the channel buoys and out into the open sea. The Quiberon Bay stretches out in front of us. We can see the Teignouse lighthouse and the obscure outlines of two islands, Houat and Belle-Île. I stand at the helm and don't think that anything can cast a shadow over or tarnish my happiness. I am wrong.

It starts with a hard cracking sound. The oak shroud extension had snapped. Everything then happens very quickly. The mast wobbles, then, under the weight of the sails, snaps clean at its stem.

I will not linger over this grim memory. We begin to gather the rigging in a heavy silence, since no good will come of cursing or shouting at a setback, however big. Curses and recriminations are just a waste of time. Luckily, a friend who is sailing in the same waters throws us a line and tows us back to La Trinité.

It is a hard blow for me. I don't have any money left for repairs to be made on dry land. I have already run up quite a bill with the Costantinis, who have unbegrudgingly extended me credit: 'Pay us when you can.' Each month I went to the yard with a meagre offering. These ended in 1963.

This was one of the rare occasions in my life when I felt a little discouraged. To repair the mast footing, the upper mast and the shrouds is beyond my means. In fact, I don't have any means at all.

We drive back to naval college.

It is there that Gilles gets in touch with me by phone in order to announce in his warm and sonorous voice: 'A client asked me to carry out the repairs to *Pen Duick* at his expense.'

'Who is he?'

'He asked to remain anonymous. Someone who likes you a lot and who knows what you have been through to relaunch *Pen Duick*.'

I am fairly sure I know who the generous benefactor is but, since he prefers to remain anonymous, I feign ignorance.

The mast and all the new refurbishments are set right in record time by the yard.

One weekend *Pen Duick* is transported to Bénodet. The next, the beginning of May, we pick up the buoy reserved for him by the Manoeuvres Unit at Poulmic, following agreement with the naval college authorities. I am the only pupil at this august establishment to have his own boat. I am also granted an exceptional favour. Rather than having to return at midnight on Saturday, following the afternoon's leave, I am permitted – together with any of the fellows who come as crew – to go at noon on Saturday and to come back on Sunday evening.

Six on board is the limit for a cruise that, on account of Poulmic's position, tucked into the Brest peninsula, remains almost unchangeable. More often than not, confronted with a westerly wind and on a rising tide, the afternoon would be spent tacking so as to get out to sea. In the evening we usually moor at Camaret or close by. Occasionally, wind and tide permitting, we go as far as the Île de Sein or Molène.

I have regulars who come aboard, no matter what the weather. Hubert de Lépinay hardly missed a sail; Malézieuz, Foillard, Véricourt and some others frequently volunteered for a soaking. But quite a few of our colleagues hesitated to join us. Each week I made the rounds of the stations to canvass for crew, without always achieving a full complement. Only later did one of the guys point out: 'They're wary of accepting because of lack of experience.' I explained that I didn't expect a battle-hardened crew, just that two or three should have some experience – all the others needed to do was to look and learn.

My first year's studies at the naval college are concluded with some sea trials at the end of the summer. My marks just sufficed to continue on to the next year. I scored an average of twelve, the absolute bare minimum. The class of 1958 is allowed one month's leave in September.

Our first cruise is to the Scillies' archipelago, with its hundred or so little isles, formerly known as the 'Cassiterites', on which grow exotic plants that you would not expect in such an environment and on whose jagged, teeth-like rocks plenty of boats used to come to grief in the winter. In the windy English Channel *Pen Duick* makes his commanding way. Each movement of the old gaff rigging is a pleasure,

Memories of the Open Sea

if a test of strength for even well formed young biceps. At the yachting Mecca of Cowes the outstanding beauty of my boat is confirmed. Keith Beken, the doyen of marine photography, notices us as we pass by under sail. Straightaway, he jumps into his launch and then circles us, armed with his celebrated plate camera. Not a bad way to have the first photos of *Pen Duick*, which I preserve like relics.

The second year at naval college begins. I return to my hammock in the dormitory and my place with our station, No.14. I am summoned by the director of studies who addresses me in a firm voice:

'Tabarly, you've got a harder head than this desk. I am well aware that if we continue to enter you for the Thursday afternoon cross country you will not go. It won't do to carry on putting you into the cooler. We should be forced to think of more severe sanctions, including expulsion. That is not what we want. I have given orders that this year you may go your own way. But I wish to count on your participation for the big meetings and competitions, for example against the other colleges.'

'Principal, you can count on me.'

In this way, running no longer caused me any bother. Nor, even though I was far from being a star pupil, were my studies a concern now. On the other hand, my troubles with *Pen Duick* had not ended.

The weekend before Christmas we went out in fairly bad weather. We had made a few tacks along St-Matthieu's Point. There was a swell and we were enjoying ourselves. It was on the way back that things started to go wrong. Hemmed into the Brest inlet by a strong westerly, I warned the helmsman several times that he was on the wrong side of the wind. 'Careful! You are overreaching.'

A waste of breath. Then, critically, and without meaning to, he jibbed. The boom flashed like a meteor from one side to the other and the mast cracked at the level of the jib spreaders. Or, to be precise, just below.

Eric Tabarly

On the slithering boat we gather in the upper rigging, but the remaining stump of a mast has neither shrouds nor a halyard. They all stayed attached to the upper – fallen – part of the mast.

We have to fix an emergency halyard. I shin up the smooth, slippery timber. By fixing a block to the new masthead I can secure a halyard. In this way we start to put this little saga behind us and regain the route to Poulmic. So long as we remained on a beam reach we made progress, albeit slowly. But once we reach Pen Ar Vir Point we need to head up into the wind: impossible. With our little jib, we are not able to tack. We would still be there if the school manoeuvres staff had not seen us in difficulties and dispatched a launch to tow us back to our mooring.

Once again, I find myself laid up.

By chance, as I was wandering along Lauberlat cove, I came across a big mast, abandoned for years, high up on the shore. It is quite something, probably an old mast from a barge. I say to myself: 'With this piece I should be able to fashion myself a mast.' I go to Lauberlat in one of the school's launches and get some information before locating the owner and doing business with him. Then, towing my ample spar behind, I return to Poulmic. Having taken it out of the water with a crane, it is stored in the naval college's workshop.

'Happy Christmas and have a good holiday,' my colleagues hail me, as they set off for their seasonal leave. My own leave will be spent alone at the college, adapting the mast to the right proportions.

As it rakes the harbour the winter wind whistles furiously. Wave crests, known to the ancients as devil's skin, stretch into the distance. The trees too are wind lashed. The sky is a moody grey. Once inside the carpentry workshop I do not see this winter landscape. I plane and sand the mast into a square, and then into a hexagon, before rounding off the edges. The pitch pine wood is good. I have now got myself a good mast. It is still standing on *Pen Duick*'s deck.

I could have broken all my bones on account of it, or even met my end. The new mast had just been put in place and I was right at the top – eleven metres up – halfway through fixing the rigging

Memories of the Open Sea

once more, when one of the college launches arrived and, in its wake, churned up the sea. *Pen Duick* starts to pitch and roll and pull on his moorings. The mast, which is not yet fully secured by shrouds and stays, bends impressively and I do not think it will hold with my weight at the top. I need to get down quickly. In my haste, and with the rigging swaying, I miss a hold and head down quicker than planned, head first into thin air. By pure chance, I manage to catch hold of a shroud that is already installed. My fall is curtailed, fifty centimetres above deck level.

Gérard de Véricourt, who was right by when this happened, turned pale. After the incident when, clearly shaken, I was standing next to him, he said to me in an astonished tone: 'My dear fellow, you have a fistful of both strength and luck'.

He is right. I am reasonably strong. But it is my strength which, paradoxically, costs me the naval college's sports prize: a pair of binoculars or a stopwatch, I no longer remember.

The director of studies summoned me to explain this decision: 'Tabarly,' the 'widow' says, 'I am personally opposed to your receiving this prize. I feel that with your physical attributes you are obliged to represent the College more than you have done!'

I did not get the sports prize. I also risk not graduating from naval college. I have to admit that I am not very enterprising in the vast area of studies. My application is limited – to just avoiding, as we put it, finding myself below the mean, this being the non-negotiable requirement of an average of twelve out of twenty – and so consider myself to be safe. But I failed to take into account what is known as the director's 'verbal rating', so called, it is ironically suggested, because it relates to just how lippy the examinee has been. The director judges the pupil according to his own particular criteria, foremost of which is the number of days accumulated in detention.

I should point out that, at the party to celebrate the end of the course, one names the student who has spent most nights in the little cell 'top con'. Officer Cadets' tradition demands that, to attain this not very prestigious title, the transgressor should scratch his belt once for each night spent in the cooler. As the accolade did not interest me, I hadn't marked my belt in this way and so couldn't be ordained 'No.1 con' – even though it was obvious that I was better acquainted with the cells than any of the others. I forget the number of days' punishment I amassed, whereas the Commander knew exactly what the total was. The 'personal report' he pins on me is a calamitous eight out of twenty, which takes the shine off my average. At a meeting of the institution's governing body, various teachers made their positions clear in relation to my case. Some are for sacking me, others support me – including Lieutenant Nœtinger.

As part of his defence of me, he noted: 'The one time we get a trainee officer who understands the sea, we cannot show him the door.'

The Operations Officer, Commander Jaouen, then made his own intervention on my behalf: 'Thanks to Tabarly, most of our students have understood the role of wind and current and have been accustomed to life at sea. The class of '58 is the most *bouline* – or practical – there has been.'

For the uninitiated 'bouline' is old sailors' argot for those who have sailing in the blood.

The 'Pope' – sailors' slang for the Commander – gave himself some time to think and revised his personal report from eight back up to twelve.

I graduated without acclaim, last in my year, with the rank of Ship's Ensign, second class, equivalent to Second Lieutenant. I am twenty-eight.

As custom dictates, I embark with the rest of my year for a tour of the world on the *Jeanne d'Arc*. The original training cruiser of this name, with the four funnels which contributed to the reputation it had in colonial countries for speed, had ended up in the breaker's yard in the thirties. Me and my mates took our stuff on board the ten thousand ton cruiser, launched in 1932 and designed as a training ship. It would be replaced, shortly after our voyage, by the third *Jeanne d'Arc*, a helicopter-carrying cruiser.

Memories of the Open Sea

There is never a dull moment on board. There are theoretical classes but the training is, above all, practical. Learning by doing. There is watch on the bridge and other command posts on deck. We are inducted into all the duties and chores. Drills come thick and fast: combat stations, safety, and man overboard; drawing up to a wooden raft in the water after manoeuvring correctly to approach at the right speed and distance, so that the crew can lift it out of the water with their boat-hook. Last, but not least, we trained on the dispatch boat which escorted the *Jeanne*, that was in use the whole time by a group of pupils.

Custom also dictates that, one hundred miles prior to each port of call, the big sloop, known as the 'galley', will be lowered into the water. It is small – ten metres long – with three masts. Aboard are a compass and chart, sextant, chronometer and tables. The crew, consisting of a dozen pupils, must manage to bring him to port under sail.

I was lucky. My group – the first on board – let me take the lead on the galley to get to Les Saintes. The West Indies' trade winds were blowing nicely and during the night we proceeded at a lick. When we got to Saintes in the morning we were only a few hours behind the *Jeanne d'Arc*. The extent of our luck can be contrasted to those unfortunate enough to be dropped one hundred miles short of Valparaiso. They were not helped in this becalmed corner by contrary northerly currents. On that occasion the galley barely caught up with the anchored *Jeanne* before it was time to move on again.

Occasionally, the training cruiser makes a circuit of the globe – hence this trip's name 'world tour' – but not necessarily. Duration at sea and the number and length of dockings vary. My year goes to the West Indies, Mexico and New Orleans. We cross the Panama Canal and head south to the equator, then carry on down the Peruvian and Chilean coastline, through the Straits of Magellan and back up to Buenos Aires, Montevideo and Rio de Janeiro. We then cross the Atlantic and berth at Dakar. From there we should have gone to

Eric Tabarly

Algiers, via Gibraltar. But because of the putsch we were re-routed to Ajaccio. Then Istanbul and Venice, before returning to Brest.

An incredible journey and an emotional return: *Jeanne* is coming up to the narrows. All of a sudden to starboard there appears in front of us a superb yacht under full sail, *Pen Duick*. My father at the helm with my brother Patrick at his side have come to greet us. I had never before seen my boat under sail. *Pen Duick*, according to form, raises the tricolor three times to salute the *Jeanne*. Hers is raised once in response.

CHAPTER 6

'PAY WHEN YOU CAN...'

Like the ways of the Lord, the subtleties of the armed forces are sometimes unfathomable. Having spent three years at naval college and on the *Jeanne d'Arc,* I reasonably thought that I would rejoin the Fleet Air Arm. On leaving my squadron to go to naval college, my Commandant had called me into his office to say goodbye. He had said: 'I know you are partial to boats but the Navy will not want to waste your flying hours from the *Jeanne d'Arc*, and you will without doubt go into the Fleet Air Arm.'

Actually, no. I am posted to the Cherbourg mine sweeping division. Strange. But orders are orders.

As I anticipate discovering le Cotentin with its apple trees and drizzle, the Navy allows me to go on leave. At the beginning of August members of the class of '58 went their various ways. I do not realise how many will later cross my path.

For us it is the end of three years studying that will remain a good memory throughout my life. I never got bored. It was a pleasure even and I had experiences of real friendship and hope, peculiar to one's twenties when life, one feels, is opening out before one. A page in my life had turned.

'What are you planning to do on this month's leave?' Foillard asked me as we left.

'Race *Pen Duick*.'

'You have my address, so you know where to get hold of me,' he said, as we shook hands.

Eric Tabarly

On the coast it is enough to watch kids attending sailing school in their mini dinghies, starting with reading the wind, setting their sails and reading the currents. They do not mind the cold, getting blisters on their hands or getting yelled at by their instructors, because they are fascinated by boats. Since ancient times, a small number of men has always been drawn to the – always one step beyond – horizon.

I was one of those who had fallen under its spell. I am twenty-nine with a long leave in the bag. I am the owner of a legendary yacht. I want to compete against more modern, stronger yachts to see what *Pen Duick* is capable of. I also want to improve my performance in the delicate matter of skippering. I want to know what I am made of.

The profession of sailor teaches humility and demands a long apprenticeship. The sea deals with braggarts and sailing is not a suitable pastime for posers, unlike a fair number of professions in which it is possible to fake it and bluff with impunity. On a boat, you either know what to do or you don't. It is hard luck on con-men. The ocean is pitiless.

I had started to learn my profession of skipper a year before in September 1959 in races organised by the RORC, for which I had entered *Pen Duick*. That was before setting out on the *Jeanne d'Arc*.

At the time, there were still a few yachts like my cutter with gaff rig: a quadrilateral mainsail crowned by another, triangular, sail, the topsail. I had reckoned that my boat would be able to compete against them with distinction.

But when I registered him for weighing by the British organisers, I got a nasty surprise. To appreciate my disappointment it is necessary to go into some technical detail here. The RORC's weighing procedure was designed to handicap yachts relative to one another and, in theory, to put them all on the same level. To achieve this, a series of hull and sail dimensions were taken. These were taken into the class formulae and calculated to give the boat's handicap which, set against the actual time taken in completing the course, gave a compensated time and result for the boats. To this general formula were added other handicaps to put boats of various vintages on an equal footing. These relate to age and also to rigging. In practice, Bermuda rigging performs less well per square metre than the Marconi equivalent, which has a more aerodynamic mainsail. But *Pen Duick* did not benefit from these handicaps because, the RORC's class official explained to me, the hull had been re-constructed and I was not entitled to them. In my opinion this is not logical, since the objective of the handicaps is to place boats of a different design on the same level. Now *Pen Duick* actually dates back to 1898. In one fell swoop, they had put me on the same footing as, for example, *Bloodhound*, with its 16-metre waterline, 20m overall, whilst *Pen Duick* measures 10m and 15.10m. The rule, that had been categorically made in order to give different kinds of boats the same chance, cannot be said to have been properly followed.

There were five under my orders. My father, who was crew for the first time after a long time as boss on board and Patrick, my younger brother. The 13-year gap between us had prevented our being close during his childhood but, as he got a bit older, we had got to know one another and become proper brothers. And the band of brothers from naval college: Foillard, Malézieuz and Véricourt.

'This time we are in order,' Foillard had exclaimed, climbing on board.

My companion was alluding to the Sunday morning when we had launched *Pen Duick*. This was at La Trinité-sur-Mer. For a number of days my academic year had been taking part with trainee army officers from Coëtquidan. During the night Foillard and I absconded and headed for Costantinis, where the brand new *Pen Duick* awaited us. The kind of risk we were running goes without saying.

Going back to that September, before embarking on the *Jeanne d'Arc*, we had competed in the Channel Race, then Cowes–La Coruña, in which we were pleasantly surprised to find ourselves at Ushant, after two days of tacking in light northerly winds, just behind *Striana*, one of the finest French racing boats. Then the mainsail ripped in the Bay of Biscay. This piece of nautical ill luck forced me to carry on with an old storm trysail, which dated from the time my father had bought *Pen Duick* – and to arrive in La Coruña very late.

So I had this month of leave between the *Jeanne d'Arc* and Cherbourg. In August 1960 me and the crew make our way to Beaumaris, just off the Welsh coast, on the Isle of Anglesey, to take part in the Irish Sea Race. Once again, I can see what a fine boat *Pen Duick* is. We are just about neck and neck with an international eight-metre, up until the south coast of Ireland. At which point, with a following wind, our adversary raised his spinnaker. I do not have one. We hoist a little balloon jib but are left floundering. In order to race one needs a full set of sails.

This bitter truth is confirmed soon after the start of the Fastnet Race. Thanks to a south westerly, which had stiffened impressively during the night, the only jib we have on board rips. *Pen Duick* halts at Brixham. 'I am going to find a sail maker to repair the jib for us,' I tell the crew, galled by this latest setback. Out of every bad thing comes good, the saying goes. The local sail maker's prices are so low that I not only ask him to repair the jib but order a replacement for it and a mainsail at the same time. *Pen Duick*, who only had old fashioned cotton sails will now display new sails of synthetic material. They will be ready for the following spring.

The holidays come to an end. Cherbourg is now my home. Ensign Tabarly climbs the gangway and salutes the colours flying at the stern of the naval minesweeper, *Castor*, the Section Commander's ship. While on board I am second in command of everything to do with the ships. While at sea I keep watch. Our job is to drag mines lying on the sea bed or attached to buoy ropes. *Pen Duick* is moored directly opposite Cherbourg Yacht Club. Each weekend, no matter what the weather, my Cherbourg friends and I go for a little sail. One Sunday the wind blew up and, being unable to return, we sheltered

Memories of the Open Sea

at Guernsey. I telephoned the Commander to let him know and he advised me against moving rashly. The division was due to set off on Monday morning but, because of the weather, the exercise had been cancelled. I arrived on board on Tuesday morning and had a six-day arrest slapped on me.

I cannot remember the exact date but one evening in June 1962, as the only officer living on board, I am reading a yachting magazine and come across the announcement for the British organised single-handed Transatlantic race and say to myself: 'This is a challenge I would really like to undertake.' For me this race represented the most complete competition for yachts under sail. The accounts of the participants in the first single-handed Transatlantic in 1960 had grabbed my attention.

I wrote to the organisers, the Royal Western Yacht Club of Plymouth, asking them to send me the rules. In their reply they let me know that the departure had been fixed for Saturday May 23 1964. As to the practical details, they consisted of an itinerary: departure from Plymouth, England; arrival in Newport, Rhode Island USA. Size of boat did not matter. It was stipulated that they should be propelled solely by wind – and the yachtsman's muscle power. The engine should be used only to supply electricity, and entrants did not have the right to any outside help while at sea. Stops were, however, permitted, for repairs and taking on new supplies.

With each day I became ever more involved with the idea of this long race. I obtain copies of the logs of the five 1960 entrants: Chichester, the winner, Hasler, Lewis, Howells and the Frenchman, Lacombe. According to these, three routes are possible. North, as chosen by Hasler; orthodromic – the great circle – taken by Chichester and Lewis; or via the Azores, the choice of Howells and Lacombe. There was a lot to think about in considering each of these routes. At sea, the shortest journey is not necessarily the quickest. Running against the current, too strong or light a wind, or predominant headwinds can all bear down hard on a boat's progress. All the time the sea and the atmosphere are changing.

Eric Tabarly

These variations are linked to the season, the latitude and barometric pressure. To assist the mariner in his choice there are charts specific to each sea and for each month. It is thanks to these pilot charts one knows that in the Gulf Stream waters flow towards the northeast at a rate of three knots and that the cold Labrador current carries icepacks along Newfoundland. After pondering and analysing all the information, I decide on the orthodromic route.

I just need to decide on the boat I am going to take. None is more important to me than *Pen Duick*, with his rigging lending him an inimitable aura. But I know very well that this style of ancient rigging is not suited to a solo transatlantic crossing. One man could not handle it.

By the end of the summer I decided on the course of action to follow. I left Cherbourg on a Saturday leave at lunchtime, destination the Costantini brothers at St-Philibert. I was conscious of their feeling of friendship towards me, proven by their help and sustenance during the rebuilding of *Pen Duick*. I knew enough about the way they worked and the professionalism of their yard. But, most importantly, I know that Gilles, like me, holds by light craft. Now, I am convinced that this quality must be an important factor in a single-handed race. I considered all the aspects of this race at length and was subsequently assured of the need of two apparently contradictory characteristics: speed and ease of handling. Given that it is a race, speed is vital. So is handling. Without any help on board, I will have to helm and manoeuvre, navigate, cook and generally maintain the boat. Impossible to do on too big a boat, with too great an expanse of sail.

In Gilles' office I explained: 'In order to be quick it needs to be long. We both agree about this. Since the surface area of sail depends on its displaceable weight we are bound to use light – but strong – materials.'

'OK. And what will the length be?'

I had given this a lot of thought along the following lines: without actual experience, I was not really in a position to establish the size of boat compatible with my strength and attributes; therefore I must rely on others' experience, that is to say Chichester the winner's and the runner-up Hasler's. The former had been drained handling his twelve-metre cutter. The latter had raced well on an eight-metre folkboat.

'I think the right length will be ten metres,' I say.

'All right,' agrees Gilles.

The Costantinis built a Tarann plywood boat. During another meeting at St-Philibert, the twins proposed building one for me, at their own expense, which they would lend to me for the Transat and later use themselves.

'We are going to call her *Margilic V*. It is the name we give our family boats.'

Once Gilles had drawn up the plans, the yard began work in October 1962.

In this kind of race, obviously one's physical condition assumes fundamental importance. Whilst waiting to sail *Margilic V*, I train. Whenever naval service on the sweeper permits, I go to the stadium. Athletic strength is indispensable to a single-handed sailor. The four hundred metres is a long sprint which familiarises one with the pain barrier. I invariably practise the long jump and continue, as always, rope climbing. Every day I go through a routine of press-ups. The various activities which sailing involves – carrying sail bags, hoisting or gathering in sails, climbing up the mast – are muscular ones which do not permit one to be out of form or weak. I continue to sail *Pen Duick* as much as possible to stay in form. The human body is a remarkable machine which, when well maintained, can be unbelievably resilient.

My grand designs are suddenly put in jeopardy by an unforeseen circumstance. I receive a new posting: the Navy is sending me to the base at Bizerte. So all my plans are futile because I cannot see how, from Tunisia, I would be able to get involved in the future boat, and train and race. I am somewhat downcast, even though the

Commander of the Cherbourg dragon division, who knows of my plans, reassures me:

'Don't be too concerned, Tabarly. The officer at the postings office in Paris is an old training college friend. I have written a letter for you, explaining your situation to him. He is going to find some other posting for you. Everything will be OK.'

So it is with confidence that I go to The Nursery barracks in Paris, with a reference in my pocket. I stand in front of the officer as he reads the letter. He lays it down on his desk and looks up at me. Not an accommodating look. Sternly, and with finality, he tells me: 'Tabarly, you are not in the Navy to go sailing. The Bizerte posting will assist your development as an officer. So you will go to Tunisia. You may go now.'

I leave The Nursery very concerned and needing to find some way out, quick. I walk the Paris streets asking myself who might help me. Suddenly, I have a flash of inspiration. Kerviler – a skipper well known throughout the Navy, an author of a treatise on manoeuvres which is a naval college text, a yachtsman known for his skill at the helm, who often represents the Navy in Dragon Class races – might be able to lend me a hand. We know each other, since I crewed for him a few months previously bringing a Naica, purchased by the Navy for Brest Sailing Club, back from Gosport to Brest. Kerviler is the sports director and my final chance. I do not have far to go in The Nursery to find his office. We do not waste time on sailing reminiscences. Kerviler is a man who likes to get straight to the point.

'What can I do for you Tabarly? You appear somewhat anxious...'

'Yes, Commander, I am.'

I explain my troubles to him. Once I have concluded, he simply says, 'I will endeavour to sort it out.'

Which he does. Three days later, at Cherbourg, I am informed of my new destination. I am being posted to Lorient, where I will command an EDIC 9092 – a landing craft for infantry and tanks – which is 60m long, with a crew of fifteen.

Memories of the Open Sea

Besides a few landing exercises with the regiment based at Vannes, my duties are to reconnoitre the region's beaches suitable for EDIC landings. Each week I put forward a route to the staff for the following days. Quite often La Trinité serves as the night's port of call, so I am able to check on *Margilic V*'s progress and, later, that of *Pen Duick II*. From April 1963 *Margilic V* is in the water. I train, I sail and, with the Costantini brothers, take part in local pre-season races, before entering those of the RORC, the Fastnet being the most important. Whether in a crew or solo, these voyages teach me two things. On the one hand, *Margilic V*, given his dimensions, handles well whatever the weather and however his sails are set – if the RORC results were average that was due to the RORC's handicapping system which penalised boats with a light displacement. On the other, I demonstrate that there is no problem handling him alone and am confident that I could do the same with a notably larger boat.

'We need to design a stronger boat for this race,' I tell Gilles. '*Margilic V* forms the basis on which we must conceive *Pen Duick II*. What we need is a longer waterline, but – in spite of this – a lighter displacement, real sturdiness combined with a responsive helm, greater sail area whilst maintaining steady handling.'

From now on Gilles and I spend our time perfecting this wonder of the waves. I make pencil sketches in a school notebook and then Costantini adjusts and refines them.

At the outset, our ideas were somewhat at odds. I had learnt a great deal aboard *Margilic V*, a type of design incorporating a simple, straight-edged bilge. This is the part of the hull, usually curved, running between the keel and the topsides. An angled, rather than round, bilge is sharp. I personally preferred multiple bilges, comprising lower and central sections and a third along the vertical planking. Gilles baulked at this solution but I, the customer – without a penny, nevertheless still right – dug in and prevailed.

I will never forget this period, one of the most intense in my life. I had to concern myself with *Pen Duick II* the whole time and

Eric Tabarly

I had to keep myself in tip-top condition. The Costantinis had put *Margilic V* on sale on account of the costs due to be incurred with the new boat. In the meantime, I continued to prepare on board. If I feel lasting nostalgia for this time that is because it was marked by loyalty and friendship. Yet again, Gilles and Marc reassured me: 'You can pay when you can...' Admittedly, in the small world of traditional yachts, where everyone knew everybody, I was known to be a serious sailor. Beyond that I was unknown. And besides, the general public barely knew about the single-handed Transatlantic. It was our love of boats, and friendship, that served to bring the Costantini brothers and me together on this project.

'I am concerned about the sails' practicability,' I say to Gilles. 'I need size for speed, but not so much as to be unmanageable. They must be designed in such a way that I am not forced into complicated, back-breaking sail changes.'

I am influenced by reading Chichester's book, where he frequently laments his difficulties in manoeuvring and I do not want to find myself in the same situation.

We consider the question of rigging. I do not spend too long over the sloop or cutter options. Their mast heights and mainsail areas will demand too much physical effort. The ketch arrangement, of forward main mast and smaller mizzen at the stern, seems to me the best solution. Each sail has a smaller, more manageable surface area. Plus one should remember that with the North Atlantic wind the boat is sufficiently under-canvassed by design. Ketch rigging allows one to trim the boat from the helm, an important consideration for the single-handed sailing operation of automatic steering. Last of all, because of the light displacement allowing us a long deck and economy in sail size, we can have a large gap between the mainsail and mizzen, an effective arrangement.

If the design of the boat is almost settled on, the process of construction has yet to begin.

October passes by. Then November. As December begins, *Margilic V* is still not sold. It is not long since I finished paying off my debts to the Costantinis for the restoration of old *Pen Duick* and my finances are close to zero. As the end of December approaches, work on my new design has still not started. The start date for the second Transat is the following May 23, that is to say, less than six months away. Insidiously, morale ebbs away from me and I foresee having to stand down from participating.

Raised in the faith, for a long time I was a practising Catholic. Then one day I asked myself how come a loving God would permit so much crassness and misery in this life. Maybe he will let me know the answer in the hereafter. Whilst awaiting – not too intently – a reason, I do not call upon him in times of danger with the prayer, 'My God, do something...' If He has got me into this jam, then why would He then come and get me out of it?

Sometimes, however, I question my doubts. In fact, sometimes I have the impression of benefiting from His divine mercy and goodwill. Not long before Christmas 1963, when my chances of being ready for the Plymouth departure would seem to have vanished for good, friends let me know that they are advancing me 20,000 francs, no interest payable. This sum will only pay for part of the work but, when I tell the Costantinis that I now have this unexpected loan their smiles are unrestrained and Gilles says to me once again: 'Let's build your boat. You can pay the remainder when you are able.'

From now on, things go quicker. Gilles and I together agree on the following dimensions for the boat: a 10m long waterline and an overall length of 13.60m; 2.20m draught and 3.40m beam.

Thanks to the multiple bilges, the hull would narrow in a significant manner, well above the waterline, giving the penetration of a slim boat, but, if it listed, it would have the stability of a wider boat. This hull's design was the result of the endless evening conversations Gilles and I had during that interminable end of year.

The start of 1964 seemed similarly never ending. Never ending and stressful at the same time. Whilst the yard is ready to fit the 15m-lengths of ply planking onto the wooden frame – reinforced by metal members – I must organise the provision of various materials: the rigging, the deck fittings, the sails.

On New Year's Eve, I slip on a beam lying around in the Costantinis' yard and twist my ankle. My entrance on crutches at the Paris boat show draws attention. After the normal kidding and good wishes for a speedy recovery, I am due to profit from the dispute between two recent nautical reviews. Sometime before, my friend Alain Gliksman, editor in chief of the magazine *Neptune*, had convinced me to sign a deal with his publication, giving him the exclusive rights to my account of the race. His competitors from *Cahiers de Yachting*, since I am at the show, do not delay in forming a group around me.

'Éric, you should have signed with us. We are in a different league from the others and, what is more, we will prove it to you. Do you need equipment? Ask and it's yours.' They take me from one exhibition stand to the next. They can provide me with everything I need and I do not have to spend a penny. No need to coax me into accepting these amazing gifts: masts and booms, rigging, winches, sail material, lines, blocks.

'You see,' says one of the *Cahiers du Yachting* team to me. And again: 'You see, thanks to us, you can get everything you require. That is the proof that we are more influential than *Neptune*.'

'That may be so but I signed a contract with that publication and I am not able to cancel it. Thank you for all your kind attention. I am very grateful!'

CHAPTER 7

SAILING SINGLE-HANDED

Time drags. Time flies by. Time is short.

Three variations that I have experienced, been subjected to, suffered, while getting the boat ready. It seems a long time ago now, almost frozen in time, that the project had been taken on without knowing how it would be financed. Time unravels when one crosses the dividing line from dreaming or hoping to encountering a reality full of stumbling blocks. It slackens or seems to acccelerate as the date of the deadline approaches.

The hull finally starts to look like a boat. The cabin has been fitted out with two bunks, a galley, the chart table and storage for supplies and equipment. To save money, I spend each weekend painting the hull interior with the help of my father. I'm stressed out by the building of the keel, with its bulb shaped design. The foundry, which was originally meant to deliver it by the end of March, has now assured me it will be ready by April 5. This delay is not without consequences. It means that I will not, through want of time, be able to get to know my new boat, practise, and get on with changes and alterations.

April 5 is nevertheless a significant date. That morning *Pen Duick II* was launched. I am on deck. The boat glides with an impressive air, down the rolling track, running from the yard to the sea. The hull lowers into the churning foam, the stern immersed to the cockpit, before righting itself. Then the boat, still without any ballast, bobs about like a cork. Carefully, he is towed as far as the

Eric Tabarly

La Trinité quay, where a mobile crane signals the end of his first, short navigation. He is lifted out of the water and placed on a trailer. Wedged and strapped, he takes to the road. Destination: the naval shipyard at Lorient.

Gilles Costantini is strong both in person and character. With his father, and then running the business himself, he has built more than six hundred yachts designed for racing and winning. Boats which compete with the rest at La Rochelle and Bénodet and whose owners – bankers and industrialists – are audacious enough to confront the British in their home waters – not without honour.

As teenagers, Gilles and I had crewed together and sometimes competed against one another. Our friendship goes way back. Boats are our passion: their form, function and looks. Each time a new construction leaves his boatyard, Gilles is unable to hide a hint of emotion briefly clouding his clear-eyed gaze. He is an artist. At that time there were no computers to impose their design criteria. It was a time when boats bore their architects' imprint. There was Nicholson, and Cornu. There was Costantini. Each had a particular style. Gilles without doubt inherited his artistic talent from his father but, even more, he claimed, from his paternal grandfather. His name was Virgil. A native of Mestre, on the outskirts of Venice, he lived by his painting, a calm Italian of few words. Some of his works had even been exhibited in Paris, London and Tokyo. Virgil loved to travel. Having criss-crossed Italy and Switzerland, he was drawn to Scotland and England. It was on a thirty-metre yacht, *Aziadée* – the purchase included crew! – that he dropped anchor at La Trinité-sur-Mer at the start of the century. At that time, the town lived by its merchant vessels. The Trinitains filled their holds with wooden props which they re-sold in Cardiff, and returned with a freight of coal, cheaper than the equivalent mined in Northern France. Gino was born and married a girl from Vannes. From this union came the twins, Gilles and Marc. When Gilles talks about his grandfather, Virgil, and his father it is always with pride and affection. 'Artists,' he says, reflectively. Like him.

Memories of the Open Sea

Just before *Pen Duick II* was loaded onto the trailer, he surveyed him jigging on the water. 'You've got a pretty boat, Éric,' he said to me. In his voice you can catch the contentment of the father recognising his offspring.

Not long before launching, the Navy flew to my rescue by facilitating various finishing touches to be carried out by a unit of the shipyard dealing with general responsibilities. One of its tasks is the maintenance of the Navy's sailing club boats and its head, the 'IDT' – works engineer – Henaff, is a big yachting enthusiast. Things pan out well. To tell the truth, it is rather more than the finishing touches which will be attended to: fitting the keel is, for example, a significant piece of work. I would never have been ready on time without this vital support. As for myself, I had withdrawn from my duties on board the EDIC in order to devote all my time to preparations.

After several days work, the bulb-shaped keel, deep and narrow, is in. The chart table and kitchen, the electric circuit and drawplates, the dinghy and anchor chain-pipes, masts and rudder, sails cut by Victor Tonnerre: everything is in place.

The naming ceremony takes place in an almost empty shipyard on Saturday May 9. *Pen Duick II* is a name with a ring to it, which I like and which saves me from racking my brains for something new. 'No.1' is laid up in a corner of the Costantini yard. Gilles' wife, Odile, performs the christening. The champagne bottle breaks unequivocally against the bow: a good augury according to sailors' superstition – and rubbish, as far as I am concerned.

On Sunday May 10 *Pen Duick II* casts off from Lorient to head to La Trinité. A significant moment, long in the waiting. For all that, I do not feel anything special. We are first and foremost ready to test this new boat, to verify if he is actually what I expected. It gives me the opportunity to note that, because of the material's elasticity, the mainsail is rather too concave. Victor Tonnerre, who is on board, accepts this and tells me:

'Don't worry. I'll fix it.'

'You'll have to get a move on.'

'I'll get a move on.'

I have only a few days left to finish preparing before heading for Plymouth. I mount the self-steering. A few hours trials to see what it is like: no problem close to the wind, but not so good on a beam reach; anyhow, I no longer have time to set this problem right. With Gilles, my father and brother, I once more check that the blocks are running smoothly and that certain equipment, for example the highfield levers, are correctly positioned. Some re-sawing of protruding bolts and the filling of a few suspect looking cracks is required as is the storing of reserve sails, hinge greasing and deck scrubbing. I chip in, inspect and check. Time flies by at a dizzying pace.

My mother asked me to install an emitter-receiver radio set. I go along with this. She says the set reassures her. From my perspective, there are two drawbacks. Firstly, it gets through a lot of electricity. Secondly, if it stops working and I cannot contact her, Mum will worry even more.

May 16 I am ready to head off to Plymouth. The boat is ready. Well, almost.

My mother had come on board to kiss me and to place a medal bearing the image of Our Lady Star of the Sea on my chart table. At that moment, in the way she looks at me, I comprehend the measure of her love and tenderness towards me.

'I've got to go Mum ... '

I take her back on shore in my dinghy. She climbs out. She forces herself to smile but her eyes are brimming with tears. All at once I feel that I am to blame for inflicting all this on her.

'Don't worry Mum. I am coming back; everything is going to be all right.'

The sky is a magnificent blue. La Trinité-sur-Mer goes about its business as usual and barely seems to notice *Pen Duick II* as he heads into the distance. On the slipway my mother's frail silhouette fades and then vanishes from view.

CHAPTER 8

VALENTINE IS NOT A GIRL; CHICHESTER IS THE FAVOURITE

It was Whitsun Monday. Leaving the Mewstone rock and Yealm estuary behind him, *Pen Duick II* headed into the tree-lined harbour at Plymouth. With my father and Jean-Paul Aymon, the *France-Soir* reporter who came aboard as we briefly docked at Brest, we catch sight of Charles II's old citadel, a fortified lookout from long ago.

Under sail, *Pen Duick II* made his way silently along a coast, in whose bracing waters only British bathers would splash about, enjoying themselves beneath a menacing sky. Suddenly Drake's Island appears as though it has been unhooked from the land. The island holds a certain fascination for me: on account of its name, that of Francis Drake, Admiral and pirate and legendary sailor who, three centuries ago in this harbour, anticipated the approach of the invincible Armada with his concealed squadron. Drake, fêted and ennobled, before falling into disgrace, was one of those sailors who filled my dreams as a boy.

Soon we are at the far end of the harbour. The port stretches along each side: starboard, towards the old barbican quarter, and to port, towards the Stonehouse dock basin, behind the swing bridge to Millbay. Boathouses and cranes and deserted quays form a rather lugubrious bank holiday scene.

Eric Tabarly

'We're not going to moor here,' says my father under his breath: 'It's depressing.'

He is right. We carry on, under reduced sail, hoping to find a more welcoming spot, and finally we pick up a mooring in deep water in front of the yacht club. Beneath the citadel's walls, bathers are scattered around the municipal swimming pool, determined to get a tan beneath a very pale sun.

It is May 18. We leave in five days time. You might believe that I had all the time in the world but, as the saying goes, I am in fact chasing the game. *Pen Duick II* is a long way from ready. Although I am not much of a worrier, I am a little concerned now. There is a wide range of things still left to organise: fitting metal runners to take an upside down compass above my bunk, so that I can check on my course without getting up; putting a coat of anti slip paint on the deck; finalising provisions; placing a plexiglass cover on the astrodome I got off an old Sunderland flying boat, found at the Poulmic aeronaval base, so I can keep an eye on both rigging and sea; getting a Hermes speedometer, which I was unable to do in France.

These five days will pass quickly enough – partly because I need to attend meetings and receptions with the other competitors. It is not a time for dilly-dallying.

'I am going ashore to get the lowdown on the race rules.'

'I'll come with you,' Jean-Paul Aymon tells me.

'I'll hold the fort,' says my father.

The honorary secretary of the Royal Western Yacht Club is a gentleman with a very British moustache, rather like Daninos' *Major Thompson*. Drawing on his pipe, which gives off a mild aroma, he welcomes me from his position at the bar and hands me all manner of documents. He then points out that mine is the only boat moored in the harbour.

'Your rivals are in the dock basin. That is where,' he expressly tells me, 'the inspections and weighing will take place.'

Who are my rivals? Apart from the five who participated in the first Transat, whose faces I know from yachting magazines, they are unknown to me.

We meet at the reception given by the Commander of Plymouth Naval base, Sir Nigel Henderson.

The first I observe – not without admiration – is Francis Chichester. There are men with a destiny and he is one of them. A strong, square chin suggests his forcefulness. He was a forester, founder of flying clubs, a pilot, originator of a particular navigational method, author, record holder in 1931 for early long distance solo flights and, during the war, editor of navigation instructions for the Air Ministry. A seasoned sailor, he has raced since 1954. After winning the first Transat, of his own accord he made another solo Atlantic crossing aboard his famous *Gypsy Moth III* in thirty days, an achievement praised by both President Kennedy and the Duke of Edinburgh. Once more he is using *Gypsy Moth III*, a cutter constructed with mahogany planking on an oak frame. Overall length: 12.06m; waterline: 8.43m; beam: 3.10m; displacement: 13 tonnes. He has not changed his great circle route for this second race.

Valentine Howells had prompted a silly misunderstanding on the part of some non-specialist journalists. Not being particularly well known, a few reporters, on account of his first name, had referred to him as the 'mysterious woman skipper'. However, Valentine is not an exclusively female name amongst Anglo-Saxons. Howells is big boned, 6'3" tall, with a slab of a face and weightlifter's arms, known by Chichester as 'the black bearded Viking'. Not exactly a 'mysterious woman skipper'. His *Akka* is a 10.70m steel sloop, weighing twelve tonnes, and will be setting off again on the orthodromic route. Thirty-eight years old and formerly in the Merchant Navy, he now farms in Pembrokeshire. On top of this he has fished for crayfish since the 1960 race and owns a restaurant with his wife at Saundersfoot.

I see David Lewis, a native son, having been born in Plymouth. He was then brought up in New Zealand, before returning to

Eric Tabarly

England to finish his studies and take up medicine. In 1963 he had a catamaran built. Following some problems sailing off Ireland, he has plumped for a cutter's Bermuda rigging and bowsprit. He lives on his boat. Of independent character, in the wake of this second Transat, he would go on to sell his cottage and practice, in order to make a three year circumnavigation. *Rehu Moana* is 12.30m long and has a 5.18m beam – but a catamaran of his weight cannot, one imagines, be all that quick.

Bill Howell is the only Australian in the race. Aged thirty-eight, he gave up his dental practice in Wimbledon to sail from Europe to Vancouver, via Panama and Tahiti. He holds the record of twenty-four days, for the fastest South Atlantic crossing. His *Stardrift* is a 10.40m long cutter with a 2.50m beam, 1.54m draught, weighing eight tonnes. It is a nice looking boat of classic design, somewhat old now, having left its boatyard in 1937 – built to last.

With Jean Lacombe, a forty-eight year old photojournalist based in the US, I can contemplate a proper conversation. He was the only Frenchman involved in the first Transat and I am immediately at ease with him. He is a relaxed man, who is self contained and observant, and who likes to be alone at sea.

His first Atlantic crossing was in *Hippocampe*, a little boat he designed himself: 'I had set out from Toulon. It took fifteen months to get to the other side...' In 1960, his boat *Cap Horn* was the smallest entrant at 6.50m. This time he will helm the same size of boat again, a plastic sloop, weighing 1,300 kilos, called *Golif*. It stands to reason that Lacombe will come in last. He is aware of this but it does not bother him. He is a strong minded and brave man.

There is quite a variety entering this Transat. For example, Alec Rose, at fifty-five among the oldest, was a market gardener and then a grocer at Southsea, on the south coast.

Following five years spent transforming a salvaged dinghy into a yacht, he sells his shop and sets off for two years in the North Sea and the Baltic, then returns to sell the boat and upgrade to *Lively Lady*, a 10.97m cutter, weighing nine tonnes. He takes up the reins of his business once more and trains every day, whatever the conditions.

Hasler is a retired naval officer and national hero, on account of his involvement in the World War II 'Operation Frankton', a sabotage raid with canoes on Bordeaux port, intended to destroy cargo ships enforcing the blockade. In a boat that was barely eight metres long, Hasler finished second in the 1960 Transat. *Jester*'s wooden mast is rigged with a junk's battened sail and without shrouds. He is 7.89m long and weighs 2.50 tonnes and, with no cockpit, has all of his competitors wondering. Lieutenant-Colonel Hasler, notwithstanding, is optimistic: 'This is the boat in which I competed in the first single-handed race. Whilst he is not that quick he is extremely easily handled by one man. I am taking the northern route, where I hope to find favourable winds'.

Together with Bob Bunker, Mike Ellison is one of the youngest participants. Both are twenty-eight. Ellison is in the Merchant Navy. He was due to take part in the first race, but had to pull out at the last minute because of various glitches. For the 1964 race a friend has lent him his 10.90m long schooner, *Ilala*, constructed in plastic and notable for having a junk's two sails and no shrouds.

Bunker, it has to be said, is a law unto himself. Employed at the Guinness brewery in Park Royal, London, his voyages to date have been in a sail-assisted canoe. To compete in the race he has ruined himself with the purchase of *Vanda Caelea,* a clinker built sloop, 7.62m and weighing five tonnes. Following his engagement on the eve of departure, he received forty-eight bottles of Guinness from his brewery. Bunker wittily said: 'For my first attempt, I can survive at sea for fifty days even though I only have beer for forty-eight.' Then there is Michael Butterfield – not his real name – a thirty-two-year-old lawyer who, signing up for the race, declared that: 'For various reasons I wish to remain anonymous.' *Misty Miller* is an 8.84m catamaran and, with seven hundred and fifty kilos of ballast, weighs 2.65 tonnes. He chose the southern route, with its favourable winds, and is amongst the favourites.

Eric Tabarly

First a planetarium keeper, after that supervisor of a dairy company, next an architect and, finally, promoter of a twenty-four-bed hospital, Geoffrey Chafley, born in Calcutta, is new to single-handed racing but not afraid to buy *Ericht II*, a twenty-eight-year-old cutter of 9.50m and eight tonnes. He also took the decision to go via the southern route.

Derek Kelsall, a good looking oil engineer operating in Africa and Texas, is a trimaran enthusiast, sailing them in the Pacific. About *Folatre*, 10.66m long with ketch rigging, he does not appear one hundred percent certain. Built in a hurry, only five days remained for trials. Concerned, he confides that: 'This boat is an unknown quantity for me.' All the same, he was designed by the most reputable trimaran architect of that period, the American Arthur Piver.

Both Axel Pedersen and Robin Macurdy are forty-five years old. The former, a Danish emigrant to New Zealand, made it back to Europe at the end of a two year voyage on his 8.54m ketch *Marco Polo*, but radioed to say that he would not be able to make the departure date on account of adverse winds. The latter is a doctor. To acclimatise himself to solitude he had sailed his 12.35m ketch, *Tammy Nucie*, to the Faroe Islands. The shape of his head, a receding hairline, and glasses give him the air of an intellectual; he harbours few illusions about his likely finishing position. Sipping a whisky, he philosophically admits that: 'My boat is the heaviest in the flotilla. I am not expecting to win, rather to arrive at Newport in a respectable position.'

Sloops and cutters, schooners and ketches and multihulls reflect the full spectrum of competitors' – not ordinary people's – temperaments.

When I moor at the basin quay for the formal checks my adversaries are intrigued by *Pen Duick II*. Some wonder whether he is not too light, and therefore too fragile, to face up to the ocean's furies, whilst others reckon him too big for a solo sailor. I am in no doubt: my boat has been built very solidly, following consideration of the substantial pressures he will have to withstand. The ply used is multiple and significantly stronger than the standard type. The sail sizes have been the subject of detailed conversations with Victor Tonnerre, the Lorient sail-maker. I wanted a relatively small mainsail so that reducing it would not be too tiring. To do this I had chosen a screw operated rotating boom; a fundamentally sound system, though I had also stipulated reefing points in the sails, in case something went wrong with the winder.

I am happy with my ketch sail set-up, which will be the best bet for solo sailing. I realise that this sail arrangement will entail several more manoeuvres for me. But the ease of manoeuvre with its consequence – less tiredness – make up for this.

Francis Chichester wanted to look over my boat. Elegant as ever, in a double-breasted navy blazer and white shirt and club tie, he steps on board. I act as his guide.

Chichester is both a very correct and a very tall Englishman. The maximum standing height beneath the deck head is only 1.50 metres, so, to move about, he has to hunker somewhat. As a seafarer, he knows that in a boat's cabin one is either sitting down or in one's bunk. I did not want a cabin roof protruding too high above the deck. Standing in the way of the wind, it would act partly as a fair drag on the boat; also, it could get badly damaged by a breaker.

My visitor has a knowledgeable look at the steering station positioned inside, to the right of the entry steps, surmounted by the plexiglass dome and nips through to the cabin amidships, which contains a galley, equipped with stove and folding table, mini-sink, and motorbike saddle to sit on. Directly opposite, my chart table and, again, a motorbike seat are positioned on the starboard side. It is a solid ensemble design, allowing the chair and table to swing on its axis; thanks to a braking system, it can remain horizontal in relation to the roll.

The single-handed Transatlantic tests one's endurance and I was not neglecting anything that might help life on board. This boils down to navigating, eating and sleeping. Light enters the cabin via four plexiglass squares screwed onto the deck. Twelve millimetres thick, they are positioned above the chart table, the kitchen, the amidship cabin and the fo'c'sle.

On his way up and out, Chichester notices a narrow, empty compartment to the side of the ladder and beneath the hatch. He looks at me quizzically. I explain: 'While sailing, I like the cabin hatch to remain open. This is where I am going to put sails and also my oilskins dripping water, and keep the cabin dry.'

Thanks to Howells, I had an introduction to the Mashford brothers' boatyard, some distance away, in order to modify the mainsail dimensions. That was one concern. The speedometer was another. I absolutely need one so that I can gauge *Pen Duick II*'s speed. I do not yet know him well enough to gauge it from effects like the sound of water against the bow, the length of water streaks along the planking, or the strength of the wake because such signs vary from boat to boat.

My Aunt Mony came to join me. She shops for final provisions – fruit, eggs, matches – which the Naval Services at Lorient had not been able to organise in time for the La Trinité stocking. This had all been done by my father, down to the storing of charcoal, placed in paper sacks by my mother and destined for my stove.

Aunt Mony frets about how tired my father and I look. It is true that, for weeks now, preparing the boat has hardly left a moment for relaxation.

May 23 1964. The race commences at 10am. I still have an hour to spend fitting the Walker speedometer, which was delivered late last night. Following various controls, I had left the Great Western tidal docks in the afternoon and am now moored, like the other competitors, in the outer dock at Millbay.

Installing the speedometer is not a cakewalk. First, I have to fix the instrument to *Pen Duick II*'s transom, by the self-steering. Then a hole is required in the deck, to lead the transmission wires to the meter, attached to the stern deckhead. But, between it and the transom, there are a number of other compartments that need to be drilled through. Access is difficult. The clock is ticking towards departure time. I work with maniacal intensity.

The speedometer is fixed at 9.30am. Without these last minute jobs I would have had the rigging up for a while. The others are on the move – slowly, on account of the light breeze – to the harbour. I remain a good mile from the departure line and my father is still on board, together with two journalists from *Neptune*. The launch, which is meant to come and pick them up, has gone to refuel on the opposite side of the harbour. At 9.50am it has still not appeared.

My predicament is beginning to get embarrassing. My father and the two reporters remain with me. I cannot make out if the cannon blast I hear is the first or the second: annoying, because the third shot starts the race.

Pen Duick II makes his way across the harbour. I take a quick look at the dominating feature of the esplanade. A large crowd has gathered for the event. All the way to Drake's Island, the sea heaves with a diversity of boats: private yachts, dinghies, motor launches, old tubs and an amphibious car. An impressive flotilla, almost overflowing with passengers, which will follow the competitors as far as the high sea. My father and the journalists quietly curse the launch, of which there is still no sign, for not picking them up. As for me: a decision is required – from the third cannon report there is ten minutes' grace before the race rules take full effect. I can't really turn up at the starting line for a single-handed race with a gang on board. The reporters came with a rowing dinghy, which I am towing. This prompts me: 'I am going to luff a bit to slow the boat down, so that you can get into your dinghy,' I say to my *Neptune* associates.

As *Pen Duick II* approaches a standstill, my passengers – not without difficulty – take their place in the dinghy, which is barely three metres long and totters beneath their weight, not far from capsize. One last handshake. The three of them, using an oar I lend them to scull, cast off. I pick up speed to head to the departure line, a quarter of a mile between a Navy sweeper and the Melampus buoy.

Eric Tabarly

I am not on time, and still too far away to hear the warning signal indicating 'ten minutes' or to see the jury boat's flag being hoisted, at the same time as the cannon report.

Fifty metres from the line, I luff up, as sailors like to say, allowing the sails to flap against the headwind. There is a reasonably strong northerly wind. Close by me are both Chichester and the black *Gypsy Moth* and Hasler aboard his canary yellow *Jester*. Beyond, I glimpse a group of contestants describing circles in the water.

I do not feel any great emotion. Thirty-three years old, this is my first Atlantic crossing under sail. Many times I asked myself if, at the moment of heading off into the wide ocean, I would experience doubt. As it happens, nothing. When everything starts to happen I do not have time for feelings and their analysis. I feel as ready as if I was heading off on a cruise. The mental element is not an issue for me; being alone holds no fears.

CHAPTER 9

THE UNDERMINING INFLUENCE OF A DROP OF WATER

Ten am. At the same time that the cannon shot explodes and echoes, the jury boat flags are lowered: departure is signalled. Kelsall's trimaran is the first to cross the line, followed by Hasler aboard *Jester* with his junk rigging, shrouded in spray. *Pen Duick II* is side by side with Chichester's *Gypsy Moth*, with Valentine Howells' sloop close behind.

My departure is not all it might be. Following my last minute alterations, I did not know my chronometric reading and, more immediately, I did not have time to organise and put up my eighty-metre-square red and black spinnaker. I would have been able to set up the pole, get the light sail out of its bag and attach the sheets. I wouldn't have been reduced to slapping the halyard. In fact, I would have been able to have been first across the line. The point is I should have been ready on time. I get the self-steering started. There is disarray all around, on the sea and up above. A hybrid armada, one hundred strong, is dispersed about the harbour, swirling around the competitors, impinging on their manoeuvres, risking collision.

There is a light wind but my spinnaker, nylon and light, fills out and, straightaway, *Pen Duick II* picks up speed. The manoeuvre took me ten minutes. The passengers on an overtaking launch appear genuinely impressed and applaud. With my sheets in order and having turned off the self-steering and taken the helm again, once out of the harbour, a slight following wind and the hindrance of lapping water combine to make him roll. Although it is barely filled with wind the spinnaker pulls *Pen Duick II* along nicely, so that I soon pass both Chichester and Ellison, on his schooner, *Ilala*. Now only Kelsall's trimaran is in front of me. As my boat picks up speed, to starboard I notice Valentine Howells' sloop swinging about like a weathervane. He has been hit by some Sunday sailors who came too close. I am not sure if his boat has been significantly damaged. Finding Valentine, with his colourful personality, both interesting and sympathetic, I hope that he can continue in the race.

The gap between Kelsall's trimaran and *Pen Duick II* narrows, and *Jester* is now trailing in his wake. All that can be seen of Hasler is his head, rather like an officer standing in a tank's turret. He handles the boat from inside the cabin, in which he has made an opening. I am told that the ex-naval officer was considering having a dentist's chair installed, capable of being inclined for navigating, cooking and sleeping purposes and no need to move.

Fully loaded motorboats, ploughing through the water and augmenting the uneasy swell, continue to follow the competitors. I take a long look at this collection of boats to check if the launch my father should have been on is there, but it is not.

It is now 11.30am. The accompanying flotilla goes about and heads back to Plymouth. The rain starts to come down heavily. In spite of the poor visibility, it is still possible to tell that Kelsall's trimaran is falling even further behind me. Only Chichester seems to be sticking close to *Pen Duick II*. Before long he fades away too. The coast has been swallowed by open sea. I am truly alone in this corner of sea.

When I sit on my Harley-Davidson seat, positioned by the stove and the larder cupboard and the soft water pump above the basin, everything is within hand's reach, including the ravioli I am re-heating, and fresh fruit. At 2pm I grant myself a little siesta. Lying on the windward bunk, so as to be protected by a curtain against the boat's roll, rather than being knocked to pieces against the planking, I periodically cast an eye at the upturned compass, screwed to the ceiling, and listen to the noises made by the boat. The hull, whose acoustics leave something to be desired, magnifies the noise that the running sea makes against him. Sounds I am going to become familiar with.

I get up at 3pm and tidy up on deck. Since the tack has changed, the boat's motion has become more comfortable, with the current from astern. All of a sudden a muffled engine noise emerges from the fog and a big launch arrives at full speed, spray flying around its bows. Without delay, she is directly alongside *Pen Duick II*. I make out the two reporters from *Neptune*. And my father. 'You have had some chance finding me in this pea-souper!' I exclaim happily.

'I was not going to leave you like that!' cries my father.

'Do you know where the others are?'

'Other than *Folatre*, about five miles behind, we didn't see anyone,' my father shouts out.

We say our final goodbyes and the launch heads off back to Plymouth, vanishing into the haze. This is the moment in which I experience a genuine feeling of loneliness. The meeting with my father has moved me. But then my thoughts turn one hundred percent to the boat and getting the same out of him, particularly when the wind, like now, is capricious. It subsides at the end of the day, forcing me to reinstate the spinnaker, which blows about ineffectively. In the still sea, the boat rocking me just a little, I reckon that, since there is nothing else to do, I might as well have something to eat. Night has fallen. I am ensconced on my motorbike seat devouring my spaghetti with onion sauce, when the wind resumes from the south west. The night is humid and, as for visibility, 'you can't,' as another sailor put it, 'see your own hand from five metres'. *Pen Duick II* is heading west, in the main shipping lane. Ships heading in from the ocean or the Irish sea and bound for English southern ports, the Baltic or North Sea cross my bows or pass me by almost continuously. Only their lights are visible in the mist – white, green or red, depending on their direction – plus those illuminating the superstructure.

The international marine code decreed that sailing boats have priority. In practice, freighters and tankers need to see me long enough in advance so as to change course. A yacht's lights are not exactly powerful and, quite often, they are not spotted before it is too late for a big steamer to do anything. So I remain at the helm until daybreak. It is 5am before I feel confident to allow myself to lie down and freshen up.

The self-steering engaged, I set the alarm for 7.30am before slipping into my bunk.

Sunday May 24. The vibration suggesting a propeller wakes me at the same time as the alarm starts ringing. This noise is discernible in calm weather and signals the presence of a boat.

Even before I am up on deck, I can tell the fog has thickened and that there is no point in straining my eyes in order to make out – absolutely nothing. By contrast, one can hear a concert of foghorns booming into this eerie atmosphere from all directions. I can safely say that I do not feel relaxed. The knocking sound of the propeller becomes louder as it gets nearer; it is joined at regular intervals by the sounding of the ship's horn. I feel helpless. The wind has died completely, leaving a wake-less *Pen Duick II* as if nailed to this part of the sea, sails swinging listlessly.

The horn blasts become deafening, so it is difficult to tell which direction the vessel is coming from. I am also using my fog horn but am aware that it stands little chance of being heard.

The suspense is nerve wracking, almost to the point of physical pain. I can only hope that I am not in the way of the ship's course, whose engines make an impressive din. I feel like a cyclist who has erred onto a motorway, floundering in the fog and weighed down.

All of a sudden the racket is so close that I divine that he is now passing in front of my bows. I say 'divine' purposefully, because I cannot see it. What makes me realise that it has passed across my bows is *Pen Duick II* being lifted up on its wake. Slowly the rumbling presence moves away. I let out a big sigh. Ouf!

I am spared having to mark time only because of the two to three knot current which, thankfully, heads me in the right direction. I still need to negotiate the Scilly Isles. A light west-northwest breeze picks up and *Pen Duick II* is able to make his way out of these rocky regions without incident. I could count the hours of sleep I have had on the fingers of one hand. In this kind of race fatigue is the fearsome enemy you cannot concede ground to. I snuggle into my bunk.

Monday May 25. The breeze, which had become fresher during the night, stiffens again and *Pen Duick II* ploughs a seven to eight knot furrow through a fog which continues to stop me from taking a reading. By the afternoon the wind gives out and I am obliged to head further south.

There are chores to attend to of tidying up and carrying out inspections. At the same time I wait for light to penetrate through this atmosphere's dense blanket.

I am lucky to be able to take part in this race. Chance can take the form of a guiding hand. If it had not been for Captain Kerviler, I would currently be stationed in Bizerte. Without him there would be no *Pen Duick II*. I had already been fortunate when an anonymous benefactor had made the restoration of my veteran *Pen Duick* , stagnating at La Trinité, possible. I have always known that, as I grow older, this classic boat will stay with me and that, whatever is required, I will ensure he keeps going.

Tuesday May 26. A sailor's moods are variable. When, early in the morning, I put my nose outside, I am conscious of a sharp fall in the temperature, as the cold bites into me. My teeth might not be chattering, but I am shivering in my marine jersey which I wear next to my skin till about midday when the sun finally bursts through the clouds and disperses the fog, to reveal a splendid blue sky. Immediately, my spirits lift. A big coastguard plane – a Shackleton – flies over at low altitude, circles me and heads off. His dropping by delights me and means that my position will be transmitted to my parents and my mother will know I'm OK. A little later on a cargo ship, the *Factor* of Liverpool, makes a detour to greet me.

And then, not long after that, my self-steering starts to play up. Having just disengaged the autopilot and fastened the helm, I lift the equipment up and discover that a wooden collar has worn out. I am not in a position to repair it. This is the worst complication that I could be faced with. It is clear to tell that if my autopilot cannot be used – the direct consequence of what has happened – I will have to stay at the helm throughout the day and, at night, take the boat out of commission so that I can sleep. In which case the single-handed Transatlantic is lost before it has begun. With my morale at rock bottom, I step back into the cockpit. And there I make an unexpected, very welcome discovery: with the helm fastened, *Pen Duick II* maintains his course. I would never have thought that boat design might be the source of such joyful revelations. My happiness, however, is checked. Who can say whether such a true course could be held in strong winds in the same manner as when the weather is, more or less, favourable?

At the same time that I was pondering this, the weather keeps changing. The morning was overcast, humid. At midday the sun shone. Low clouds return in the afternoon, bringing an icy drizzle and a southerly wind. The barometer fell drastically. Amongst the rigging the wind began to whistle hard. Aided by a crosswind *Pen Duick II* accelerates.

Sensing that it would be a lively night, I stretched out on the starboard bunk, but was unable to sleep. A full scale din rages in the cabin. Waves grind and knock the boat and I feel as though I am getting mixed in a cocktail shaker within a drum. In spite of my efforts to curl up, *Pen Duick II*'s kicks are so violent that my eyes remain wide open, fixed on the overhead compass registering each swerve.

Memories of the Open Sea

Outside, the wind does not let up. The time arrives at midnight to let the 29.58m yankee down and replace it with the No.1 jib, which measures 12.70m. The Genoa staysail of 16.40m gives way to a small – 11.20m – staysail. These operations are not casually undertaken with a force six wind and the boat pushing along at ten knots on a choppy sea. The drenched rigging needs to be hauled in and the new sails raised from a spray lashed deck in constant movement beneath my feet. The wind having altered its force and shifted to the southwest, I trim the sails as best I can to remain on a westerly course. I am soaked through and knackered, too. When, at 2am I turn in, the pandemonium on the boat doesn't stop me from sleeping.

Wednesday May 27. The wind has slackened; I put the mainsail up again. The raging wind has quietened. *Pen Duick II* moves on at a more sedate pace.

Thursday May 28. The roll, the thwack of the sails, the boom swinging from one side to another making the blocks creak, all combine to wake me. These irritating sound effects are accompanied by the hammering rain pouring down on the deck. If it is not the ocean spray then it is the heavens opening that keeps me constantly soaked.

The swell is big and *Pen Duick II* moves up and down like a seesaw. Having lowered the jibs and trimmed the mainsail, the wind dies down and I take advantage of the calm to attempt to fix the self-steering. It almost goes without saying that it is not an easy job. Lifting the apparatus up and onto the deck does not present a problem. The next thing is to replace the gudgeon bearing with a plastic tube end, held in place with copper wire. This involves stretching across the back of it and leaning over the instrument panel to get to the broken piece. Beneath my oilskins I am conscious of the chilling effect of water drops, malignly making their way down my spine. The downpour does not let up. With the boat heeled right over, the gunwale digs into my stomach and sides. As the boat sways in the swell, my arms and even head get fully submerged in the sea. It is the clip securing the self-steering wire that is worn. The only way to bring this little game to an end is to put a small section of plastic pipe in the tube and secure it with the copper wire. I lose track of the time spent on this repair, but finally I get it done. How long it will last remains uncertain, but for now it works. The rain keeps pouring down. Entering via the oilskin sleeves, water trickles down my stomach and back. The cussedness of a single drop of water which, unerringly, takes the most discomforting route.

Back in the cabin I change. I put on moist clothing, for nothing will dry below decks. For morale, and in order to observe the naval tradition of something special for Thursday's menu, I let some pre-prepared chicken chasseur simmer gently and treat myself to a fine meal.

Pen Duick II is now about four hundred miles from Ireland, the closest land to me. Climbing back on deck, I find a little bird with bluish feathers and a yellow, pointed beak, protruding from below a round head. It is not a seabird; most probably it had the misfortune to be cast up by a current of rising air and then driven away from land by the wind above. He is dying. When I make towards him, he is not much more than an inert blur beneath the storm.

There is never a dull moment on board. When the sun puts in an appearance again, I decide to put up the aerial of my radio set. I try to call, without success; perhaps I should admit to a certain aversion to all things electrical – and even mechanical. All the voyages I had previously made were aboard boats without this equipment and, nevertheless, I acquitted myself reasonably well. All the same, I would have liked to have got in touch, so as to reassure my parents.

It is a calm night. In the log I record that, 'Sleeping only one and a half hours at a stretch, I am not running too big a risk of being blown off course should the wind change.' To give an example, if the wind moves from north to northwest, *Pen Duick II* will change course, veering in a south westerly direction, rather than heading west. At an average speed of seven knots, after an hour I will find myself four or five miles south of my plotted course. This is no catastrophe. Everyone has to sleep now and again; in this respect my competitors and I are all in the same boat. The important thing for me is, as far as possible, to sleep in little stretches, so that this particular problem does not affect me any more than it does the others.

Pilot charts are the result of serious work and can be used for reference with confidence. Having gathered innumerable empirical data they are categorical that, at this time of year, in these waters, the dominant winds are westerly, a fact that informed my conception of a boat that could sail close to the wind. On waking up, Friday May 29, I note that the wind is directly from the east. Who can you trust? It is clouding over and the barometer is inclined to such a point, I question putting my spinnaker up. If things carry on developing this way, I run the risk of not being able to haul it in quickly enough and therefore of tearing it.

I like manoeuvring a boat as much as anyone, but everything has its limits. With goose-winged yankees, *Pen Duick II* seemed to prance on the waves. Because my self-steering did not function at this speed, I was at the helm the whole time, until the wind swung round to the north, obliging me to lower the yankees and replace them with the single heavy yankee, appropriate for a beam reach. My labours are not yet concluded. The wind picks up again and, without going any faster, the boat's list is accentuated. The reason for this is clear enough: *Pen Duick II* is still oversailed. Once more, I get the mizzen down and exchange the heavy yankee of 29.95m for the No.1 jib, which is only 12.70m. The weather was turning stormy. After nightfall the wind stiffens to a force seven and shifts back to the east. Now the boat is hammering across the long waves, sliding down them like a very big toboggan. With the speedo stuck at twelve knots, I suddenly feel very good and therefore morally revived.

This session at the helm lasts for hours. My arms ache and I feel tired, but because of this miserable self-steering, which goes haywire in a following wind, I have to stay at my station.

Eric Tabarly

Occasionally there is some compensation to be derived in the midst of a tricky situation. Mine arrives towards midnight, when a large school of dolphins surges towards the boat to play about it. I knew that these marine mammals produce sounds sufficiently varied for certain zoologists to qualify as a language. It is the first time that I have heard them. They are playful. For hours on end, squealing and snorting, they mess around. They could be gourmands too – since on the Saturday morning, May 30, I see that the screw of the milometer line has disappeared and with it the miles covered. Did one of them swallow it? Straightaway I worry in case the counter has been damaged by this gourmand but, having replaced the line, I can tell that it is still working OK.

This Saturday, the rain bouncing off the deck, and the spray whipping into the cockpit and my face – the whole conjunction of liquid elements – left me tired and wanting to live on dry land. With the cabin helm extension engaged, I hunker beneath the plexiglass dome where, at least out of my oilskins, and as though in a hothouse, I feel revived.

The first week of the race is over. *Pen Duick II* is a fair way south of the orthodromic route but I preferred to extend it in order to find the quickest, most accommodating path for the boat. In spite of the cold and lack of sleep, I do not really feel tired.

CHAPTER 10

MY SELF-STEERING PACKS UP AND I FEEL LIKE DOING THE SAME

My big chrome alarm, which is of a cheap kitchen design and which I bought in Prisunic de Lorient, is beginning to show rust spots, rather as if it had the measles. Its noisy tick-tock and penetrating bell allow me to sleep regular hours and reassure me. After two hours it ring-rings at top volume, piercing my ears and getting me out of the bunk. Its hefty appearance is confidence inspiring. This is a reliable alarm, which doesn't kid you with the hour or lose time. Wind him up and, once again, he will steadily eat up the hours.

In spite of its readiness to ring almost to the bitter end, on Saturday May 30 my sleep was so deep that I did not hear it.

When sailing, the boat's familiar sounds lodge in the brain. You can be dead with fatigue and imagine yourself sleeping like a dormouse but, subconsciously, one continues to check on any noises, ready to sound the alarm. That morning it is flapping sails and a boom swaying from one side to another which wake me. *Pen Duick II* is once more in calm waters, nosing forward.

My unintended lie-in plus the lack of any wind do not make for the best of moods. The problem vexing me is knowing just how long *Pen Duick II* has been whiling away the time and what my position is relative to the others, in particular Chichester who, according to my calculations, shouldn't be that far from me – either in front or behind. I get up on deck. The sails swing about like washing on a line. All I can do is to haul them in and be ready to raise them again the moment the wind is good enough to get up again. A waste of effort, so I resort to bringing my jibs up on deck, ready to be hoisted once the wind consents to pick up. There is nothing else to do other than general chores, in particular tidying up. For me, order aboard a boat is essential and everything must have its place. This is basic, not some kind of obsession.

When I poke my head outside again the wind remains idle. The boat sways on the ever-present swell. Without having anything else left to do, I decide to oil my self-steering.

There are days when nothing goes right. First nasty surprise: the self-steering has lost its blade. This does not rile me too much, as I have a replacement and all I have to do is mount it. The apparatus clicks onto a pin within the mounting and is then held in place by a bolt. Optimistically, I tell myself all that is required is to take out the bolt, insert the new rudder's pin into the mounting tube and tighten the bolt. I heave the apparatus on board where a second unpleasant surprise awaits me. Inside the tube, the old pin is broken and cannot be extracted. I need to make a hole in the blocked tube and take it out like one would a bottle stopper. I need a tool that I don't possess so I'm stuffed. Standing beside the useless contraption, dark thoughts assail me. Without autopilot, I can't see how to continue the race, as I will have to be at the helm continuously. And I have to sleep, too. In the few hours sleep I will permit myself *Pen Duick II* will be merely bobbing about, while the competition heads on. I picture Chichester, ensconced below decks with a gin and tonic or Guinness, as he pens: 'My second single-handed success'. I also think of Kelsall, with his trimaran *Folatre,* or Butterfield, aboard his catamaran *Misty Miller*, both boats quicker than mine with a following wind, making for Newport.

Here at sea my luck – or lack of it – is going to cost me victory. Insidiously, the thought of abandoning begins to occupy me. Since there is no longer any hope of winning, why not abandon and head

Memories of the Open Sea

to Newfoundland, where I can act the tourist, while my autopilot is fixed? Reasons and excuses for withdrawing from the race are not lacking. Quitting now would be the reasonable thing to do but, viewed another way, would be an easy option. The thought of returning to La Trinité to explain all my misfortunes to friends, who had believed in me, is an unappetising one. This demoralized moment passes and I give myself a little pep talk: you will finish the race, no matter where you are placed. To give up a competition because there is no chance of winning runs contrary to the sporting principle.

How long has the self-steering part been broken? Most likely since last night's strong winds. The big sea and a high speed must have combined to play havoc with the gear. Subsequently, a number of hours have passed and the boat has taken good care of itself during the night. And that means that, if I find an appropriate method to hold the tiller in place, the boat will hold its course. Meagre consolation seeing that, unless the wind is up and constant, I will need to repeatedly re-align the tiller.

Sailors are frequently asked what they think about at sea and their replies are, invariably, self conscious. Personally, I am not thinking about anything. Or, rather, my thoughts relate uniquely to the boat, listening to any sounds he makes, interested only in ensuring that his progress is as rapid as possible. I am preoccupied with the boat because of the relentlessness of tasks on board. Contrary to popular opinion, boats do not represent liberty. Navigation is the acceptance of constraints one has chosen for oneself. It is a privilege. Most people have to put up with obligations life has imposed on them.

The sky clears as, at last, the sun comes out after days of drizzle and fog. The wind has shifted and *Pen Duick II* rides effortlessly along a following swell. For the first time in this race sailing is once more a pleasure. The moment has come to take my sextant out of its box, take some bearings from the sun and calculate my exact position. Up until now, without any sun, navigation has been by dead reckoning. Using my Cras ruler-compass and a pencil I was marking successive points along my proposed route, and risking a potentially large margin of error.

The trouble is, on little boats, in anything but flat seas, using a sextant, too, is uncertain. Equilibrium is affected by roll and pitch. The lens and mirror can get soaked with spray and the navigator, situated almost at the same level as the water and its swell, can have a problem picking out the horizon.

So I make use of the good light, the light wind and the boat's steadiness to take observations. If my calculations are correct, I am halfway between Plymouth and Newfoundland.

Having put the sextant back in its box, I am back on deck just in time to catch sight of a bird, uneasily perched by the stern. He has ash coloured wings, a white breast, and around his neck a black and white collar. His beak is orange, with a black tip. This is a Cape Cod bird, the sandpiper. I recognise him, having seen a photo in the American magazine *Life*. My visitor has big feet and trouble keeping his balance on the deck. Then he gets a drenching from the sea.

A British plane flies overhead and the bird takes off. My log line has gone again and I have no further replacements. From now on, as well as navigating approximately, I will not know my speed. Cruising, this loss would not really matter, but not knowing how fast you are going in a race is extremely trying.

Monday June 1 does not prove to be a particularly noteworthy day. In the cabin I have a quick look at four books I have brought along: Chichester's *Solo Racing*, and Lewis's *Atlantic Adventures*, *Vertue XXXV* by Humphrey Barton and Jean Merrien's book about solo sailors. Since Plymouth, I have not opened them once and there is little likelihood I will be reading them between here and Newport. By contrast, Chichester and Lewis had both brought veritable libraries on board and, with their self-steering working properly, I imagine them having plenty of time at their disposal to read. The times I have for relaxation come in very small measures. My time is taken up with sail changes, adjusting the sheets and helming. A ten minute break every now and again whistles by

Memories of the Open Sea

and cooking also has a reasonable claim on my attention. While there are those happy to eat whatever comes to hand, I prefer to eat things I like: it is good for morale. Pasta and rice form the basis of my diet. I like to prepare a flambéed omelette or a rice pudding with cherry jam. Cooking is not actually a waste of time. In the galley, one is aware of everything that is happening on deck and you are immediately on hand for any manoeuvre that has to be made.

As well as food one must get some rest. Weight loss when sailing single-handed varies, according to the individual, between a few hundred grams and a dozen kilos as a result of physical effort and nervous tension and lack of sleep. I am not sure if there has been any change to my normal weight of sixty-six kilos. Alone, one becomes conscious of various manias. I make myself sleep without any clothes because if I get inside the covers fully dressed my sleep is neither so profound nor relaxing. It may take a bit longer for me when I have to get back on deck but I don't feel off-colour, having slept badly.

June 2 is a short night. Towards four o'clock the wind is blowing force five and I have to get up in a hurry, throw on oilskins and boots, and clamber about on deck. *Pen Duick II* impresses me with his strength. Like a thoroughbred in a race, he clears any obstacles that the sea places in front of him. Spindrift is whipped onto the deck by the wind and gets mixed up in the obscuring spray. Without a speedometer any longer, I don't know the boat's precise speed but I do know that I am going quickly, very quickly. Suddenly the heavens open and the rain, blowing about in another heavy squall, lashes into my face.

This fine progress across the waves continues till about midday, at which point, in spite of the boat's objections, it is clear that he is overcanvassed. I take in the yankee but, once again, the wind strengthens and the mizzen and staysail represent a surplus. I get busy again bringing them down, the squall sluicing down my oilskins. Sea and rainwater stream down my face and under my pullover. Shuddering, I set about the next task. I still need to take a reef in the mainsail, as the boat runs the waves, veers on their crests, before being engulfed in their trough. Not a walk in the woods. First of all I have to bring the sail in, so that the first row of reefing points are ranged along the full length of the boom. Then, when the fold in the sail is ready, I raise it again. Heavy weather: the barometer's needle is all over the place as the sea, in the shape of breaking and foaming waves, swoops down. *Pen Duick II* forges on unperturbed, climbing up the expanse of green then heading down the other side of the maritime mountain with a deafening knocking, snorting and shaking in this rollercoaster entertainment. Inside, the drenched sails make everything wet and everything is in a damn shambles – because that is the way things get in heavy weather. But it is not the moment for housework.

The whole night long I was getting in and out of bed, undressing and then dressing again, according to the whim of the wind. To those soft headed dreamers who fantasize about freedom at sea, I suggest they look elsewhere.

In the course of the night the gusts moderated, with the wind settling down and the sea becoming more even. The boat heads on slowly but surely. The sun is close, warming me like a hot water bottle. After showering and a towelling down, I savour this idyllic scene, at the same time as sorting out sails which had been thrown down into the cabin, drying clothes and ventilating the interior that sweats humidity.

Regrettably, calm reigns once more in this part of the ocean. Once again I go through my usual routine when becalmed. That is to say, I lower the jib, then hoist it again at the first sign of some breeze, and try to get the spinnaker working – but it flaps about in a sad fashion. I collapse it and, in its place, put up a staysail whose effectiveness is only sporadic.

I feel exhausted, sickened even. My efforts achieve six miserable miles. My eyes, made red by the sun and saltwater, are giving me trouble but, however I feel, I cannot afford to lose more time. Not having succeeded in obtaining radio contact with Plymouth, I do not know the position of any of the others. I have the sensation of being the only person in the world.

The wind has swung astern, which means that the boat's course cannot be fixed by securing the tiller. Racking my brains to think of a substitute system for the broken self-steering, I note in the log: 'The only possibility is to settle the tiller's position using the jib.' Because when the boat is luffing, relatively, the wind presses and increases the tension on the jib sheet. This is the opposite of what happens when the boat is bearing away. I further note: 'Set up the jib sheet with a windward block connected to the tiller and balance the sheet's tension with a pair of bungees to leeward, with the result that the tiller should move to either side, depending on the relative tension of the stay and the bungees.'

I set about this task and confirm that *Pen Duick II* heads on without yawing. The system works in an acceptable manner, except in that it demands constant adjustment of the bungees, depending on whether the wind picks up or abates. Which is to say that, the whole night long, I was acutely sensitive to the boat's noises – noises which will suggest to me what the boat is up to. I barely get any sleep, having to go back and forth between my bunk and the deck. Nevertheless during the morning (Thursday June 4) it is clear that I am not in bad physical shape. Which is no bad thing since, almost as soon as I had finished my breakfast, the barometer was heading for an uninterrupted fall, whilst beneath a cold, lugubrious sky the wind rose sharply to force six. In the time it takes to bring in the big yankee and the genoa staysail and raise the No.1 jib and smaller staysail in their place, the sea develops and swells and roars and the boat shakes about violently. A draining period. *Pen Duick II* nimbly scales the swell but coming down the other side can be brutal. He hurtles down into the wave troughs with a smashing noise. I am aboard a toboggan, tossed about by a choppy sea extending as far as the eye can see.

The slate grey sky is packed with moody looking clouds. Not much less moody and unwelcoming is the sea with its troughs and white crests coming from all directions and pounding *Pen Duick II*. The barometer continues its descent and I wonder what is coming up weather wise without really knowing the answer.

The hours I have spent at the helm seem like an eternity and my arms are beginning to ache. I am cold – and wet. And then, shortly before midnight, I decide to take in a reef, so as to have a little more peace of mind when I go to bed. Well, well! No sooner had I finished the operation that fixes the sail onto the boom, than *Pen Duick II* viciously heeled over. Straightaway he picks up speed as I re-enter the cockpit, hanging on as I go, so as not to be swept away by the slabs of water breaking all over. My boots are full of water and my marine jersey drenched, in spite of my oilskins.

The wind is now force eight. It has shifted to the east and is pushing me in the right direction which is cause for celebration. On the other hand, the prospect of spending another night at the helm is bleak. I am already exhausted. Whatever strength I had recouped the previous night has been left behind in the course of this tough day. But, on such a shambolic sea, there is no possibility of fastening the helm in order to sleep.

I feel worn out. Tiredness gains the upper hand. Because I have to remain at my post and in order not to be lifted overboard by the crashing sea, I tie myself in with a line round the waist secured to a sheet cleat. Safety harnesses do not provide me with a sense of security. They get in the way during manoeuvres, particularly when single-handed. One is moving from the bows to the stern and the security rope, running through its drawplate, must be long enough to permit the sailor to move from one task to the next, with a certain freedom of movement. It almost goes without saying that, together, the line and its guides present frequent possibilities for getting one's feet caught and for stumbling over. Furthermore, the man who falls into the water when his boat is moving along at upwards of seven knots is, more likely than not, going to be left in its wake and unable to get back up on board. In order to do so, he will have to somehow be swept by the wind to the boat's side, directly opposite the gunwale.

Memories of the Open Sea

You might as well hope for a miracle. The sailor thrown overboard is a sailor whose concentration lapsed. There is an old dictum: 'One hand for the man, the other for the boat' – which is true. During a manoeuvre or going up on deck, one must always consider having something within reach to grab onto, which it would be almost impossible for the sudden force of the sea to rip off.

Helming, on the other hand, one is vulnerable. When the boat lists, the sailor finds himself almost standing up, without being able to use the tiller as a support. Even a violent roll can catapult a man into the sea. At large in the North Atlantic there is not even time to say a prayer. Straightaway, almost, you die of cold. I am fond of living and do not wish to go that way, which is why I use strong rope to lasso myself in.

I remain in the cockpit until 3am, at which point the wind, ever capricious, softened and shifted to the north, as some stars appeared. Although tired I let go of the tiller, secure it and go back on deck to raise the mainsail with a reef. Once *Pen Duick II* gathers momentum on a beam reach, I have only one thought in mind: bed – sleep.

Days pass by without resembling one another. Friday June 5 I am able to triangulate my position, on a once more amenable sea, and am pleased to learn that *Pen Duick II* has passed the half-way mark. This is good for morale. I am now sure that I will be able to reach Newport without the self-steering. For a while doubt had worked itself into me. But I know I can cross the finishing line and am hopeful that it will be in an honourable position, not knowing at this point where the other contestants have reached.

Days pass by without resembling one another. Saturday June 6 starts badly. Sleeping like the dead, I did not hear my alarm bell and it was only at 12.30am that I awoke with a start. I checked the sails and course: everything OK. The ringing next woke me at 3am and again at 4.30am, at which precise moment I had a moment of clumsiness. Pulling on my sweater, a loose sleeve swipes the prized alarm which falls and stops. In spite of my efforts at resuscitation, a small metal part drops out from it: the end of my clock. Following the self-steering and the speedometer, it is the third instrument that has given up on me – it is written that I will lose everything essential. The alarm's demise is a disaster for me. Because, if its ringing had always intervened to wake me, how am I going to cope without it? At the same time, I curse myself for having forgotten to provide a substitute amidst the madness of the final preparations.

It is not long before a price for this mistake is exacted. The same morning, instead of getting up at 6am, I only stir at nine, to find that *Pen Duick II* has changed tack and is marking time according to his fancy, the jibs blown back by the wind. This concludes the second week of my race, and I fortify myself with a bowl of cereal.

In single-handed racing, if one is not involved in a manoeuvre, eating or sleeping or studying the sky and listening to the boat, then one is thinking things over.

The last few days the prevailing wind had inclined me south. If the pilot charts are to be trusted, *Pen Duick II* should be entering an area dominated by south westerly winds. That would be ideal – both for the passage towards Newport and in order to cross the Grand Newfoundland Banks in the south, thus limiting the likelihood of confronting an iceberg.

The outlook is both very grey and very cold. Under spinnaker it is not possible to leave the helm in order to revive myself with something hot, so I must make do with a bar of chocolate. On the crest of each wave the boat loosens itself for a controlled glide down, a pleasant experience, if only it was not bucketing down with an icy rain that, in spite of my oilskins and a washing up towel tied round my neck, works itself insidiously in. My teeth chatter.

By the end of the day I am fighting cold and hunger. I haul in the spinnaker and raise first the staysail, followed by the big yankees which I pole out. With the tiller aligned by a bungee, I go and settle myself in front of the cooker on my motorbike seat. Happily ensconced with a big helping of chicken and Vietnamese rice set down before me I take the first few mouthfuls. Suddenly *Pen Duick II* heels right over, the boom having gybed on account of some unforeseen breakdown in my system. The rice flies in all directions. In the time it takes to undo the strap securing me to the seat, I am back above decks to resume the helm. It is 11pm. Above me an impressive storm rages. Lightning cracks the night sky and thunder rolls lugubriously across an unwelcoming environment. The boat is moving along like crazy; it tears down towards the bottom of each wave; the soundtrack of the wind in the rigging is a crescendo. As it reaches at least force seven, it sprays the spindrift into the air. The wise thing to do would be to lower the extended jib that keeps me running before the wind but on this point of sail there is no way to fix the helm without the boat yawing. Yes, I am feeling cautious and, while I hope that the storm should move on as rapidly as it has appeared, I cannot help but notice the leaden sky following me, full of dark clouds moving around menacingly. The wind accelerates from thirty to forty knots. I know that, being as tired as I am, I do not have another night in me to spend at the helm, controlling *Pen Duick II*'s plunges and nipping his swerves in the bud. So I will not be going where I want to go. I will be going where the wind wants me to go, something that I do not like.

Again the wind grows stronger. Everywhere the sea has come to the boil. It is impossible to continue in these conditions. Coming off a crest, I spontaneously decide to luff, in order to draw the sting out of the side wind biting the yankee, so that the boat slows down, and I can subsequently bring it abeam, rather as if I had heaved to. Taking advantage of *Pen Duick II*'s being almost stationary I make towards the bows, having loosened the kicking strap. A little too loose it would seem. Because after battling with the yankee, blown out by the incessant wind, the sail collapses as, brutally, does its pole, pulling off a stanchion footing and ripping a piece off the bulwark next to me. Had I been below it, it would have been my head that shattered.

The storm lets rip. The noise and wind force reach a new pitch but in this kind of situation you do what you have to do. I have to bring the mizzen and mainsail down in order to get going again on a broad reach with the staysail. I take down the yankee, fold the sails and sheet out. I put away the extension pole and generally tidy up.

At one in the morning I am able to come down off deck to get some rest.

Sunday June 7 is glacial. Inside the cabin there is so much humidity that, rather than using butane or petrol which, though good heaters, would intensify the situation, I decide to light my stove using coal. The former are better inasmuch as they are straightforward to light. My choice requires more patience. In spite of following the instructions closely – moisten tampon with alcohol to light charcoal – it requires several attempts before the stove gets going. Within a few minutes the temperature in the cabin is fine in spite of the hatch above the steps being left open in order to avoid any risk of asphyxiation. As my wet clothes are allowed to dry out, I sit by the stove and, savouring its warmth, think.

I have not been able to take a sight for three days and I am concerned to know my position. The Gulf Stream worries me. I would not want to get drawn into it, as it would run counter to the favourable Labrador current.

The wind lightens and in the evening I am able to hoist the mainsail for a port tack. The wind has lightened but it comes from Labrador and is glacial. These are punishing conditions to be in the cockpit. When, at night, I raise the yankee and mizzen it is so bitterly cold that my fingers are soon numb. This wintry Sunday the wind helps to disperse the fog. Thanks to the unplanned detour south of my route, I am out of the Newfoundland fishing zone. The sea is free and collision not a risk. The humming stove brings warmth to body and soul.

Monday June 8. Since the beginning of the race no two days have been the same. Yesterday I was shivering. This morning there is a superb sky. Dominated by the sun, there is not a single cloud and a warm breeze blows. Under full rigging, including the topsail, *Pen Duick II* continues on his way at five knots along a beam reach.

Memories of the Open Sea

The sun, transforming my surroundings into a sublime, monochrome blue, does not just warm me through and act as a stimulant but, finally, allows me to make observations in order to ascertain my exact position. The sextant ready in its box with the chart table, I pick a position south of my most pessimistic estimates. I think the fine weather is thanks to having entered the Gulf Stream, which runs at 0.9 knots towards the east while I go west. *Pen Duick II* lies right at the southern limit of his route, eight hundred nautical miles from Nantucket Island and the approach to Newport. I ponder that if I carry on this route I am going to lose twenty miles a day and I will require around a fortnight to reach the Nantucket lightship. If I veer off towards Sable Island, in order to regain the favourable Labrador current, I will be able to make the lightship in six days. To continue on my current course, adding at least one hundred and eighty miles to the route would be rather like going up a down escalator: lots of effort producing a negligible result. My choice is therefore clear – *Pen Duick II* must head back to a higher latitude. The pilot charts indicate that we would then be in an area where the dominant south westerly wind will be able to take me away from this wretched current. Initially it is from the north, which does not help me a great deal, but in the afternoon it swings round one hundred and eighty degrees to the south, beautiful and hot. By evening I will be shivering in the arctic cold, but for now it is fine and the spray that douses me is warm like in the trade winds.

June 9 is a gloomy, uninspiring day. All sails up for a feeble wind, the sky filled with squally clouds that make it impossible to take a reading, nothing to celebrate. And always the same question: where are the others? I am convinced that being without the self-steering has cost me a lot of time. And then there is the unreliability of the wind forcing me up on deck the whole time to deal with luffing, flapping sails, the boat moving about chaotically, not to mention ill-timed breakdowns. It's not good. Nevertheless, it is not too bad – with clement weather that allows me to move about barefoot on deck in my pyjama bottoms.

Eric Tabarly

In this kind of race one loses touch with dry land and with worldly concerns. One occupies a sort of alternative reality, foreign to most people. Set in a circular, watery landscape, one's thoughts – and one is almost living within one's head – are for the boat alone. I am far from humankind, wholly preoccupied by the fact of not knowing the distance I have covered or exactly where I am going, by *Pen Duick II*'s yaws and my own yawns, the struggle against fatigue. Everything is provisional. At nightfall the wind is sleeping and I feel grumpy – even though the water temperature is much colder than in the morning, allowing me to reckon that I have finally got out of the Gulf Stream and into the Labrador current. Somewhat at ease again, I head for bed, determined to buck myself up.

I leap up instinctively because of a terrible fracas. In my sleeping state I had not been able to identify it but had been convinced that I was on the verge of disaster. Panicking, I belt up barefoot on deck but, as far as I can tell in the black night, everything is OK and *Pen Duick II* is steadily continuing on his way, pushed along by the gentle breeze. After my eyes are accustomed to the dark, I make for the bows, where I find that the yankee is half-collapsed, its bottom trailing in the water. Only with the sail hauled back on deck do I realise the cause of the commotion. The halyard block at the top of the mast has come off. Normally it is fixed thirteen metres up by a shackle made of stainless steel, but with this working itself loose the block absconded.

There is no way of making a repair in the dark. Satisfied to know the origin of all the noise and there being no real damage, I bring the yankee down and go back to bed. The prospect of heading right up the mast to replace the block at dawn does not appeal in the slightest. I'm going to have a rough time.

On awaking June 11, I find the boat navigating in a thick, icy fog, carried along by a light south easterly breeze. There is a swell coming from behind and *Pen Duick II* rolls easy.

According to Pierre Dac, the humorist, 'Thinking is no good. You need to reflect in advance.' I reflect. The boat's movement

Memories of the Open Sea

should not make going up the mast too dangerous. But first, to be ready for the repair, I need to send my bosun's chair up to the top of the mast, together with a block and shackle, the yankee halyard, tools and a strong rope which I will be able to hold onto. The whole bundle goes up using the spinnaker halyard. I glance up at it, once it reaches the top, swinging around and have some presentiment of my uncomfortable position once I am up there.

My climb begins. With one hand I cling onto the doubled rope and, with the other, whatever comes to hand – shroud, stay, spreader – so as not to swing around with the boat's roll. My feet have a role to play too, pressing against the mast or against a shroud and helping me to maintain stability. Although the roll becomes relatively bigger the higher I am, everything goes well enough up to the top spar. Ten metres above the deck the boat's movements become so exaggerated I fear that I will be tossed into the sea at any moment. Perched high up on this stressful swing, I realise that I will never be able to get onto the chair's little plank. Above all, I see that, with the boat now abeam, the wind will knock me about even more forcefully. Clinging to the spar, I naively anticipate his swinging back to a following wind but, of course, the mulish *Pen Duick II* does not grant my wish.

I climb down to re-set his course myself. I take a few deep breaths and begin a second climb up, this time without hindrance. I swing my legs above the chair and sit down. The spinnaker and flag halyards and the block and rope, agitated for an hour, have become entangled and it takes quite a while before I am able to unravel them – largely because the swaying of the boat is so violent and abrupt that I am obliged to use all my strength to avoid being either thrown off the chair or against the mast. Then, at last, I manage to fix the block correctly. Feeling satisfied, I come back down with all the materials. I look up and inspect my work. Ay! Ay! Ay! Bemused and annoyed, I see that the jib and spinnaker halyards have got twisted above the top spar. As the proverb says: 'He who does not have a head, must have legs.' What I need for a third knackering climb are arms. When I regain the deck once more it is almost midday. My tightrope act has lasted more than four hours and I am spent. Behind the fog the sun is heating up. I recuperate with a shirtless lunch on deck. *Pen Duick II* is going at an average of two knots, less like a racing boat than a barge.

There is a fine drizzle. It is grey and faintly depressing. The wind is getting on my nerves, getting up momentarily, only to then die down again. I am obliged to make constant adjustments to the sheets. The highpoint of the day comes at midday when the sun makes its second appearance, just as I was giving up on it. I have just enough time to jump down into the cabin for the sextant and rush back up on deck to get my precise latitude. The sight is in line with the point I had assumed in the morning. Manoeuvres, trimming, and spells at the helm succeed one another before a sudden nightfall and sharp drop in temperature. *Pen Duick II* heads northwest towards Sable Island.

South of the Island by less than fifty nautical miles, it is not exactly the Côte d'Azur. It is bitingly cold. Once I have taken down the yankee, torn by the pressure of chafing against the shroud, I lose the feeling in my fingers, which are absolutely frozen. By the heat of the coal burning stove I bring some life back to them, before putting on first some woollen and then waterproof gloves – the only way to keep them warm. Ready for work again, I send up the no1 jib and replace the genoa staysail with its standard counterpart. I go about to head southwest.

Here I am in the region of Sable Island, but calm because *Pen Duick II* is sixty miles to the south of this fearsome sailors' graveyard. Confident of my position, I know the boat does not risk becoming the two hundred and fiftieth wreck bogged down in these troublesome waters with me an unwilling guest at the local lighthouse.

Actually, I feel quite good. To have got to this stage after twenty-one days racing – despite various setbacks with unpredictable equipment and being forced too close to the wind and sometimes having to set course as if on a whim – is not so bad. I still have five

Memories of the Open Sea

hundred miles – or four days – to go, if I maintain my current average.

I would be very interested to know where Chichester has reached, and also the multihulls, that can go at dizzying speeds. I ask myself the question. I don't have the answer. My bed awaits. End of the third week of the race.

CHAPTER 11

WINNER WITHOUT KNOWING IT

This fourth and final week of solo navigation starts like Jacques Prévert's poem *Racoon*. That is to say, with a whole series of manoeuvres, multiple mischief on the part of the wind, a thickening mist, calm followed by rainfall ... and me.

To start with, a dying wind requiring all sails raised, then a change of tack, southwest, in order to avoid getting sucked into the Gulf Stream counter current. And me at the helm.

Then an unconvincing sun lightening the greyness. And me with my sextant, getting a rough sighting. Next the wind becomes a little more encouraging. *Pen Duick II*'s bow heads up towards the Nantucket lightship at dawn June 14 as a depression begins to take hold, the barometer falling amidst growing squalls and stronger winds. The wind later becomes more constant – but, before long, fades away. And me involved in manoeuvres or at the helm.

Following lunch, more of the same. Returning up on deck I notice, in plain view, an opening of fifty centimetres along one of the mainsail seams, caused by too much chafing in the calm, and so the sail needs to be taken down. And me, rather like the dressmaker's apprentice, with my sailor's sewing kit.

The day ends in fog, visibility reduced to fifty metres. The boat pulls itself forward on shallow, lapping waves to the accompaniment of knocking and vibrations. It rears up with the spindrift thrown

Memories of the Open Sea

off a rolling sea, provoked by this confrontation of wind and the Labrador current.

And me, thanks to *Pen Duick II*'s chaotic movement, unable to close my eyes the whole night. His sudden jolts push me around my bunk, head drumming against the bulkhead.

June 15 dawns magnificently. It is still fresh but the sun illuminates a clear sky and the mercury is rising. Whether Canadian or American, I don't know, but I pick up a station on my little wireless set playing jazz and Beatles' tunes. This music seems to sing 'Land Ahoy!' All of a sudden my impatience to reach the finishing line becomes more pressing. I grow eager to hurry the boat along but the wind subsides and he crawls through the water, before stopping. As usual in this predicament, I lower the foresails and trim both mainsail and mizzen, ready for the moment the wind is kind enough to do its work. I set about tidying the galley, changing over the soft water canister, and airing the smelly interior that oozes humidity. The plexiglass hatch only permits a thin stream of air.

Still calm. In order to be doing something, I settle down at the chart table and trace my route. Following changes of course it represents a curious series of zigzags since Plymouth, via Lizard Point, Land's End, the Scilly Isles, the Longship lighthouse, the Grand Newfoundland Banks and Sable Island before, according to this morning's point, coming just northeast of the Georges Bank. *Pen Duick II* is now less than one hundred miles north-northeast of Nantucket.

A relaxed sail is out of the question. In these waters the seabed is etched with sharp folds, most notably along the edge of the underwater plateau, in the shape of a hook, that stretches all the way along the Canadian coast and south of Boston.

The Georges Bank forms the central section of this plateau. Its limit looks down onto a trench two thousand to four thousand metres deep. So now, after negotiating the shoals of Newfoundland and Sand Island, here I am at this bank and then that of Nantucket.

Eric Tabarly

These ill-reputed, often sandy, plateaus make for dangerous seafaring, as they are only visible from a few metres.

If the approach of land excites me it also leads me to be extra careful to avoid going aground. I still have no idea where the other competitors have got to, particularly Chichester, made favourite by the British press, but I sense that my finishing position will be creditable. Whatever, I will have achieved my objective: to finish in less than thirty days compared to Chichester's thirty-three in 1960. I rack my brains, imagining the multihulls progress. If they have experienced the same weather conditions as me, then they cannot be far from finishing.

Useless to speculate, given that I have no information about the others, but it will not be long before I do, as Newport is fast approaching.

June 16. Wishing to take advantage of the sky's brightening to check my latitude, I got soaked beneath an avalanche of spray. More annoyingly, so did the sextant. It is when I am methodically drying it that I notice several fishing boats around me. During the morning a four-engine Argus, followed by a twin-engine Gruman, had flown over me, back and forth at low altitude. It leads me to think their purpose, humming overhead, is to survey the race. If so, that must mean that I am amongst the first to finish. One thing is for certain, my parents will be glad to know that I am OK and near the finishing line.

Pen Duick II moves along on a strong breeze. The sea is as blue as the Mediterranean and flecked with white horses. But I am worried. I cannot make out the second Texas tower, which should be visible above the Georges Bank. Using the goniometer, my triangulation suggests to me that it should be five miles to starboard. I take a good look, but am still unable to make out Texas No.2.

This tower was placed there on account of the cold war and belongs to a series of military installations, intended to detect the purpose of assailants in advance. Each tower, with a triangular platform mounted on tall piles rising from the bank, has a number.

Memories of the Open Sea

Number two, located at the highest point of the Georges Bank, is approximately one hundred miles from the Nantucket lighthouse and I can't understand how, given the excellent visibility, it is not possible to make it out.

The boat is pushed along in the force seven at about seven knots, with pretty white horse spindrift everywhere. *Pen Duick II* plunges down into the troughs, throwing out a flurry of foam, before riding up the next slope, snorting and spitting out water as he goes and, with a deafening noise, then bravely dives back down. There are swathes of water washing over the deck while I, eyes stinging with saltwater, helm most of the time to prevent the hull taking too much punishment. I am getting as drenched as the boat but the water seems less cold and I feel intoxicated by this mad sailing, comparable to a long, straining final sprint. If *Pen Duick II* has been relatively slow in a following wind and moderate weather, when sailing close to the wind and in big seas he has justified the confidence I placed in him. I have not cosseted him. Rather, I have pushed him to the limit. He hasn't complained.

As one might have predicted, the wind drops during the night and I have to stay at the helm. It is cold. I pull on a thick sweater, a pea jacket and oilskins. Still I am frozen. I fervently hope that one hundred miles away in Newport it is hot.

The wind keeps varying – changing direction, rising and falling, it surges and dies down – each time I am obliged to do something with the sheets. For a second successive night my presence is required at the helm. However, I don't feel tired. Drawing close to landfall and the Nantucket light and finally finding out my placing keeps me in a wakeful state.

My physical shape is a revelation to me. I have barely had more than four to five hours of sleep, in snatches, per day, since the failure of my self-steering.

As the moon rises to lighten up the night, I see that I am still at large in the aquatic desert. I also have the impression of dragging along slowly so, to take advantage of the least change in wind direction, I make small tacks.

A-ha! At bang on 1am I finally catch a glimpse of the glaring light which is then intermittently lost amidst the waves. *Pen Duick II* is on the right track, about three miles west. One thing remains unclear: there being no sign of Texas tower No.2 on the Georges Bank. I still did not know then that, no longer considered necessary by the US Air Force, it had recently been destroyed. The demolition did not figure in my list of lights. I was anxiously looking for something that no longer existed and putting myself on edge for no reason.

The lights of Nantucket switch off at 4 am June 18 as day breaks. The boat glides slowly along with the help of a gentle breeze. What I am looking for now from the helm is some sign of the lightship on the horizon.

If I don't have any news of the others, they, equally, do not have any of me. My one attempt at establishing radio contact dates back to May 28 but, not being a success, I had decided not to waste any more time getting in a state over the set. The last time my position had been given was at dusk on June 4 when a cargo ship passed me.

All I know is that in Newport an armada of about one hundred and fifty boats is getting ready for the start of a race to Bermuda and that the town is currently known to be the capital of international yachting. There is one French contestant, called *Brigantine*, in this race, which is as legendary as the Sydney–Hobart and almost as prestigious as the Fastnet. It is a pity that it is due to leave so soon after I arrive, otherwise I would have happily jumped aboard as crew.

At 10.45am on June 18, six hours later than I had calculated, I pass by the Nantucket lightship. Her crew, noting my approach, put a red launch over the side into the water, and come over to circle me. A sailor notes down my boat's name and number.

'How many boats have arrived so far?'

No reply. The launch is now almost alongside *Pen Duick II*. I repeat the question, this time using my imperfect English.

Memories of the Open Sea

'You're the first!' shouts the sailor with a notepad. He does so with complete indifference, lacking any idea of the significance of these words for me. Dubious, incredulous, not wanting to give myself over to a false joy, I lean out on a shroud and ask him to confirm this reply.

'You're the first!' he shouts hoarsely, clearly put out by my insistence.

Again the American opens his notepad and, biro poised, starts to ask me some extraordinary questions.

'Where have you come from?'
'What?'
'Where have you come from?'
'Plymouth!'
He carefully notes this down.
'What is your destination?'
'I am sorry?'
'What is your destination?'
'Newport!'
'Are you travelling alone?'
'Well... Yes.'

He carries on taking notes, before putting his biro and notepad away. The launch turns away and charges back to the lightship.

His damned attitude makes me question what he said. I suggest to myself the possibility that more of the single-handed Transat contestants could have arrived in the night, without being seen.

The weather is fantastic. The sea laps very lightly. The wind is rather tired. This does not stop *Pen Duick II* from ploughing on at four to five knots. I fetch towards the finishing line under a hot sky, which warms me through after the night's shivering.

Midday. Overhead, a light aircraft buzzes back and forth, not much higher than the main mast. Through the pilot's window I can make out somebody using a camera.

3pm. The wind picks up a bit. Just as I am sheeting in, a pair of twin motors appear on the scene, circle the boat a few times and then move away, just as another moves in. All this attention directed my way allows me to think that I am among the leaders. If I was last it is unlikely I would be receiving so much interest.

The superb weather, a light crosswind and smooth sea allow the boat, tiller secured, to light-heartedly follow his own line. I do some proper tidying up. To start with I spread my clothes and sail bags and sails on the deck, so they can dry. I also bring up the cabin floorboards, which are mildewy with humidity. I scrub them with sea water and then arrange them on the foredeck to dry. The plexiglass hood above the cabin centre is unscrewed, in order for fresh air to displace the humidity. Finally, I carefully place my remaining bread, grown damp, above deck. For the last few days I have been obliged, before eating it, to scrape off the mildewed crust. Cleaning up now seems more important than manoeuvres. Night falls. The breeze remains steady as, all of a sudden, the blinking of the Cape Gay lighthouse on Martha's Vineyard becomes visible. I am accompanied by its light right up to daybreak. Worried that I might fall asleep, I stay up on deck all night. I have not had any shut-eye for thirty-six hours and, if I were to drift off now, God alone knows how long it would be before I woke up. To turn in would be dangerous in these waters, courting the possibility of coming aground on one of the Isles I was passing by, should the wind change direction.

Every now and again I shake myself. In spite of my eyes being wide open, I could still slip into semi-consciousness or sleep. These eyes are stung by saltwater and prolonged wakefulness. I pass by the cliffs of No Man's Land to starboard and then Vineyard Sound. Journey's end is less than fifteen miles.

Almost without announcement it becomes hot; I helm without my jersey. As I do so, I see a launch crossing my bows. She makes an elegant turn, to tuck in leeward of *Pen Duick II*.

'You're first!' shouts a joyful woman's voice. It belongs to Aunt Mony, who has arrived from France and joined the launch hired by my friend, Jean-Paul Aymon of *France-Soir*. Then other launches put in an appearance, bringing with them French Press Agency reporters and other French and American journalists.

With the helm secured, I give the first interviews in my life on the open sea holding onto the mizzen shrouds. It is obvious that these guys know next to nothing about sailing and I am astounded by the banality of their questions. They all ask: 'What did you think about when the sea got wild?' Brought up short, I mumble, 'Well... uh...nothing special...' They are visibly disappointed. Personally, I would have liked to have talked about *Pen Duick II*'s attributes, the way he performed and his bravura, about this *Pen Duick II* who, all the way through the weeks of this race, showed that he was an exceptional boat. What did I think about? Pushing him forward, getting him to perform to the maximum.

The renewal of relations with other people at first only accentuates my natural reserve.

The finishing line is close. Down in the cabin I fill in the little form I was given in Plymouth, outlining the basic rules of the race, to confirm that I have respected them: my progress has been solely wind assisted; nobody came to my assistance while I was at sea; I was genuinely single-handed.

Back on deck, the wind having swung astern, I hoist the spinnaker. Launches head towards, and circle, me; their wake bobs both me and the boat about. Aboard one of these motorboats are the French Consul from Boston and the Captain of the *Chatel*, who is the Naval Attaché in Washington. Through a loudhailer the Attaché shouts to me: 'The President of the Republic has decorated you Chevalier of the Légion d'Honneur.'

This recognition – why deny it – flatters and affects me and I project my voice in order to express my gratitude, but I am drowned out by a symphony of klaxons and foghorns, sounding from the flotilla of multi-varied craft that have come to meet me. In a dignified manner, the boat makes its way between the Brenton tower and buoy to arrive at the finishing line. So there we are. Finished. In first place. I go and take down the spinnaker.

Eric Tabarly

Pen Duick II enters the long gulley that leads to Newport. This is flanked by steep, grassy banks, above which mansions are lined. Ahead of me, just at the harbour entrance, I can see the one hundred and fifty yachts which are readying themselves for the start of the Bermuda race. Their crews sound their horns and 'hurrah' me with brio. Such esteem shown by top sailors touches me, but it is not the time for emotion. I have to make ready for berthing.

I want to carry out this manoeuvre as though I were on the parade ground. First of all the mainsail and yankee are lowered. Then, without much delay, I let down the mizzen and staysail. *Pen Duick II* eases along and slowly settles beside the quay length. Impeccable! It would have annoyed me to fluff this berthing in front of so many spectators.

Having fastened the boat, what follows is hard to describe. Straightaway, I am stampeded by officials and then, hot on their tracks, reporters and photographers. The first to arrive in front of me is Charles A Hambly, the Mayor of Newport, whose path is cleared by two well-built policemen. With a certain degree of solemnity – that sticks out amidst the general confusion and crush on my boat – he declaims to me a single sentence in laboured French that he must undoubtedly have learnt by heart:

'I have the pleasure of granting you the honorary freedom of my town and I hand you the seals.' This is the cue for a manly handshake. I am then engulfed by a wave of journalists. Again and again they want to know, on this first meeting with me, everything concerning myself, my family, my life, the race. Regarding the last, all questions home in on the trilogy: icebergs, storms and solitude. I am something of a disappointment. À propos icebergs:

'I didn't see any.'

The reporters are let down. Storms:

'The boat wasn't damaged at all.' This frustrates them further. Solitude:

'Since I was a boy I have been used to sailing on open seas; being alone at sea has never worried me. Even when, not much beyond the starting line, the competitors' flotilla broke up and disappeared, as though swallowed up by the ocean, I was not particularly affected.'

How to explain that, for a sailor, the sea's expanse is as natural an element as is the void below for a mountain climber. I equate being at sea with being on a boat and that is where I feel at home.

My main concern had been for my mother, with her anxieties for me throughout the race. I could not forget the poignant image that faded into the distance of her on the quay. My one fear had been letting down all those who had supported and helped me to build and fit out *Pen Duick II* in record time. Otherwise, it was the boat and his advance which received one hundred per cent of my attention. If you want to win a race, then you are always on deck performing, without the time to indulge in feelings. No doubt this is an approach lacking romance or poetry but, if you are not right on the ball, anticipating what the wind and the ocean will do next, then quite rapidly you will find yourself at the mercy of events.

Before lunch there is a reception for me at the wonderfully situated – on a rock, approached by a path – Ida Lewis Yacht Club. Here I am presented with a magnificent silver salver by the President. Next, the offices of the French Consul ensure that it is to the best club in Newport that I am taken for a sizeable steak, welcomed by my stomach, last invigorated by breakfast at dawn.

I just had time to put on a clean sweatshirt and trousers before falling in with the officials. I did not have time either to shave or to stow away the sails. I am asked if the race was not too draining. The truth I reply is 'No' and, actually, I still have a fair amount of energy left, allowing me to say that I could have carried on at sea for considerably longer. The race I have just won corresponds exactly to the life I have wanted to lead. Doing what one wants to do increases resilience tenfold.

CHAPTER 12

IN NEW YORK'S GREY-BLUE WATERS

On arriving in Newport, and with my moorings secured, the immigration official had almost choked with indignation when I affirmed that I did not have any ID on me. It had required the French Consul's intervention for the diligent functionary to permit me to step onto American soil. In the mayhem of my final preparations, I had clean forgotten both my passport and visa request. By the time I realised my oversight I was in the middle of the Atlantic. 'Too bad,' I had said to myself, 'if they do not allow me on land then, as soon as I have crossed the finish line, I'll head back to La Trinité.'

I had thought of just about everything for the return voyage to France. I had sufficient provisions on board of pasta and tinned food, wine and coffee and coal to cross, in a relaxed fashion, the Atlantic once more. All I needed to stock up on was fresh vegetables, eggs and drinking water, and do the small amount of washing my modest wardrobe of two pairs of blue jeans, some T-shirts and marine jerseys, required.

I had planned for everything other than finishing first and for what that entailed. I thought that, after a brief sojourn in Newport, I would head back to Old Europe at the double. However, my stay in this pretty town with its pastel shaded clapboard bungalows would stretch from June 19 to July 2. That is what is known as the price of fame. My beard, well developed during twenty-eight days at sea, initially served as cover. Then, having shaved, I looked different and hard to recognise until the local papers re-printed old photos of me from which I was easy to spot. I reply in my schoolboy English to everybody and, smiling, sign autographs for strangers who, like me, are sea- and boat-lovers.

I am taken to Washington. The limousine makes its way down wide, mansion lined avenues that are liberally interspersed with greenery and lets me out at the French Embassy. His Excellency M. Hervé Alphand received me as part of a reception and presented me with the insignia of the Légion d'Honneur, which the Head of State had, exceptionally, awarded me.

I am driven to New York. There I am presented to the President of the New York Yacht Club and the commanding Admiral of the Coast Guards. The Club is without question amongst the most hallowed spots sailing knows. Ranged against a backdrop of craftsman's wood panelling and classically restrained furniture are the cups, trophies and flags that evoke the history and role of this yachting holy of holies. More than just a yacht club, it is a museum. The walls are decorated with relief models of members' boats. I particularly remember the hall where there were glass boxes displaying models of every America's Cup defender and challenger, impressive in size and intricate detail.

I am driven back to Newport. From my window at the Shamrock Cliff Hotel, where I am staying, I watch the celebrated American international twelve-metres train, racing amongst themselves so as to decide on the boat to be the US Defender in the America's Cup which is due to take place in September. I can see *Columbia*, winner in 1958, *Easterner*, *Nefertiti*, *American Eagle*, *Constellation* and then *Nereus*, not a contender himself, but a sparring partner.

These boats' beauty, with their outsized, supple masts that carry such an area of sail and their ability to forge ahead in all winds, is fascinating to me.

Eric Tabarly

Leaving Plymouth, I had no idea that victory would allow me, a Naval Ensign, with a yachting reputation confined to Brittany, to live through such exciting times. The dream I was living culminated one morning as I was admiring these racing thoroughbreds at their moorings. My fantasy of sailing such a fine vessel turns into reality. On *Nereus* they are one crew member short. I happen to be there and they know who I am. The head helmsman invited me to replace this absent crew member. As hesitant as a beginner, I am instructed in the basic American nautical terms so that I am able to understand orders. My station is one of the mainsail sheets.

In a race between two boats, such as the America's Cup, the start can be decisive in the outcome of the duel. Bob Bavier, who would go on to be the head helmsman of *Constellation*, was at *Nereus*' helm. He and his rival both seek to steal a march on one another. It is a subtle game that requires skill, attentiveness, perfect knowledge of the rules and a strong dose of aggression. Even as I concentrate on my sheet, which I jam and observe from just behind the winch, I am impressed by the helmsman's sang-froid. Pipe in mouth, watching his chronometer and his position in relation to the opponent and the starting line, he never appeared to be worried, tense or caught unawares. Orders for trimming the sails and his own adjustments at the helm are given and made calmly and without undue haste. Overt displays, showmanship and imprecations – in other words any kind of mannered exuberance – strike me as a waste of energy.

By chance, on June 22, a Monday, I wake at 6am. The sun rises and I move to look out of my window. At the helm of *Gypsy Moth III*, Chichester passes in front of me. He crossed the finishing line at 5.37am, just three minutes within the thirty-day deadline. Chichester must be satisfied to have completed his crossing within the time he had anticipated back in Plymouth. He shaved, combed his hair and donned his reefer, before he made his way across the line. He is just as sharp and lively humoured when I greet him on dry land as he had been at the start of the race. He knows that I

Memories of the Open Sea

have won. He gives me a warm handshake and says: 'It is an honour to have been beaten by a sailor such as you.' He then introduces me to his wife, who has come to wait for him at the berth. The two of them, happily reunited, are going to keep a lookout for their son's arrival, so that they can set off aboard *Gypsy Moth III* on a cruise to the Bahamas.

The man makes an impression on me. There is a hint of serenity in Francis Chichester's look that comes close to detachment and which sets you thinking. He has a love for the sea and for boats, which for him are an expression of an eagerness to live. I feel really sorry for those who are bored by our planet because they do not know how to participate in nature's bounty. Chichester seems to have grasped the philosophy which holds that each precious second of life should be savoured. While some comfort themselves with pipedreams, others act. Francis Chichester is one of the latter, conscious of the difference between ambition and vanity.

On June 25 I receive news that, just before midnight, Valentine Howells finished in third place. His collision in Plymouth, block trouble, and plenty of other snags, lost him time, but he maintained his combativeness and good spirits. With a jar of frothy beer, almost lost to view in his outsized paw, he recounts, in amusing fashion, the story of his night-time berthing at Baltimore, Ireland and his cross-town search for a mechanic to repair a broken masthead fixing ... people he'd woken up, encountered in pyjamas or nightshirts on their doorsteps; the mechanic's refusal to do a soldering job at two in the morning:

'Eight o'clock, like everybody else. That's when my workshop opens.'

'But I am in the middle of a race!' cries Howells, in an effort to sway the recalcitrant artisan. This meets with failure.

'Eight o'clock, like everybody else.'

I enjoy Valentine's company. His natural consideration is well matched by unusual strength and resilience. Powerful like a combat tank, Howells is nevertheless gifted with moral rigour.

Eric Tabarly

Newport's armada of yachts and grand motor cruisers are an indication of American energy and strength. A modern ensemble of boatyards and ship chandlers and marinas, cranes and dry docks seem to me, the European, to represent the American Dream, where everything is available and anything possible. I compare the means at disposal here with a typical little Breton port, where the absence of plant and capital must be made up for with a fund of ingenuity.

Victory is sweet and it conveys certain advantages. Seven of the fourteen contestants were moored in Newport: myself, Chichester, Howells, Howell, Rose, Hasler and Lewis, who arrived on June 30. I was not going to wait for the others' arrival. At the same time as I prepare to re-embark for the return journey to France, the General Transatlantic Company proposes taking *Pen Duick II* on their cargo ship *Carbé*. A rendezvous is fixed for July 8, at Pier 14 in New York harbour. As for me, a trip back on *Le France* is on offer.

I cast off the afternoon of July 2 for a jaunt of one hundred and forty miles. For a fair way up the harbour I am accompanied by a launch with Valentine Howells, Bill Howell and Alec Rose on board. After our final goodbyes it turns back. Not far on, in the narrows, *Constellation* and *Nereus*, with her spinnaker raised, cross my bows and the crew of the twelve metre yacht, which I had briefly joined, give me three cheers. It is unusual for me to shed a tear, but this display of comradeship touches me greatly – why deny it?

There is nothing more than a restrained breeze and *Pen Duick II* drags along, so that by nightfall we have barely reached Judith Point, at the extremity of Newport Bay – a mere nine miles. Just beyond this point lie the straits running through Block and Long Islands. It is a region marked by strong tidal currents and, because of the coastline's proximity, unpredictable winds and heavy maritime traffic.

A night at the helm crawls by. At dawn I come out of Block Island strait and into Long Island strait. The raised, wooded coastline has a kind of monotonous charm. I head past Jefferson, North Port Bay and then Oyster Bay, home to an impressive collection of boats. On

Memories of the Open Sea

this second day *Pen Duick II* has clocked seventy-five miles and I decide to anchor in this ample yachting centre, have a meal and sleep before setting off very early in the morning of July 4.

At 7am I hoist the sails but with such a weak breeze I struggle to get out of the bay. Having subsequently reached Little Neck Bay, I head into the East River and then New York. There are already the makings of a dog day afternoon. To the north is the Bronx and the south, Queens.

Making headway down the river is hard work. Little wind, a lot of current. Two steps forward, one step back – but, by persistent tacking, I pass under a succession of bridges and enter into not particularly appetising waters that are home to tugs, various sized barges, merchant ships, and pleasure boats filled with vocal passengers, their hubbub on the water. They regard me as though I were an interloper. In this mechanised, noise filled environment my sailing vessel's crab like progress tacking sharply under the White Stone Bridge intrigues the New Yorkers. I advance at an annoyingly pedestrian pace along by La Guardia airport then making my way by Welfare Island and Hell Gate. With a becalmed crosswind I am stuck for a time, bows facing a street whose staring inhabitants are stopped in their tracks and stare at this strange apparition of a sailing boat.

A light breeze helps me out of this embarrassing situation and, finally, the current turns in my favour and allows me to get going again along by East Manhattan. The hours are running away and night falls. Its darkness is speckled with light coming through a thousand skyscraper windows. Above my head comes the infernal din of traffic on the Brooklyn Bridge, the last of seven spanning the East River.

Now the current is rushing me forwards to Upper Bay like an arrow. I can make out on my chart a little basin hemmed in by dykes which might fortuitously provide me with shelter, away from tugs' wash and the current. As *Pen Duick II* makes his way in, a voice shouts from the far end of the jetty telling me that I am not entitled to moor here. In pidgin English when I pass I exclaim:

'Not possible anywhere else. Much current. No wind...'

Alongside the jetty, a barge looks the perfect spot to pull up to. I berth and tie up and let the sails down. The time is 11pm. As I am organising my supper, a coastguard launch alerted by the dock watchman draws alongside *Pen Duick II*. They want to know who I am. I decline to say. What am I doing there, they ask? I explain that I am intending to be at Pier 14 around dawn, but that it is difficult for me to make my way under sail at night, given the strong current and there being no wind. The functionary asks for instructions on his radio.

'OK. Good night.'

When I wake up I resume my struggle with the current beneath the inscrutable glance of the Statue of Liberty. I will pass over my latest confrontation with the currents of the East and Hudson Rivers when I reach their confluence. With some difficulty I draw closer to the piers built along the opposite bank. I pick mine out a little further along the other side and, following a quick calculation, tell myself to go past it, so that *Pen Duick II*, pushed by the current, will be brought back in line with Pier 14. I do as I tell myself. And I cock up. Having gone about, when I cross the river my drift is such that I end all the way back at Pier 13 ... missed! Somewhat grumpily, I moor and lower the sails. The Transat personnel whom I had radioed in advance of leaving the basin of the previous night come to my aid, pulling me along the quay. Ouf! I am not about to repeat my cruise in the glaucous waters of New York. I infinitely prefer the high seas.

The following day, July 6, using *Carbé*'s jib crane I dismast the boat and two days later *Pen Duick II* is soaking up the sun on the cargo deck.

CHAPTER 13

FAME IS NOT THE SPUR WHEN I RACE

Man is ungrateful. My old *Pen Duick* has been left waiting for me in a corner of the Costantini yard – wintering him in a boathouse being beyond my means – and I have scarcely thought of him. I intend to sail him at some unspecified point in the future.

More immediately, on my return from the US, once I have politely undergone the demands placed on me by the fame of my solo victory, one thought dominates: to compete in the big, open sea races such as the Fastnet, the Morgan Cup, Plymouth–La Rochelle, Plymouth–Santander and, further afield, the Bermuda and Sydney–Hobart races.

My speedy return to France, thanks to the General Transatlantic Company, is a godsend. *Pen Duick II* and I are re-united at Le Havre, just in time to take part in the last two main races of the 1964 season: Yarmouth–Lequeitio and Lequeitio–La Trinité. With my unyielding hunger for all forms of sailing, I rate these two tests as being particularly interesting opportunities to put *Pen Duick II* up against the racing cruisers. The weak point of my ketch, I know, is that, conceived for single-handed sailing, he is undersailed and, unless I encounter perfect sea and wind conditions, any chance of winning is remote.

Once a controller acting for the Royal Ocean Racing Club (RORC), organiser of these races, has weighed *Pen Duick II*, we are placed among the Class II contenders. The purpose of this weighing is to calculate a boat's handicap according to various measurements that are multiplied or divided, according to a single formula that pertains for all contestants, so as to place different boats on a more equal footing. Whether that is what actually occurs is another thing.

I had telephoned my mother as soon as I had arrived in Newport. Her happiness following all the anxiety caused by my radio silence had overwhelmed me. She was an extraordinary mother. I phone my parents again and then Gilles Costantini. He and my father are going to be members of my crew.

I shan't linger over this race. Having crossed to England on August 8, *Pen Duick II* is on the starting line. At the outset, the wind, a stiff force six, causes all the other competitors to reef in. My boat is under full sail and takes his place at the head of Class 2, close on the heels of the Class 1 *Outlaw* who has a reputation for performing well with a fresh wind. This wind drops during the night and, undersailed for the calm, *Pen Duick II* is overhauled, finishing in the middle of his class.

The return leg from Lequeitio to La Trinité is initially marked by a moderate breeze that then pushes on, developing into a force seven. Straightaway, *Pen Duick II* wakes up, galloping across the waves and into the lead to give us, it seemed, victory. But then the combination of a squall and an agitated sea led me to confuse the Belle-Île and Île d'Yeu lighthouses. So we make an uncalled-for detour and lose the race. Instead of arriving as victors, as we should have done, around 6am, we come into La Trinité at midday, defeated. The rushing wind is not able to block out the acclamation of the crowd come to greet me. I had left the Trinitaian harbour to what almost amounted to indifference, save a shout of encouragement here and there. My return received much more recognition. But it is not glory I am after when I race.

One has to always analyse cause and effect – such is my character, or obsessiveness. During the course of these two races I studied the boat's performance and what I noted confirmed my original hunch. When the wind was up *Pen Duick II* was on top form, whatever its direction, but when it slackened he was a cause for consternation. It is clear what has to be done: make the sail area bigger.

I took on a big project and sacrificed everything else to the restoration of *Pen Duick*. I heaped another responsibility on my shoulders in the construction of *Pen Duick II*. Now I am cooking up more trouble, the need to have a bigger boat with schooner rigging so as to rub shoulders with the leading racing boats – a new boat that will be called *Pen Duick III*.

For the time being it is just a project. Whilst waiting to bring it to fruition, to test the validity of my idea, I decide to transform my current boat into a schooner. This modification has the added bonus of not costing too much: the mainmast will stay where it is, becoming the foremast; and then all that will need to be done is to replace the mizzen with a taller mast, placed further forward.

From the autumn, when I return to the base in Lorient, the Navy wants me to undergo a specialist marine commando course anticipated to last a year and that is when the Costantini yard will take care of the alterations to *Pen Duick II*'s rigging.

There can be no doubt that someone is looking over me in this life, helping me at critical junctures in my career to profit from chance meetings or fortunate decisions.

Towards July 1965 my marine commando training is nearly over when I am summoned to the Naval Staff at Lorient. The officer by whom I am received passes on a proposal I have scarcely been expecting: 'The Minister for Sports and Young People has asked the Navy to second you to his department. Needless to say, that is on the understanding that you are amenable to this detachment. What do you say?'

'I accept.'

Maurice Herzog had come to welcome me on my return to Le Havre and congratulate me in the name of the Government. I had subsequently met him at official receptions. I was confident in assuming that he was offering me a position which would allow me to pursue my sailing ambitions.

It is a lucky end of year for me in which events conspire in my favour. The project of a third, bigger boat is now in the forefront of my mind. It is with the next, 1968, Transatlantic Race in mind that I want it bigger. I knew that I had experienced no difficulty manoeuvring *Pen Duick II* and was now certain that I would be able to handle a significantly bigger boat. But building him will cost. With the royalties from my first book, *Victoire en solitaire*, published by Arthaud, I have a tidy sum in the bank, but still a long way from what I need.

Providence once again smiles on me. Passing Maurice Herzog along a corridor one morning in his ministry, the hero of Annapurna says:

'Tabarly, if you were to sell your boat, I would buy it for the school.'

The school in question was the National Sailing School being built at Beg Rohu in the Quiberon peninsula. I had not yet put *Pen Duick II* on sale. Nevertheless I knew that in order to fit out another boat he and I would have to part.

'Actually I am considering doing so, Minister.'

'In that case, go and see M Chartois, the school's future director, and sort things out with him.'

A rendezvous is made and I find myself at the Ministry of Sports, received by Chartois. He is a little fellow, smiling, hospitable, almost ingratiating. His question: 'What price are you asking for your boat?'

'I think that ten million – old – francs would be a fair price.'

Chartois does not haggle. Rather, with a nod of his head, he indicates his agreement, before replying: 'That's agreed then. The only thing, as you know, is that the school is not yet actually ready to open, so nor do I have a budget yet. All the same, let us agree that the boat belongs to the school and that, as soon as I am in a position to, the account will be settled. In the meantime, any cost you incur in maintaining the boat we will add to the purchase price.'

Memories of the Open Sea

There are no signed papers. Chartois' word is all I require.

Following this interview I continue to use the boat, having consulted the director, who has included *Pen Duick II* in the school's inventory.

Converted into a schooner, the boat is put into the water to take part in some pre-season races in Brittany and at La Rochelle. Short distance, they serve to fine tune the modifications. The crew's nucleus comprises my father, Guy, brother, Patrick, and Gilles Costantini. We bag first places but, come July, after a good showing in the Cowes–Dinard race, our subsequent results are not so good. In a light, following wind I observe that the jib is too small as is an undersized spinnaker. These analyses help me to think through an appropriate rigging for the boat under consideration: *Pen Duick III*.

Meanwhile, and obviously with Chartois' agreement, I ready *Pen Duick II* for the big American race to Bermuda. For a second time, *Pen Duick II* is modified in order to conform with US handicapping, not the same as British rules. The rigging is changed and the boat reverts to a ketch, the main mast fore rather than towards the stern, now occupied by a very substantial mizzen. The addition of a bowsprit allows the jib's foot to be extended and for an increase in the spinnaker size from 70 square metres to 110 square metres. As for the hull, I sever the long transom. A loss in looks is the price to pay for more power.

My new sailor's status, on detachment to the Ministry of Sports, does not bring any financial benefit. Unlike the other fellows, my original salary is not increased in line with inflation. But this drawback is made up for by not being inhibited in where I go. I can live wherever suits me best, especially at my parents' house in St-Pierre-Quiberon and thereby close to La Trinité where the Costantinis carried out *Pen Duick II*'s transformation. A single race in the spring of 1966 assures me the new rigging is definitely more efficient.

At the end of March I cast off from my mooring at La Trinité for the US. I decided to deliver him alone and keep myself up to the mark with a view to the next single-handed Transatlantic in which I anticipate taking part once more; I like having projects in reserve. I had bad weather during this crossing and a ventilator breaking down forced me to pull into Fayal Island in the Azores. I mend. I move on.

The sun keeps me company almost the whole distance but, with land in sight, fog descends around me. The route into New York is busy with merchant ships and liners, the wind is negligible, the swell undulating and, by the narrowest of margins, a trawler avoids colliding with me, pulling up hard before the point of impact. Finally, feeling knocked out with tiredness, I make it into Oyster Bay towards the end of the afternoon. I stayed up for three nights. The first I listen out for sirens and fog horns, the next struggling against the worst storm I have ever encountered, the last finally beating along Long Island Sound.

This time I have my passport and visa. I therefore have the relaxed attitude of the man who considers he is in order. To announce my arrival I phone through to New York Customs covering the Oyster Bay area. The official politely asks me, as a formality, to pass by his office. Not having a car, the return journey will take a day using public transport.

I get on a bus the following morning and go to the immigration officer's post. He inspects my papers. Everything is fine and dandy before he asks: 'When are you leaving Oyster Bay?'

'I am here to compete in the Oyster Bay–Newport race, which starts on June 12. I shall cast off then.'

'Good,' he says blandly. 'I will hold onto the boat's papers. The day before you leave, come and get them together with your pass into Newport.'

At this time in the United States a pass was mandatory when you were moving from one area to another. What puts me out is having to make the Oyster Bay–New York trip once more, a second loss of time I would like to get round.

Memories of the Open Sea

'I do not have a car,' I say, trying to win him round. 'It takes a day to come here and return to my boat. Seeing as my papers are in order and you know my departure date, you could issue me the pass now.'

He shakes his head in disapproval.

'I will look after the papers,' he repeats decisively.

What was bound to – did – occur. I am joined by my crew of Gérard Petipas, Michel Vanek, Alain Glicksman, Philippe Lavat and Jurgen Romer. With every attention to detail, *Pen Duick II* is readied right up until departure time. Fatally, I completely forgot to go and get the boat's papers and pass in New York.

So on June 12 1966 the start is signalled in Oyster Bay. In spite of the participation of the East Coast champion, the redoubtable Ted Turner, a headwind blowing at thirty-five knots helps us to arrive as clean winners at Newport under just jib and mizzen. And, by a cruel little trick of fate, the immigration officer who had handled my arrival with neither passport nor visa in the single-handed Transat is on duty once more. A good memory for faces perhaps being part of the job, he immediately recognises me, remembers my papers not being in order two years previously. I feel his eye upon me.

Authoritatively, he says to me: 'I trust everything is OK this time.'

'Almost!'

And I explain to him my oversight. The fellow went almost berserk.

One would have thought that, in a modern country like the US, one could organise the boat's documentation to be sent from New York to Newport in a matter of hours. But no! The start of the Bermuda Race is due to take place ten days later. So we stopped in Newport for these ten days. Well, each of these slow moving days, I wait for the precious documents to come by post. Day by day relations between the immigration officer and me deteriorate. The day of departure I come across a note left lying on my chart table. Written by the functionary in big letters it says: 'If you cast off without having visited my office, you will be boarded and searched by gunboat.' I go and see him and soothe him and he lets us go.

This time victory beckoned us but then thumbed its nose. On the penultimate day we are, in fact, well ahead of the rest of our class and not so far behind the other boats. I am reasonably sure the traps of the Gulf Stream – capricious current whose meanderings cannot be predicted – have been negotiated successfully. Depending on which part of it one is in, the current can be favourable or adverse; its central section runs at a rate of four knots. The only way to ascertain the direction of this vicious current is to test the temperature in the knowledge that the main section, or centre, is the hottest. We find the current we want and, pressing on, make a valiant advance in spite of the violent storms and moody sea that are typical here. Twenty-four hours from the finishing line victory is ours for the taking. The lead is significant. But a forty-five degree shift in the wind loses us the race and our class position plummets to fifth.

As a footnote to the little saga the boat's documents were waiting for me in Hamilton.

Hope springs eternal. The crew and I think that we can make a good showing in the Bermuda–Copenhagen Transatlantic. The race seems tailor made to bring out the best in *Pen Duick II*, along a route where strong, following winds tend to be dominant. And so it is that after four days, with a nice breeze blowing, we are hammering along on a broad reach, on a silver blue sea, feeling optimistic. It is me at the helm. The spinnakers are fully blown out from each mast, the water lapping along the hull; no need to check the speedometer to know that we are moving along very nicely. Without warning, the tiller goes flabby and, without my being able to do anything to prevent it, *Pen Duick II* luffs: the rudder locking mechanism has come loose – the obvious cause being metal fatigue. By joining a spinnaker pole with some cabin planks taken out and brought up to me by the crew, I concoct a jury rudder. Faster than five knots it is hard to hold and it requires the muscles of lads like Philippe Lavat and Michel Vanek, working in tandem, to handle it.

As a boy Éric wanted to be an Admiral. Once he discovered the amount of studying he would need to do, this less than brilliant, but realistic, pupil gave up the ambition. His passion for boats remained.

Tabarly dressed for the bush. At Tann Son Nhut, during his service in Indochina.

Saigon. Tabarly making a solo flight in a Cessna.

Tabarly (left) with fellow trainee pilots and a Lancaster at Agadir air base.

Trainee officers on the deck of the *Jeanne d'Arc*. Éric (standing, left) finished last in his year. He was now a Lieutenant, nevertheless.

His first – and only – Naval sea command : an EDIC 9092 tank landing ship. The job he was given involved finding beaches where the craft could land.

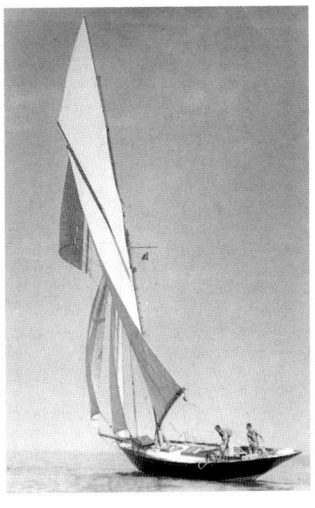

A timeless boat – *Pen Duick* aged one hundred years.

Pen Duick returns to the sea. His hull has been re-cast in fibreglass and, before long, he will be sailing again.

Drawn from a young age to the boat's appearance, Tabarly consented to years of sacrifice and devotion on his behalf.

It was *Pen Duick*'s combination of elegant lines and traditional rigging that made Tabarly think of him as a noble old gentleman.

Tabarly's friend, the boat designer Gilles Constantini, standing in front of a sketch of *Pen Duick II*.

Winner of the Single-handed Transatlantic. During the race, *Pen Duick II*'s radio silence had caused concern for his parents, now able to congratulate a son, who did not always get on with mechanical devices.

Washington, 1964. Wearing a borrowed Naval Officer's uniform, Tabarly receives the Légion d'honneur from the French Ambassador.

Aboard *Pen Duick III* with the all-winning crew of 1967. It included his father, Gérard Petipas (left) and Olivier de Kersauson (second from right).

Sea trials: against *Pen Duick III* and his crew, the new trimaran proves to Tabarly that he is quicker – but not, yet, as reliable. *Pen Duick IV* would later be bought by Alain Colas. Re-named *Manureva*, the multihull sunk without trace during the 1978 Route du Rhum.

Pen Duick V going into the water. He was the first water ballast boat.

The first Whitbread round the world race, 1973: *Pen Duick VI* in a rough sea. Originally conceived for this race and a crew of fourteen, Tabarly won the Single-handed Transatlantic with him three years later. He was without doubt the fastest boat, on all points of sail, of the time.

Tired but happy – Tabarly following the 1976 Single-handed Transatlantic.

The five remaining *Pen Duicks*. From left to right : *V, II, I* and *III*. Behind them, *VI*.

Éric with Jacqueline and their daughter, Marie. He used to say, 'I will never marry and have children. I don't want any dogs'. The old stone barn he found by the River Odet was home to a dog, too.

Memories of the Open Sea

Thus the race ends for *Pen Duick II*. Having abandoned it, we require five days, sailing in thick fog to reach St-Pierre-et-Miquelon. Within this cocoon-like corner we make our way to the invisible port with the aid of the lighthouse foghorn, the sound of waves breaking on the rocks and the depth sounder. There are five days of repairs and five more, having cast off, spent in a pea souper. The sun reappears for us to return to Granville under spinnaker. On balance, 1966 has been a disappointing season. Nevertheless, *Pen Duick II* mark 3 has shown what he is capable of.

I am out of money. All my royalties went on the boat's modifications, but these reduced circumstances do not perturb me. The completion of *Pen Duick II*'s sale to the National Sailing School is imminent and I will then have access to the payment.

Once I am free of money worries relating to my second boat I can cause new ones to come into being, building *Pen Duick III*.

CHAPTER 14

FREE TO INCUR NEW DEBTS, HAVING PAID OLD DEBTS

I am not contemplating marriage or starting a family or even owning some handsome hound – having too great a fear at the age of thirty-five of bidding my freedom goodbye. I am interested in political and economic affairs just as I am in marine paintings, cinema and theatre and also, when I have the time, mountains and unspoilt countryside, fine buildings and old châteaux, gothic cathedrals and houses dating from the Middle Ages. I am not indifferent to world events and social crises, nor to the misery and hunger that prey on certain continents. All this by way of saying that I am neither misanthrope nor misogynist, that I am not a dropout and that I am interested in what goes on in our world. But, in truth, sailing is the only thing which grabs me, which sparks my creative spirit and subsequent projects. Anything to do with increasing the speed or improving the performance of a boat, regardless of sea or wind conditions, I find fascinating.

Before setting off for Oyster Bay, I had finished and given the basic design of my future boat to La Perrière boatyard at Lorient so that they could work out the detailed structure. I had chosen this yard because the Costantinis only built in wood and I intended that *Pen Duick III* should be in aluminium, or, to be exact, duralinox, a lightweight metal La Perrière yard had experience using.

Once I am back in France, following minor alterations, the final outline is decided on. Next, in the ENSM's Nantes hull tank, tests are carried out on the hull and keel under the supervision of Professor Ravilly. The results correspond to my criteria: *Pen Duick III*, even if he was the identical shape, would be better than his predecessor and, since he is actually bigger – a thirteen metre against a ten metre waterline – he will be unquestionably faster. The yard starts work. All that remains for me to do is to go and collect my money from M Chartois.

I return to the Ministry of Sports and Young People, rue de Châteaudun. I have the feeling that the business will be briskly conducted. Chartois gives me an affable reception and, when I tell him how I am hoping the situation can be made regular now that the Bag Rohu school is formally set up and that I need the money for the new boat I have under construction, he replies:

'That is OK. The money has been set aside. You will get it soon – within the next few days.'

In a trusting state of mind I return to my parents at St-Pierre-Quiberon. To wait. For days. Weeks. For months. Still no news. I set off again to Paris. I seek out Chartois again. On seeing me, he raises his arms in a weak gesture of impotence: 'My poor friend,' he groans, 'I am truly sorry, but the National Institute of Sports bursar does not want to hear another word spoken regarding the purchase of your boat.'

This I find a bit off. Believing him to have been sold, I had not tried to find any other buyer, so I still have *Pen Duick II* on my hands. The changes I undertook to enhance his performance do not alter his market value.

It is one of the few times in my life when I shout out my frustration. My raging is heard by Colonel Crespin (ret), the Director of Sports at the Ministry, who asks me to come into his office. This bald headed, stockily built man has an old soldier's natural authority. He asks to know the reason for my anger and I explain my predicament. Indignant, he straightaway picks up his phone and calls the bursar at the INS.

'I am told that you no longer wish to buy Tabarly's boat?'

This is flatly denied: 'I do want to buy it, but Chartois opposes the purchase.'

The Colonel cuts in: 'Tabarly was told his boat would be bought and that can't be gone back on. I order you to buy it!'

I leave Crespin reassured. Naively, I say to myself: 'In a fortnight this will be sorted out and I will have my cheque.' Once again, weeks pass by and nothing happens, aside from work starting at La Perrière yard and Chartois' continued obstructionism in the face of further directives. I am furious. Crespin himself is hopping mad. In January 1967 the Colonel, beside himself, takes the bit between the teeth and calls the various parties into his office.

'Mon Colonel,' groans Chartois, 'the Sailing School budget cannot support the maintenance of a boat *Pen Duick II*'s size...'

'Monsieur, that is something you should have considered in advance,' came Crespin's glacial retort.

Not accepting defeat, Chartois attempts a final dodge. He says: 'Mon Colonel, the students cannot do without electronic equipment. The boat needs this apparatus before going to Quiberon.'

The Boat Show organisers had presented me with a speedometer and electronic weathervane – a valued instrument. I had fixed both to the boat. This equipment belonged to me and I needed it on *Pen Duick III*. Cheeky of Chartois to try and grab what is mine. Lucky that Crespin is there to insist on everything being done correctly. In a tone that deters the least contradiction, he brings the discussion to a close, saying: 'Whilst no doubt your pupils need electronic equipment, there is no reason why Tabarly should give it to you as a present.'

That was that. I kept my instruments.

Pen Duick III is launched at the beginning of May. A week's sea trials go well and then the boat is involved in races to decide on the French team for the Admiral's Cup, a biannual, international event. Each country is represented by three boats measuring between twenty-five and seventy feet. Ranking is made by country, adding

Memories of the Open Sea

up the total points picked up in the course of four contests: the Channel Race, the Fastnet, and two races in Cowes Week.

My crew is made up of Philippe Lavat, Pierre English – whom I knew well from when he was a teenage friend of my brother Patrick – Yves Guégan, Daniel Gilles, my father – nicknamed 'Babar' – Olivier de Kersauson and Gérard Petipas. They are all good sailors but a boat this size takes a little time to get used to before the crew can work in harmony. Inevitably, there are cock-ups – hoisting the spinnaker being the most notable; our close first round win owes something to luck. The second was gained more convincingly, because good crew members learn fast. Kersauson and Guégan, on military service with the Navy, are seconded to me. Both are nice lads, Kersauson amazing me with his physical strength and feel for the sea not to mention his pronounced shyness. He is barely twenty years old and always anxious to know if I am happy with his work.

I eagerly anticipate June for the season's first important race, the Morgan Cup. It follows the form of a triangle in the Channel, setting off from Portsmouth to the Cherbourg buoy and then turning back towards the Royal Sovereign lightship off the English coast and, from there, the final leg back to Portsmouth.

Pen Duick III is set to perform well in it. We had arrived a few minutes before the start, just in time to get the race rules and to register the boat for his first big contest. Before the cannon report, to take advantage of the following wind, I order raising the spinnaker and *Pen Duick III* surges through this armada of more than one hundred boats. The Cherbourg buoy appears through the fog. Fore, my crew imposes itself in lowering the spinnaker and main foresail and raising the jib, staysail and smaller, battened foresail. Their manoeuvres are flawless. I am now fully confident they know their way round the boat.

From the Cherbourg buoy a headwind stands between us and the Royal Sovereign. We can either make small tacks across this line or start by making a single tack along the French coast. Because of the current I go for the second course of action, which pays off handsomely. It takes us beyond the calm which will surround our competitors in the middle of the Channel. Thanks to this stroke of luck we are far ahead of the rest of our class at the Royal Sovereign. Having been making our way for a while under spinnaker down the English coast, we cruise by the bigger boats like *Bloodhound* and *Striana*. When we pass by the jury boat in Portsmouth, they let us know by hand signal that we are first. It is six hours before the runner-up appears.

Following this victory, my crew staged not so much a mutiny as a collective sulk. I am absolutely obliged to return to France. The sailors, who were counting on going on land to celebrate this success, as is their due, were disappointed. I don't know how Olivier de Kersauson engineered this coup. Sailing at my side the shy young gentleman has developed in confidence and his humour and repartee, even when the sail is tense, make everyone laugh. On that Sunday, after we had cast off, to make their displeasure known, my crew came down off the deck in silence and into their bunks. In the cockpit I hear Kersauson's cocky jest: 'Apparently you crossed the Atlantic single-handed. At least that's what they say. Show us how you did it!'

Now I hear the others sniggering like kids, including my father, who is in on the joke. I do not say a word. I helm.

It is Gérard Petipas who takes care of navigation. The fact of being spared this work lets me concentrate harder on tactics and to be up on deck more, to direct rigging adjustments and manoeuvres, and to step in if a crew member gets in a muddle, and take over at his position immediately. As a skipper I seldom raise my voice. I let these young people who share my love of boats and racing get on with it. If it turns out that one of them lacks competence I am not going to hold it against him. It is me who brought him on board so the responsibility is mine. I knew Gérard from Cherbourg, the period of racing the '*II*'s. He was in charge of navigation on a boat berthed close to mine as we

Memories of the Open Sea

readied ourselves for a RORC race. He had been a Lieutenant for a while and was preparing to become Captain in the Merchant Navy. During his holidays he raced. When he left the General Transatlantic Company, Gérard set up as a marine consultant in Paris and came out regularly on *Pen Duick II* and *Pen Duick III*. On his chart table he plots our position and lays out the available information so that I can decide on which course we should set.

And it is a long course in order to get to Stockholm for our next start. We set foot on dry land only briefly. With the help of the crew, the business of preparing the boat is undertaken, the rigging checked and, without delay, the provisioning carried out. The July 4 departure for the Round Gotland Race is from Sandham.

As these preparations are made, I cast an eye over my crew. I am well into my thirties whilst they are mostly round the twenty mark. They are young people who are at ease with themselves, solid characters, not trouble. Like me, they are in thrall to the excitement offered by boats and racing and couldn't care less that they don't have any money. Sailing does not provide them with a career, just satisfies their hunger for new horizons for – when it comes to nautical miles – these are undoubted bulimics. I look at them. Some will go on to be skippers in due course, we will become rivals and I will be both pleased and proud to have taught them what I know. During manoeuvres which put muscles to the test, there is the calm of English, unparalleled in his adjustment of sheets, then Kersauson, like a spirited animal, Vanek, who is serious and a very good helmsman, Guégan, very dry humoured and the meticulous Sévi and Gilles. My father – the on board chef – recognises them as sailors and treats them rather as though they were his own sons, whispering to me every now and again:

'They are first class.'

He is right. Leaving to one side odd flashes of anger, hard to avoid given the trickiness of certain manoeuvres, the cramped living space and traditional rivalry between the different 'quarters' (the other's quarter always being inferior, the one that messes up etc, etc), there is a good camaraderie on board *Pen Duick III*. For sure, little quarrels always flare up amidst the adrenaline of a race. But I did not let anything beyond that take hold. I did not tolerate pettiness.

Typically for the Baltic, much of the race took place in a light breeze then towards the end it picked up. In real time we beat bigger boats than us, including *Britt-Marie*, twenty metres and *Rendezvous*, twenty-one metres. Only *Germania*, twenty-two metres long, passed by us coming up to the finishing line and on compensated time, therefore, we won. Played two, won two.

We have some time to kill before competing in the Channel Race which gets underway at Portsmouth on August 2. Like tourists, we stroll around the romantic archipelago, which runs between Lake Mälaren and the open sea facing Stockholm. After we relax on the Finnish island of Öland, home to the famous ship-owner Ericsson who maintained a significant fleet of Cape Horn sailing ships until the last war. In a museum devoted to the last of the sail powered shipping lines we visit the four-masted *Pommern*.

Having made stops at Helsinki and Kiel, we leave the Baltic feeling suitably melancholic and head for Portsmouth. Like the Morgan Cup, the Channel Race follows a triangular course: Portsmouth to the Royal Sovereign lightship, on to the Le Havre lightship and back to Portsmouth. Most of the race there is just a light breeze which keeps us ahead of the other contestants: played three, won three.

Gérard Petipas shows himself once again to be a master navigator. I do not have to intervene in the crew's manoeuvres at all since they are flawless.

There remains the Fastnet, which is the key test. We make a fetch on a flat sea to Land's End. It does not encourage *Pen Duick III*'s brilliance. Then, as the wind swings round to the south, a spinnaker led sprint to the Fastnet lighthouse off the southwest coast of Ireland. Edmond de Rothschild's powerful *Gitana* leads the way, then us, closely followed by the American *Figaro* and the German *Rubin*. On the return leg that leads to the Scilly Isles, we make a fetch beneath a stormy sky, whilst the wind continually changes in force and direction. We win by a distance, navigating this choppy sea by beating with each change of wind, the crew maintaining a near manic tempo. Passing Lizard's Point, a short way from the finish, the telegraph signallers let us know via Scott radio that we are first. I hold back from believing it. Surely *Gitana*, twenty-seven metres, has remained ahead of us? But he was hampered by halyard hassle, and it is true. Played four, won four.

We still have two races left: Plymouth–La Rochelle and La Rochelle–Bénodet. In the first, having gone round Ushant, we pull away from the Italian *Levantades* in very bad weather. The second took place with an average strength wind to which we fetched, garnering our sixth victory. In the summer of 1967 *Pen Duick III* and his crew are invincible.

This procession of victories lets me entertain the possibility of measuring up to the Australians, Americans, British and New Zealanders who, up until then, had exchanged victory in the legendary Sydney–Hobart race amongst themselves. It starts on Boxing Day.

General de Gaulle, President of the Republic, had invited me to dine at the Élysée. This was a great honour for me, but I had to decline. The reason being that the dinner's date coincided with that for the launching of *Pen Duick III* which, on account of the tides, could not be moved either back or forward. The date chosen by the General fell awkwardly!

My non acceptance caused a stir within the naval hierarchy. They were indignant at such lèse majesté from a mere ship's Lieutenant.

On returning to France a letter from the Élysée was waiting for me, written by General de Gaulle: 'Monsieur, I hope that you will be able to join us for dinner this time – tides permitting – on October 20.'

I had to get there late. My arrival was recorded for posterity by photos that show me bounding up the Élysée's steps, four at a time.

CHAPTER 15

SOMEWHAT BRUISED, I WIN

December in Australia and it is summertime. The smell of barbecuing wafts around Sydney, capital of New South Wales. At dusk, in the parks and in big and small gardens that line or look down on the breathtaking bay, the local population makes busy preparing its grilled lamb and fish including the succulent barramundi.

Australia's abundance is striking. Even the gulls that circle about and linger on the pontoons and quays are more substantial looking than their French counterparts. In the evening, the Pacific Ocean shimmers even before the Southern Cross shows. On the wooden wharfs, painted white, are exhibited white hammerhead sharks, hung by the tail, that look like torpedoes. Killed at the harbour's entrance by professionals, their appearance in death remains fearsome.

The average Australian is, to be clear, a fit and competitive colossus. From daybreak to the start of the working day, he can be observed in the act of jogging along the water's edge on Bondi Beach. At lunch, he speeds out of the workplace and takes over parks and other available green spaces to give his all in baseball and Australian rules football – amongst the most brutal of games, where the 'rules' permit just about anything.

The Australian, with his lumberjack's frame, is no delicate creature. A tough day's work out of the way, he lets his barbecue build up in the evening and carefully tends the grilled pieces without forgetting his beer or wine, the product of French or German or

Memories of the Open Sea

Italian vines transplanted to the antipodes: fifteen degree proof wine can have a powerful affect in this climate.

Yves Guégan, Olivier de Kersauson and I are in Sydney waiting for *Pen Duick III* to arrive. The previous month he was loaded onto *La Vanoise*. His unloading was put back by an Australian dockers' strike. This hold up allowed the rest of the crew – Lavat, Vanek, English, Petipas, my brother Patrick and my father – whose work commitments have kept them in France, to be with us again in time to help put the rigging back up.

There are a few days left till the race and, as usual, we are busy with final preparations, now and again interrupted by visits from the race officials carrying out inspections. The Cruising Club of Australia insists, in addition to its standard security rules, that each entrant should have a motor on board in working condition. *Pen Duick III* was equipped with a Renault-Marine.

Whilst eagerly awaiting to set off for Hobart, I continue to think about my next project. The previous December, almost a year to the day, I had sailed on an English trimaran, *Toria*, twelve or thirteen metres long, designed and built by Derek Kelsall. This little jaunt had impressed on me the breakthrough that had now been effected by multihulls. Before, they were heavy and disappointing sailing close to the wind. Having built *Pen Duick III* with RORC organised races and the third single-handed Transatlantic in 1968 in mind, I now knew that, in spite of outstanding qualities, he would not be able to keep up with the new generation of multihulls.

The winter trip on *Toria*, from Cornwall's north coast to London where he was due to be exhibited was made with a good wind and a well developed sea. It had proved to me the boat worked efficiently, could operate well on all points of sail and was quick. The next Transat, I was convinced, would be won by a multihull. I had one on which work was already underway at La Perrière yard.

Eric Tabarly

Sydney Harbour is a vast expanse of water. To get out of it you must pass through the Heads, twin greenery-sprouting cliffs with the aura of caryatids that oversee entrance into the Pacific.

Tuesday December 26. The immediate problem encountered at the 11am departure is fifty-six other contestants, camp followers and neutral observers. The thermometer reading was over 30°C in the shade, the greenery dried out and the population parched. Nevertheless, like other Australian cities, Sydney had her winter make up on. Imported pines received a layer of artificial snow while all the Father Christmases sweated and dehydrated underneath their false beards and hooded robes. All along the cliffs which circle the bay and look out to sea, people in their thousands picnic and watch the boats pass by beneath.

There is a following wind but, hemmed in amongst a marine peloton, *Pen Duick III* does not benefit. Those contestants that opted to head out closer to land receive more wind and advance a little quicker.

Before passing through the Heads, one must go around a buoy. My crew, having just lowered the main foresail, are energetically bringing the spinnaker in when I notice that up ahead amongst the leaders there is a certain hesitation, followed by genuine perplexity, intensifying into considerable hesitation. The buoy we must turn is not where the charts say it should be. No one is sure which route to take. Skippers find themselves in a shambles. The soundtrack is noise of water, wind in the rigging, Anglo-Saxon curses flying about.

Something knocks against the hull; there is shouting and insults fly about. A motorboat has knocked into us. The helmsman, losing control of himself, recklessly turns his boat about, crashing into a dinghy that immediately goes down, to leave its three passengers splashing about in the water. We do not witness their rescue because, at that moment, the wretched buoy comes into view – a fair way downwind from where she should be, but for a simple reason, that we learn about later. She had broken free from her mooring and then been pushed along by the wind. At once the boat stampede narrows

Memories of the Open Sea

in on her. Though no longer fixed, each is expected to round this moving target that seems to be playing a game with us in its refusal to stay still. I feel rather as if I am at a funfair playing dodgems. The leading boats are joined by those behind who stole their wind. It is as if in closed ranks, eight or ten abreast, that we march on. But actually it is chaos. The inner part of the peloton assert their right to round the buoy. At the same time the next section struggles to create some leeway with the boat that hems it in which, in turn, is trying to force out its close neighbour. All around people are shouting 'Water! Water!' In other words: 'Give me a bit of space!'

Pen Duick III's solid metal hull should deter others from coming too close even if *Noria* finds himself sandwiched between us and another. From this direction and that comes the sound of a crunch joined by a chorus of invective and imprecation, making it clear that fair play and rules of priority have given way in this melée at sea to the sentiments of every man for himself and *après moi le déluge*... as this intimidatory game continues, I succeed in rounding the buoy in fourth place, luffing according to the boat's taste. We pass through the Heads and into the ocean on an easterly course.

The following day there would be quite extensive coverage of this incident in the Australian Press. I particularly remember a cartoon which had *Pen Duick III* with a cannon on his bows, the crew as pirates brandishing boarding cutlasses. The caption was me saying: 'They should have warned me that down under one has to fight one's way forward.'

The forecast was that the south easterly wind would not last much longer. Instead there would be a north easterly, the dominant wind at this time of year as Gérard Petipas had told me.

' Yes, but I have heard from Australians with their local knowledge that at night this north easterly subsides, although further out one can remain reasonably confident of a strong breeze,' I said.

'And?'

'And I think the best thing to do is to head away from the coast and try to get away from the calms.'

Eric Tabarly

I take a look at what is going on around us. The majority of boats are turning south. Our main rivals though have opted for the same course as us, making a tack out into the open sea.

Our brief lead is surrendered to the New Zealander *Kahurangui*, a superb twenty-metre, but we continue to push ahead of *Fidelis*, a second New Zealander twenty-metre. After six miles heading east, I turn south. In spite of only a light wind we head on all the same then, during the night of Tuesday to Wednesday this drops away to a dead calm. As was predicted. *Mea culpa*. We have to wait until the late morning for the northeast wind to pick up once more. *Pen Duick III* idly, rather as if he was waking from a deep sleep, resumes his spinnaker led progress. The whole day we give chase to those who have got ahead of us, having headed south straightaway without any tactical complications. They include smaller boats. To beat them on compensated time we need to overhaul them convincingly. I should not have tried to be so clever.

The long *Fidelis*, which had got ahead of us in the weak breeze, is moving forward at the same speed as *Pen Duick III* now that the wind has formed some muscle, while *Kahurangui* battles on, a good way back in our wake.

On the night of Wednesday to Thursday the wind swings round to the northwest. From the cockpit comes an abrupt cry: 'The wishbone is broken!'

This type of traditional spar, which I like to use for modern day racing, curves round the head of the sail holding it out. It is attached just above the second spreader. That means climbing the mast to repair it. Guégan and Kersauson are both quick off the mark to volunteer for the climb, but I go because I want to see for myself exactly what has broken.

I am hoisted up in the bosun's chair. Once I have got as high as the second spreader, I support myself against it and begin my patching up operation. Having to hang on with my left hand for security makes it a slow, painstaking single-handed task. Every now and again I glance down and see my crew watching me anxiously from the deck. I recall Kersauson's characteristic sally: 'When a guy is at work in the masts, you must never take your eyes off him so, if he falls, you can be first to look through his pockets!' Although I am not in the most comfortable position I can't help smiling at Olivier's idea. My pockets are empty.

The repair takes me an hour. As usual after this kind of operation I am feeling pretty worn out when I come down.

'I hope that is going to hold,' I say.

And the night remains young. As we manoeuvre in the fo'c'sle, an extension pole, that had not been secured properly by the crew, falls from above my position close to the foremast. It lays me out, half conscious. My skull, chin and nose are all bleeding but I am too busy bawling out the culprits to pay that much mind. (In the spirit of charity I will not now name names.) My head is still spinning. I do not want to quit the cockpit as long as the manoeuvre is going on, but I am almost physically removed by my brother, Patrick and some of the other crew members who oblige me to settle down in the cabin. I feel pain but it is bearable. I do not intend to rest for long, not when we have yet to cover six hundred miles. I sit in front of the kitchen sink while the two medical students, English and Lavat, disinfect my cuts. I was lucky. Nothing worse – the accident could have been worse – than torn skin. My father, as ever with his long peaked blue cap, has left off cooking. Initially he was concerned, but is now reassured that my wounds are not serious.

'You going to be OK?'

'Sure.'

I take a look at all these lads with their eyes on me. I can't repress a slight smile which my aching chin twists into a grimace. Here is this race's youngest crew, average age twenty-two years. Excellent crew, perfect manoeuvres. Just as well that it had failed in its attempt to have its skipper transferred into the next world.

Thirteen knots on the speedometer, *Pen Duick III*'s top speed. In spite of the distance he has covered this season, the boat is far from being tired. He is full of spirits. Wind astern, he surfs the waves. The crew allow themselves a bathing trunk siesta on deck. Talk – no, happiness – yes. At 11pm Radio Sydney's news bulletin announced that we enjoyed a substantial lead. The Australians required that contestants have a radio set on board and that twice each day they should signal their position. So we know where the others are. If we keep going like this, we will be first in real as well as on compensated time.

'We've given it to them!' cries out a jubilant Gérard.

I am jubilant too. With the English-Lavat-Guégan watch, we listen to Kersauson's banter which he maintains throughout the day, only stopping to sleep.

Pen Duick III's lead is getting bigger the whole time. As we pass through the Bass Strait, the northwest wind strengthens and I decide to try letting out the small spinnaker and bringing down the mainsail. Together, those on watch and the others who abandon the billycan meal of salted pork with petits pois and rice salad they were half way through, carry out the manoeuvres with the kind of enthusiasm that impending victory inspires. With a stiff stern breeze pushing us along all day we crack on, drawing abreast of Tasmania, whose coast we glimpse starboard through the fog.

My father has been cooling the champagne. The 6am radio bulletin on Saturday reports that Tasmania's main Daily leads on: 'Foreigners take control in night,' implying that *Pen Duick III* cannot be caught now. And it is as if the waves are being consumed by his crunching bows all the way to the Tasman Peninsula, standing on the other side of the bay into which the Hobart River flows. It is midday December 30. We have only forty miles left before we reach the finishing line. At which point the wind plays a little trick, falling away almost entirely. For a while we beat, going about to try and make the most of any change in the wind direction. It is when there is not even a breath of air that I start to worry: 'Drop anchor!'

I have no choice but to give the order now that, besides not advancing, a fairly strong current is driving us back. And now the anxiety begins. The boats behind us draw dangerously close for, while we are immobilised, they can still count on the wind.

Nobody says a word. From sheer frustration, I give the cockpit a few kicks. 'This is just bloody stupid,' curses Kersauson. Even he has lost his desire to play the fool. To lose this race like that ... no, it's too much, too stupid. Petipas, who happens to be the worrying kind, heads down into the cabin where he can lie down and not risk seeing the arrival, out of the heat haze, of the gatecrashers. Motorboats, crowded with spectators, who offer their encouragement, make circles round us. It puts me in mind of a *danse macabre*. Gérard leaps up into the cockpit. At that moment a prolonged shiver seems to run through the sea. He shouts to me: 'Wind Éric!'

'I know!'

Without my having to give the order, the crew pull up the anchor. The time is 12.45pm. *Pen Duick III* slowly gets going again. By beating we make an average – and annoying – speed of three knots. We cross the line at 3.10pm. Thousands of people are up on the quays, applauding us. On *Pen Duick III* there are a few who start to chant.

'Shut it!'

This attention demanding glee is not my kind of thing.

Once secured to Hobart quay and before the onslaught of officials, journalists, friends and others, my father lays on the champagne. Still waiting for the final classification, we drink to our class victory. Guégan makes an appeal, which the others take up in a chorus:

'Speech, Éric! Speech! Speech!'

I would rather not but, at their insistence, I give in. Raising my glass, I say to them happily, ironically: 'I drink to the best crew in the world.'

Fidelis, who had started as hot favourite, comes in second. *Kahurangi* is third. We are both winners and, overall, second.

Eric Tabarly

Because *Rainbow*, in Class III, has got in front of us by a few minutes of compensated time. In my view the overall classification is not that important. It would be more meaningful if everybody encountered the same winds – which is far from being the case. I could go further in my criticism of overall classification, seeing how, of *Pen Duick III*'s six victories, three were achieved on compensated as well as in real time – these included the principal, Channel and Fastnet, races – where the wind favoured the big boats. In the other races, like this one, it favoured the small boats. At the moment we passed beyond Tasman Peninsula, *Rainbow* was lagging behind us by seventy miles, a far greater gap than was required for us to be compensated winners. If we had had the same breeze to carry us over the final forty miles, we would have increased our lead still further.

Instead of which we got held up in the bay by the calm as, out at sea, *Rainbow* continued to clip along and so draw closer to us. When he arrives in the bay, with the wind returned, he will not be slowed down. Just for the record, a few years later I learnt that, following a further weighing, it will be discovered that *Rainbow*'s handicap was inaccurate. If it had not been for this mistake, he would not have won.

Wearing white Polo shirts and navy blue jumpers, courtesy of Lacoste, freshly shaven and neat looking, we receive the Special Elegance Award. And with that the 1967 season comes to an end. The majority of my crew fly back to France. Kersauson, English and Guégan are now the only ones left on board. We have plenty of time before our rendezvous with the cargo ship, which will take *Pen Duick III* back to France, and I decided that we should take ourselves off on a cruise in the Pacific, entailing some tourism in New Caledonia. There is a French language teacher at Sydney University who had come to say hello before the race and who now asks if he can come along with us. He was the cook on board *Kahurangui*. We no longer have a cook and this will make a change from our standard fare. I accept his joining us.

'What is his name?' asks Kersauson.

'Alain Colas.'

CHAPTER 16

KERSAUSON, COLAS, GUÉGAN, ENGLISH, PLUS THE CYCLONE

Pen Duick III's return home via cargo ship is slated for a month ahead. The heroes of the Sydney–Hobart are taking it easy. Sea, summer and sun, everything is in place in order for us to give ourselves over to a holiday down under. The crew of four and I make our way in the manner of weekend sailors, sauntering along Caledonia's picturesque coast. We catch our fish trailing a line and sing and are happy to be together. It seems that we have hit pay dirt at the end of a racing season that brought physical tiredness and nervous tension – and required concentration – aplenty.

There is a big change in Olivier de Kersauson. No longer is he the diffident young man who originally came aboard. He acquired confidence and his natural sailing ability was soon clear to see. In manoeuvres it seems his physical strength gets a boost from somewhere within, the inner man exalting action. On board, his natural penchant for chattering away rises to the surface, irrepressible. His gags and sketches are quite original and an indication of his intelligence and culture. He is the only person I have ever encountered capable of talking about anything and everything – in alexandrines. His jests take the form of poems and provocations. They are a way for him – always on the lookout for some whipping boy – to let his irony, madcap notions and dissatisfactions spill out. On deck, he does not miss a thing, anticipating a mistake or piece of potentially dangerous clumsiness. Whereas I would step into the breach with a minimum of fuss, Olivier is vituperative – no doubt this is his excess adrenaline safety valve. If I had been a dunce at school then Kersauson had been expelled from several on account of his hotheadedness before ending up at agricultural college. He is authoritative on seeds and cattle breeds. Confiding in me one day, he said: 'Whether it's on a boat or out in the fields, I am only interested in an outdoor life.'

The trip to New Caledonia, with its warm breezes, palm trees and blue seas is the stuff of tourist brochures.

Alain Colas, on first view, does not have the appearance of a sailor. He is a polite and friendly lad who does not pounce on his billycan meal with the voracity of the others, who gorge themselves like ravenous dogs. English, who observed him with an insider's eye, suggested humorously to Kersauson: 'You must follow his example and chew sedately. It's excellent for the journey ...'

The apprentice Colas is an enigma for me. As we exchange cockpit badinage, there he is, in his swimming trunks, already developing the yachting theories that will set him apart from sailors of my generation. He had been in the United States and was impressed by the Anglo-Saxon way of doing things which had left its mark on him.

He explains to us that a number of sports in America, such as basketball and American football, had only developed with hefty sponsorship from big business. We listen to what he says and he watches us go about our business. He is still a greenhorn, not used to big boats and apt to make mistakes. To give an example: on a small boat, too close to a sheet which, without warning, de-tensions, one might get a bruise from the whiplash, but nothing more, it is just a line. A sheet on a big racing boat is far more dangerous and its force can injure or even sweep you overboard.

Kersauson, a good guy, shouts to him: 'Alain, move away from there. You'll get your head – or unmentionables – knocked off!'

Memories of the Open Sea

Watching us, Colas learns quickly. One can tell that he is someone with the necessary ambition to stand out from the crowd.

Pen Duick III left Uvéa, the little island at the north of the Loyauté archipelago. We make our way southwest to Nouméa where we are going to drop anchor. There is a good south easterly crosswind pressing against the foresails.

Having veered too far westerly, we find ourselves close to the coral barrier which we should have skirted to the south. The barrier is five miles from land but, on a choppy sea with visibility not being what it might be, we only sight these reefs when we are close by them. Too close, even.

'Going About!'

I had scarcely finished giving the order. My crew sheet out, helping the sails to swing to the other side as quickly as possible and we clear out of this tight spot like thieves, heading east. I order the mainsail to be raised, with two reefs, for a fetch. No sooner done than, without warning, the wind shifts all the way round from southeast to southwest; and picks up force.

'Lower the jib!'

Kersauson and Guégan launch themselves towards the bows. Their bodies are hooked in the sails they haul in with devilish intensity, as the rain comes bucketing down on us. The wind is continually gaining in strength till it is more than seventy knots (around about a hundred and thirty kilometres per hour). Even under reduced sail *Pen Duick III* marches on at eight knots.

And always more wind. Spray is swept this way and that across the surface of the sea by the wind, or thrown up and back by the bows. This and the insane rain produce an atmosphere that is hard to breathe. So one has to turn one's back against it or be asphyxiated by these cataracts, which at the same time crucify one's eyes.

The seascape is impressive. Above the blistering white ocean, clouds of spray swirl and rise as if the sky, in alliance with the wind, wanted to draw up the sea itself.

Eric Tabarly

The wind is still getting stronger. It is beside itself with rage. Valiantly, *Pen Duick III* resists in all directions the waves' brutal assault. No one says a word. Each asks himself whether or not the storm has yet reached its limit. I am at the helm. Half suffocated by this air, and the fuming jets of water which speed their way to the cockpit from the bows, I notice that two of the mainsail slides have come loose.

'Strike the mainsail!'

There is always potential for one's fortunes at sea to take a turn for the worse. In the time that it takes my crew to free the halyard winch ratchet, more slides break loose and the sail comes loose – sideways, just above the boom. Inevitably, then, it tears away from almost the full length of the mast, blowing horizontally from the masthead, where it remains secured by a halyard that needs to be cut to let it go completely.

We carry on a beat, with the small staysail. *Pen Duick III* makes good headway, sailing up into the wind at an angle the textbooks would recommend. But in spite of being under drastically reduced sail he lists unwontedly. We could keep going, but the question is: is it worth it? In this weather, not being able to see a thing, we cannot go via the reef and channel our way through the lagoon, scattered with blocks of coral. Therefore, take down the staysail.

This is easier said than done. To try and get to the bows is to enter a battle zone, looking throughout for something with a solid deck fixing to hold onto. This terrain has to be conquered step by step. One must hold onto the guard rail running round the boat as one struggles against the force of the wind at the same time as taking hits from the big waves which, in their fury, come sweeping across the deck.

I let Colas take over at the helm. One metre at a time I head forward with my crew, but up at the bows, which writhes savagely, just to stay upright in this whirlwind is an acrobat's act. Everyone knows what their task is and we are able to bring the little sail down. My crew has skill and guts; even Colas, although he is a near neophyte, gives a good account of himself.

Memories of the Open Sea

With immediate effect, the wind no longer has *Pen Duick III*, all sails down, in its grip. Where before his list was quite extreme, and he was shaking and vibrating in his struggle with the sea, now he seemed calm. There is no knocking sound, no water rushing across the deck. Of his own accord, he lies ahull and, thanks to the short design of his keel, he then drifts at will. Beneath the wind force in the rigging he lists lightly; this and his design keep him from rolling side to side.

Back in the cockpit, the crew make inquiring looks my way. Around us the ocean is nothing more than a whitish sprawl in movement, whipped up by the wind into something resembling Chantilly cream. There is nothing more that can be done other than wait for this to blow over.

'Let's get some sleep,' I say.

We get out of our dripping oilskins and dry ourselves. I take a look at my cyclone travelling companions, exhausted and done in like myself, almost in a state of shock in the aftermath of this apocalypse. Each of us is picturing those immense columns of spray, rising malevolently into the air like snakes. Quite a spectacle, one can't help but marvel. Kersauson, who is fond of the word, says 'magic'. I was not personally worried. *Pen Duick III*'s handling was wholly reassuring and I know that, if he had been called upon to run with the wind in such conditions, he would have been able to.

English, Guégan, Kersauson and Colas talk away, exchanging their impressions. Exactly what they are saying I don't know. Once I lay down in my bunk I was out like a light. Round midnight, the wind relents and its din dies down. Following six tumultuous hours this relative silence wakes me. I get up.

'Everyone up on deck!'

I hear yawning, groaning, some protests. At twenty, my crew's age, one sleeps soundly but waking up is a delicate process.

One after another, they lazily arise and haul themselves up into the cockpit. Once again the stars take up their place in the South Pacific against a dark grey-blue sky. On an ocean that moves with a long swell we raise the foresails and, beating, make our way once more towards Nouméa. Daybreak, when it comes, reveals, for as far as the eye can see, vegetable debris uprooted and then strewn across the water. The cyclone's work has given this area a dejected look.

CHAPTER 17

I HAVE A DREAM: A FLYING BOAT

Once more it is *La Vanoise* who is going to transport *Pen Duick III* back to his home waters from Sydney.

As for me, I had barely set foot back in Brittany than I head straight for Lorient and La Perrière yard, which has already started building my trimaran. Let me go back a little. Earlier, in September, I had got in touch with André Allègre in Sète. He is the sole French architect specialising in multihulls. News was spreading amongst the sailing community, letting it be known that there will be some useful multihulls at the Transat starting line. Since the eye opening experience aboard *Toria*, my conviction grows that victory in the coming single-handed contest will go to one of these craft which were being described as spiders of the sea. As is my wont, I had given the matter a lot of thought, and had decided on a trimaran, not a catamaran – a pacy design with an annoying tendency to capsize.

Allègre, like me, prefers three hulls. With long distance racing in mind, we both drew up plans for a twenty-metre trimaran. By the standards of the day, this was a monster. We had studied various float forms and, following tests in the hull tank, our preference was for a symmetric rather than dissymmetric design. At Joseph Rouillard's research consultancy in Nantes, a detailed structural design was drawn up on which the whole project hangs. Particularly important is the necessity of the floats' lateral struts being both strong and light.

I will not linger on the difficulties once more encountered raising money which were surmounted. The publicity surrounding *Pen Duick II* and *Pen Duick III*'s victories helped make it easier to agree with *France-Soir*, RTL and *Paris Match* the sums required for my new boat, the quid pro quo naturally being their exclusive rights. Regarding finance, I spent my life trying to raise it for my boats, without ever, or at least rarely, losing confidence. Confidence is key. Without it, no project will come to fruition. Doubt is a mortal enemy.

Pen Duick IV is finally launched on May 11 1968 and three days later he is taken for his first sail. My nerves are somewhat on edge and the starting date for the third single-handed Transatlantic race, drawing nearer the whole time, is a cause for concern. Not everything is as it should be with the boat. In the first sea trial we are coming out of Lorient harbour, and just hoisting the sails, when the wind stiffens. I notice the masts bending to an alarming degree. Before they actually break, I order lowering the sails and we are towed back to our mooring. This is not a good debut. The masts are vane masts that turn. I am the first to install them on an ocean going vessel. To facilitate their movement, the masthead connection for shrouds and stays utilises a strong swivel mechanism. Without changing the masts' set up entirely, we cannot add intermediate shrouds. We try consolidating their rigidity with the addition of ball joints. Again, on the next trial, things do not go well. The mast is still bending. We haul in the sails as before, and are given another tow back. The next step is to add more running stays, or shrouds, that highfield levers can tauten or slacken, each time the boat goes about. All this takes time but produces the desired effect: *Pen Duick IV* can now sail. He is very pacy. I take him as far as La Trinité, where, alone on board, I test him against *Pen Duick III* with a crew. The trimaran seems to have an extra gear. I can pass *Pen Duick III* to windward, even when he is fetching – which gives rise to a few choice remarks. Quick, for

Memories of the Open Sea

sure, but so ill-disposed to make a good course that, on that day, if the choice had still been there, it is with my *Pen Duick III* that I would enter the race. Unfortunately, the choice is not still there. Before *Pen Duick IV* was launched, the workshop that made the self-steering lets me know they could not finish both sets on time. I instructed them to just finish that of '*IV*'.

So the situation was less than ideal. I was once again unable to carry out the – standard procedure – trials, required to set my multihull straight. Setting off from Plymouth, I tell myself that if I finish this race, it would be down to luck. But luck was conspicuous by its absence as, from the first night of the race, things began to go wrong.

The shipping traffic off the south coast of England was dense, very dense, with coasters and merchant ships moving in all directions. Coming up to midnight, there is a boat aiming towards me that I need to keep an eye on. Shortly, he makes a minor adjustment to his course and passes astern. At this point I make a mistake. Seeing no other boat close by, I tell myself that, following all these hours at the helm, here is the opportunity to make a coffee, and go down into the galley. I have barely had a sip when a sudden din vibrates around the boat. I scamper up. Looming above me is a cargo ship's bows. It is not a pretty sight – rather as if I am nose-to-nose with a mastodon, or a kind of dinosaur constructed out of steel.

I am sailing at about fifteen to sixteen knots. The cargo ship must be moving at twelve or thirteen knots so we were set to collide at nearly thirty knots. At this speed it is not surprising that he had surged from the horizon to where I am. Luckily, the cargo ship stopped. At the last available moment to avoid collision, his engines must have been slung into reverse. All along, my starboard float rubs and grates against the ship's bows before I can pull away and get going again. With my torch I go and take a look, to check the extent of the damage. There is a long gash which, fortunately, does not stretch beyond the first section whose foam filling guards against water flooding in. Beyond that, everything seemed intact and I think

Eric Tabarly

I will be able to finish the race, even in this state. Fat chance. At midday I have to make an about-turn. A spreader running from the mizzen mast's ball joint, probably shaken loose during the collision, has given way. To prevent it falling down completely I must go and get it repaired.

Sportingly, the Royal Navy engineering staff at Plymouth make a temporary repair to the float while the Mashford boatyard deals with the rigging. The involuntary four day stop over, I set off again. But not for long. A problem with the self-steering means the rudder is inoperable and forces me into port at Newlyn, Cornwall. I set things right and, after this latest two day delay, set off once more – but only for a few miles when the recurring problem obliges me to detour a third time and abandon. Two friends, Pierre Fouquin, who is an engineer at La Perrière yard, and the sailmaker, Victor Tonnerre, come over to help me sail, as best I can, from Newlyn to Lorient. There we discover that the merchant ship collision has seriously affected the lateral struts.

'They would not have held up for long,' remarks Tonnerre.

Victor's right. If I had gone on with the race I would have risked the boat falling apart and being lost for good. Knowing that tempers my regret.

And the possibility of a consolation prize is there: the Crystal Trophy, triangular Channel race specifically for multihulls. As soon as La Perrière has finished the repairs, accompanied by a brisk westerly breeze I set sail from Lorient. Under a jib and mizzen *Pen Duick IV*, on a fetch, gives a demonstration of his racing qualities. He makes his way through the sea with the ease of a prize animal. I feel good.

But the mood, typically, does not endure. In the course of the night, round about Glénans, the windward highfield lever instantly gives way and the mizzen mast breaks. Both masts' running stays lead to this lever. The mainmast remains standing, but with a significant bow. I will not be competing for the Crystal Trophy. Instead, back to Lorient and the yard. There is a reason for all these setbacks. For all that a boat is well designed and shows his speed, nothing concrete will be achieved without the vital setting up and sea trial time required for fine tuning.

To stop 1968 from ending on a falling note, I put *Pen Duick III* and his crew together again for the last races of the season: Yarmouth–Lequeitio and Lequeitio–La Trinité. Two victories act as a kind of salve for my wounded pride.

Ever since I was a teenager I had always been mad about and a fervent, assiduous reader of yachting magazines. From one of them, in (or around) September 1968 I learn that the Slocum Society is organising a single-handed Transpacific race. The departure will take place on March 15 1969 in San Francisco Bay and the destination will be Tokyo Bay. It is a five thousand mile excursion in which, I am informed, there are going to be fifteen competitors, four of them French Transatlantic veterans.

Entry to the race is confined to monohulls, whose overall length must be twenty-two to thirty-five feet. I really want to take part and sail in the Pacific. However, I do not have the kind of boat required. I know it is crazy but, if I want to venture on this latest 'single-handed', I need to start thinking about a new boat, designed with the Pacific meteorological conditions in mind. The problems remain the same as ever: come up with the *design* of a 10.67 metre sailing boat, raise the *money* for it to be built, find the *time* for sea trials before transportation to San Francisco – within the due date. This sailor's life of mine always comes up against this infernal triptych.

In 1968 light, resistant construction materials remain in the future. Duralinox, in the 60s, is the light, malleable metal aptest for sailing boats. And La Perrière boatyard is still one of the leaders in this field, so I turn to it a third time to find out if it can deliver *Pen Duick V*, overall length thirty-five feet, in time for Christmas.

'Yes, on the understanding that we get the detailed drawings by mid-October.'

A tight schedule. I am left only a few weeks – at the outside – to find an architect, who, in turn, would have to carry out his work in a matter of days. We will not, pre-launch, have time for tank tests on the hull, so we are running a conscious risk.

I have already mentioned that I have frequently had the luck, during my sailing career, to meet the right person at the right time. My meeting with Michel Bigoin, introduced to me by Pierre Fouquin, was one of those encounters. Amongst other projects, Michel Bigoin's portfolio included two superb yachts: the Class IV *Samourai* and *Flying Forty,* a racing boat capable of planing when running with the wind. These facts help me decide to entrust him with my fifth boat.

'My associate, Daniel Duvergie and I, will get started straightaway,' he tells me. 'Within a fortnight a design, incorporating all your requirements, naturally, will be complete.'

My requirements are simple enough: I want a boat that will be quick the whole time, whatever the point of sail, but particularly with following winds.

That is what my reading of the pilot charts tells me. The Transpacific poses the same question as the Transatlantic: should I opt for the most direct route or the one with the most favourable winds? Wind conditions in the two oceans are relatively similar. Whilst the dominant wind in the northern parts of the Atlantic and Pacific is, broadly speaking, westerly, their tropical regions are most visited by the trade winds; in between, each ocean is characterised by variable winds.

Having studied them closely, my preference is for the trade winds route rather than arcing to the northwest from San Francisco: the great circle. Although it may be approximately one thousand miles further to travel, this way might, paradoxically, take twelve days less than the shorter route. In order to seek out the trade winds, the first section will be southwest. It covers nine hundred miles amidst dominant north westerly winds, averaging force four. Arriving in the trade winds' northeast corner, one heads west for three thousand six hundred miles. Then the one thousand two hundred home stretch up to Tokyo, with variable winds. If my calculations are right, then the first nine hundred miles should take seven days, the three thousand six hundred trade winds section twenty-five days and, given a favourable current, the final one thousand two hundred miles ten days. So the whole journey could be done in forty-two days. But that depends on *Pen Duick V* being designed so as to take advantage of following winds.

If you are aiming to win a specific race, then you must have the right boat to do it with. The originality of *Pen Duick II* lay in his being rigged with single-handed racing in mind, and light. *Pen Duick III*, with his aluminium hull, took this lightweight concept further. His prototype vane mast and unusual size for a multihull, marked out *Pen Duick IV*, whatever his shortcomings. *Pen Duick V*'s originality is going to relate to an adjustable ballast, that is to say, seawater containers will be installed along the frame ends, which, with the aid of a pump, I can then fill or empty as the stability of the boat dictates. A lot of unnecessary ballast will be done away with, and I shall gain the advantage of a considerably lighter boat.

In order to pre-empt a potential contretemps over delivery times, La Perrière yard ordered the sheet metal before they'd received the plans, not to mention the reassurance that the boat was really going to be built.

The truth was that I had not yet raised a single penny for this job. Any wealth I had – salary and book royalties – was swallowed up by *Pen Duick IV*. Since he is without rigging, I am not in a position to sell. Nor am I about to sell *Pen Duick III*, for whom I have future racing plans. But there is no point in worrying – worry being more productive of ulcers than solutions. This is not a question of some kind of ethereal optimism. I am, in a more straightforward manner, confident.

The company that runs St-Raphaël's private port, which I am contracted to for publicity, rescues me with an offer to pay the sum I am after. Broadly speaking, having picked up the bill for the boat, the company has ownership until I pay it back. This could hardly suit me better. I am actually intending, once the Transpacific is finished, to sell *Pen Duick V* in Japan, to release myself from this debt as quickly as possible.

Michel Bigoin and Daniel Duvergie's sessions at the design board are relentless. Between September 15 and October 2 1968 they submit four versions for me to consider before their final sketch. This is very different to their original study, due to the ballasts I then asked them to incorporate. This innovation affects other aspects of the boat's design. To give a few examples: the draught will become 2.30 metres instead of two metres, whilst the ballast is reduced from an original one thousand two hundred kilos to four hundred and fifty kilos. The keel is narrowed and lengthened. The capacity of each ballast is five hundred litres, which provides an amazing stability: heeling at 15° or 20° and using a full reservoir, one has the same righting torque to maintain the boat in some kind of relation with the vertical position as one would have with three tonnes of ballast. Lastly, as the boat is relatively small compared to ones I have already sailed single-handed, I feel confident enough to handle a large sail area, especially in view of *Pen Duick V*'s superior stability. For this 10.67 metre sloop I have a longer mast in mind – along which halyards are placed at regular intervals to counteract the wind – standing 12.50 metres above the deck and allowing me to put up a twenty-five square metre mainsail, a genoa of thirty-eight square metres and, lightweight, the one hundred and fifteen metres big boy. Ballasts empty, the boat will weigh three thousand two hundred kilos: a sailing feather.

Since this is a race, rather than a cruise, the cabin's layout is Spartan as usual: a bunk either side, an unavoidably large chart table, and a galley kitchen, with its adjustable motorbike seat, the same as on *Pen Duick*s *II* and *III*. It helps in rough weather to make cooking less of a battle.

To avoid the stress and strain the piece of equipment had given me on my first Transatlantic, I am carrying two self-steering mechanisms. The model – the MNOP 66 – is tried and tested.

Practising my métier and really only happy on board, then it is

Memories of the Open Sea

best not to be married or have children. I could not see myself leading a family life and nor could those who, from time to time, spent time with me. Wherever I might head for, or find myself, my attention is taken up by boats. Friends in Paris occasionally take me along to Chez Castel, a tasteful, wood panelled club in the rue Princesse, where a certain Parisian type gathers till long after hours. I actually quite like this ambiance and feel as though I'm amongst friends. The habitués are uninhibited night people, the elegant women, enticing and bubbly. Nevertheless, after a few hours, I start to ask myself: 'What am I doing here?' My life is out at sea, on a boat. Maybe my behaviour strikes some as bizarre – but that is the way I am.

While the yard at Lorient builds my future sloop, November 26 1968 at 12.30pm, I am setting sail from La Trinité together with Olivier de Kersauson and Alain Colas, destination Fort-de-France on Martinique.

I want to cross the Atlantic with the 'sea spider' – *Pen Duick IV* – to demonstrate the reliability of my trimaran's performance so as to sell him in the US. I was obliged to give up on the swivel mast design. I don't have the money. Alas!

Pen Duick IV is a piece of work – all it takes is a stiff breeze to get him galloping across the waves. The crossing has endured as a particularly happy memory for me. We may not be in a race but we are up for it. Without having to worry about our class position or victory, Olivier, Alain and I are left to get this beast moving, which is a pleasure. The understanding between the three of us could not be bettered. I see that Kersauson is genuinely fond of his crew mate and note Colas' admiration towards Kersauson. When the boat is set up nicely and moving along of its own accord, we devote ourselves to a session of noughts and crosses like many a dope in France and Navarre before us. Colas, who is starting to prove himself an excellent sailor, and who has fallen in love with my trimaran, entertains us with his cooking skills, conjuring fine dishes on the hob based around the flying fish that landed on the main deck.

After putting in at Tenerife, we cross the Atlantic in what was then a record time: ten days and twelve hours, at an average of eleven knots.

After sharing a few glasses of punch in Fort-de-France, I say goodbye to crew and trimaran, needing to return to France to be on hand for his completion and then for a few trials with my new baby, *Pen Duick V*.

On December 30, I am informed that the mast cannot be delivered in time, something I am not about to accept. I borrow my father's 3CV and my brother, Patrick's trailer and drive all the way to Switzerland, snow on the roads, to Yvedon where the manufacturer Nirvana Spars is located. I then head back to Lorient in the 3CV, with the mast secured on the trailer. On icy roads, I cannot go more than 70kph without the trailer and mast turning over or ... catapulting over me. Even though I take care, the trailer starts to swing around in the rutted snow. The swing is exaggerated by the mast. The mast slips off the back. It all happens before I have time to react. The car spins round, leaving me facing the opposite way in a ditch and the trailer without one of its wheels. This is January 1 and hangovers are, by rights, the order of the day. I walk as far as the next village looking for a garage that might be open. Miraculously, there is one. The mechanic agrees to come with me. He takes the wheel off and, back at the workshop, does some straightening out and welding work on it. Returning to the scene of the accident he fixes the wheel back on. I continue on my way, exhausted, and arrive in Lorient during the night.

I am going to have a few days in which to test *Pen Duick V* before he is due to leave for the boat show. They will allow me to set everything up as it should be. In general we will be sailing every other day, the time between being spent back at port, remedying whatever deficiencies we have found. In fact, these trials have also been an opportunity for *Pen Duick V* to show me his speed, not just on a reach, as might have been expected, but fetching, too.

CHAPTER 18

THE JAPANESE SPEAK ONLY JAPANESE

I rejoined Colas and Kersauson in Fort-de-France. Together we plan to make a run for San Francisco via the Panama Canal and then up the California coast. Taking account of the trimaran's speed, I had estimated that this cruise would require thirty days given the unfavourable conditions along the way. Kersauson and Colas were of the mind that our journey will take twenty days at the outside. And that is the length of time they provisioned for. As it gradually became clear that my prediction was nearer the mark and that we risked running out of food and water, I decided to ration what we still had left. As one might have guessed, the first to be down to his last rations was Olivier who had continued to wolf down, rather than ration, his food.

We were meant to arrive in San Francisco in time to receive *Pen Duick V* who, on February 2, had been loaded onto the cargo ship *Maryland* in Le Havre. I had not anticipated that just two days after setting sail we would lose our centreboard and that, subsequently, our progress would be slow and laborious. Realising that I risked, in these conditions, arriving late, we put in at San Diego, the first American port. I try, without any success, to find a berth where we can leave *Pen Duick IV*. He is viewed as a potential encumbrance by the marina on account of his length and – particularly – beam, and none of them is prepared to welcome him. I leave Alain and

Olivier on board in order to bring the trimaran up to San Francisco. Meanwhile, I hire a car and finish my own journey by road.

At dawn on March 7 I am in San Francisco. I am told that, because of a dockers' strike, the *Maryland* is stuck in Los Angeles and that her unloading has been re-scheduled for 10am on Monday morning – barely five days before the Transpacific's departure. I cannot help reflecting that, occasionally, the fate of my boats is at the mercy of socio-political forces.

The événements of May '68 might have been fatal to *Pen Duick IV*. Just as his construction was going smoothly, the paralysis that was visited on the country during these days of agitation did not spare the boatyard. But I had been lucky. The unions had permitted a team to continue building him – but no overtime. The boat was finally finished just in time. Because of this delay with the *Maryland*, the fine tuning of my latest is going to have to be done in a hurry. As usual!

Fortunately, I am not going to be alone during my final preparations. Jean-Michel Carpentier, a crew member who has come to San Francisco to take care of *Pen Duick V*, is waiting for me. Penniless like us all, he was taken under the wing of a French resident of the town, Claude Reboul, veteran of the Fleet Air Arm who will turn out to be a godsend for me, helping me find my way both around here and on sorties further afield.

As soon as the *Maryland* arrives on the Sunday, Carpentier and I set to work. The advance part of the ballast has been damaged during handling. This is fixed using resin and sandpaper. We install the electronic weathervane and the heading repeater with its alarm taken off *Pen Duick IV* back in San Diego. The installation of the ballast water pump is completed and the mast prepared, so it is ready to be stepped.

At first light on Monday morning we go on board the *Maryland*. We come armed with rollers and anti-fouling paint to give the hull another coat, the first having faded since Lorient. Amongst sailors this coat's usefulness – particularly in hot waters – is general knowledge. It reduces the amount of algae that can stick to the hull and act as a brake.

Around midday, Customs formalities concluded, I am standing by the sliding pontoon crane as, from the hold, it unloads not just *Pen Duick V* but also Jean-Yves Terlain's *Blue Arpege*, another contestant. The two of us immediately busy ourselves stepping the masts of our respective boats. Once we are ready, Claude Reboul gives us a tow across the bay with his powerful launch to the San Francisco Yacht Club, situated on the opposite, Belvedere, bank.

There I will meet the other contestants. Terlain is a well built fellow with curly brown hair, worn long, as was the fashion then. The boy is calm and adventurous, a charmer who knows his own mind but smiles a lot. He enjoys boats and is not afraid of life and its pleasures. We are the two Frenchmen here for this race which, despite its length and its difficulties, does not have the same reputation as the British Transatlantic. There is one German, Claus Hehner. He has had to shorten the stern of *Tina* in order to satisfy the thirty-five feet criterion. *Tina* is a very good boat and my guess is that he will be my main rival. One Belgian is taking part. René Haumaert has a Bermuda rigged yawl made of steel and is accustomed to single-handed sailing in the Pacific. Then there is an American, Jerry Cartwright, whose boat has apparently been specially designed for this race. It has a bowsprit, which permits a fairly large sail area.

We are the five who find ourselves at the starting line on March 15 1969. The night before, I taped a few jazz tunes Claude Reboul had been playing me onto a little tape recorder. I organised my supermarket casseroles and meals along with fresh fruit and vegetables and a good supply of pre-prepared pancakes eaten by Americans with every meal. All I will need to do when I feel the urge for a nourishing galette is to mix the flour with some water and return it to the hob. Served with maple syrup, it is a delicious dish. I have also tried to organise the way things will be stored, but it will be difficult to maintain order with all my clobber and such a small cabin to receive it.

I had made a sea trial to check the rigging was set up as it should be, the self-steering worked properly and that the balloon jib winches ran smoothly.

It happened on Tuesday afternoon March 12. Carpentier and I haul it, push it, try shoving it round. The boat does not move one inch. The tide is low and *Pen Duick V* is stuck in the mud. Given its modest length, my boat was put in a marina intended for small vessels with a slight draught. We had overlooked the fact that while he may not have been big himself, *Pen Duick V*'s draught was that of a big boat: 2.30 metres to be precise.

Both Jean-Michel and I were more than a little embarrassed when Jean-Yves Terlain, on his way back from a little sail with *Blue Arpege*, came to our rescue.

'I am going to get you out of there,' he shouted.

We lob a towing line to him and Terlain hooks us up for a tow. He pulls us. My keel ploughs a deep furrow in the mud. Terlain's motor bellows hoarsely, wails, then falls decisively silent:

'Shit!' Terlain exclaims. 'I've run out of gas.'

All three of us are conscious of being slightly ridiculous – are we weekend sailors? Terlain casts us off, making a gesture that eloquently conveys his regret at not having got us out of there. Drawing less water than we do, he sails over to his pontoon. In this kind of situation all one can do is accept what has happened and wait for the tide to come back in.

That means a wait of several hours, as any sailor in this situation automatically recognises. But, every now and again, God looks benignly on those who have run aground. A launch passing close by, moved to do the right thing, comes over and tows us out to deep water.

Just as planned, at 12pm March 15 precisely, Terlain and I having been towed close to the starting line by Claude Reboul, a cannon blast lets loose the five entrants from in front of the yacht club.

Memories of the Open Sea

To recite the rosary of these thirty-nine days, fifteen hours and forty-four minutes, spent at an average speed of six knots, in the concise style of a log would be monotonous. As in any ocean going venture there took place countless manoeuvres, soul searching and optimism, heavy weather, calms, squalls and fogs and, predictably, ripped sails which I sewed together again. The self-steering, situated too close to the rudder, played up every now and again, being particularly mulish in heavy seas. There were flying fish that fell awkwardly on the deck before supplementing my meals, the usual encounters with noisy dolphin schools, fatigue and, beyond that, feeling shattered – notably towards the end of the race when I was obliged to spend nearly twenty hours at the helm; the shifty current, cold, heat ... in sum, everything that goes to make up a long single-handed race.

In this long ride across the Pacific I come in ten days ahead of the runner-up, Jean-Yves Terlain, whom I often think of when I am enjoying one of the sauces – fit for a king – his sponsor had given him and which he had passed on to me, including a rabbit chasseur that, out of superstition, he had not wished to take on board. The winds were particularly unhelpful. The north westerly we should have had during the first part of the race turned out to be south westerly, on the nose. The trade winds failed to materialise until Hawaii was in view. This is to say the race got off to a slower start than expected. Nevertheless the boat's brilliance in all wind conditions was clear to see as was the ballasts' effectiveness (though filling them up was hard physical work), which, a good deal later, influenced the design of Vendée–Globe yachts. Much quicker than I had expected on a fetch, *Pen Duick V*'s only flaw was that, on this point of sail he would knock about against a well formed sea, making life aboard him grim, but without making him any slower.

Had he been set up more exactly, which was not possible due to lack of time, *Pen Duick V* would have been able to shave off another two days. Only out at sea did I become aware of the telescopic extension pole's tendency to tear (several) jibs and spinnakers. The balloon jibs were too light and fragile, since I had not envisaged relying on them so much in breezes. My role as dressmaker's apprentice is quite a big one.

What can one say about this race? For me the Transpacific is an endurance test of constant manoeuvres, occasioned by the wind's changes and its whim. Nevertheless it is not so hard as the considerably shorter Transatlantic that requires the sailor to defend himself against, and battle with, headwinds and storms and big seas. There were days on board *Pen Duick II*, going from Plymouth to Newport, when I suffered. Cold plus oceanic fury took something from me, whereas on the journey from San Francisco to Tokyo at no point were my reserves called into play.

I was not that enthusiastic about the regulation that restricted entry to a maximum boat length of thirty-five feet. The organisers most likely believed that by having only small boats enter they would get more contestants, but that did not happen. There were supposed to have been fifteen of us lining up at the departure. Instead there were five, a bare minimum for a race seeking to fire the imagination, if not rival the Transatlantic. Another symptom of this relative lack of interest was the kind of – exclusively Japanese – welcome I received on reaching Tokyo. Had the race been run in the opposite direction, there probably would have been a livelier, San Francisco, welcome.

I crossed the finishing line, marked by a small red light, 'I-sa', and situated at the western end of the little Isle of Zyo-Gasa in the evening of April 24 1969. Straightaway, I bring in the genoa and steer towards the little port of Misaki, built in the channel separating the island from the mainland. It is explicitly stated in the race regulations that competitors must carry on to the jury boat and announce their presence. Under mainsail, I enter the port. I have a look around: no jury boat. I am not bothered since the race rules have allowed for this eventuality, instructing the sailor, once he has moored his boat, to report to the little museum that can be found

Memories of the Open Sea

by the Zyo-Gasa lighthouse. The museum caretaker will then put the sailor through to the Nippon Ocean Racing Club directors by phone. Everything seems clear and straightforward.

There is a small quayside berth available just in front of a trawler. I pull into it and moor, after which, for the first time in forty days, I go and sleep without the obsessive necessity to reset the alarm to get myself back up on deck again. Straightaway, I fall into a winner's serene slumber, that is to say I sleep like a log. I awake with the light. The sun is already hot so I have an unhurried breakfast in the cockpit, looking at the quay. There is not yet a person on it. 'All right,' I say to myself, 'let's head off to the little museum.' According to my watch it is nearly seven o'clock. I step ashore.

The village is still asleep. The houses are single storey, compact. Built on the hillside in no particular order, a tangle of winding roads, too narrow for cars, somehow links them together. I am intrigued and, at the same time, a little disappointed by them. I had been expecting to find a more typical kind of Japanese house, built out of wood and bamboo, with paper *shoji* windows. No, they have nothing at all in common with the mansions one sees represented in Empire of the Rising Sun prints, most of them being made of cement or corrugated iron. There are quite a few boutiques, restaurants and shops selling fish and souvenirs, from which I reason this corner of the world must be frequented by tourists.

A noise catches my attention, that of a tradesman opening his stall. Lengthening my stride, I head over towards him. He looks at me in astonishment, not even beginning to understand the gestures with which I am doing everything I can to try and find out what the correct time is. It is what one calls a dialogue of the deaf. I speak in French and English and he replies in Japanese. Neither of us understands a word the other is saying. Approaching a dead end gesticulating, I finally show him my watch, to check what time it is here in Japan. The Japanese man's face lights up with a big smile and he points out to me a large clock that I had failed to see. It is 7:16am.

Now I just need to go and look for my little museum by the

lighthouse where I shall calmly wait for it to open. Walking along at a good pace, I begin to encounter other pedestrians as, little by little, the alleys come to life.

My route to the lighthouse takes me along a charming, narrow path that runs parallel to the sea. On a steep, rocky coastline, not wholly dissimilar to Northern Brittany, there, indeed, is the lighthouse; nothing, however, resembling a museum. Posters are not lacking but, written in Japanese, they don't help. My watch reads eight o'clock.

Passersby are on the move. Accosting them in either French or my rudimentary English elicits no response. These Japanese speak only Japanese. Time passes and I am thinking my little museum must be open now, but how to find it? A mild form of despair is starting to take hold of me when I see a small group of schoolchildren in uniform, boys and girls chatting away happily, following their teachers. In a couple of bounds I am by them. My forty day beard and tattered, unwashed jeans get astonished looks. I try my questions in English once more. One of the teachers responds, jabbering an English that is about as basic as my own and we engage in a demanding conversation, at the end of which I manage to convey what I am after. Smiling beautifully, she points out a building that looks less like a museum than a shack. Sensing my confusion, she kindly goes with me, her colleagues and the children following. Predictably, the attendant of this museum dedicated to lighthouses knows only his mother tongue. Nor is it a surprise that he knows nothing about the race. The teacher patiently acts as interpreter.

I explain to her that I took part in a boat race from San Francisco. Perhaps not doing justice to the language of Shakespeare, it takes a while before my explanation is evident for her. When it is: *eureka*! Her face lights up and betrays some admiration she seems to be feeling. She immediately and animatedly sets about the story of my crossing to the children grouped around me. But this sudden rise to fame in a hidden corner of Japan does not advance my case with the race organisers – still unaware of my arrival. Starting to wonder whether they ever will be, I pull the creased race instructions out of my jeans pocket and read out the passage dealing with arrival to the young lady. Once more we find ourselves confronted with language difficulties. I make ten readings and improvise gestures, designed to explain and emphasise. Finally we achieve communication, and she translates the regulation for the museum assistant. As he listens his face remains the mask of inscrutability that comes so readily to the Japanese.

Given that I had, literally, come from the other side of the world – I could have come from another planet – my being there left him remarkably indifferent. He points to the telephone. The teacher dials the number found on the race instructions. A few moments later I am talking with the secretary of the Nippon Ocean Racing Club, Ogimi. He assures me that he had not been expecting me so soon. He then gives me his congratulations before contacting Customs and Immigration so as to get these formalities speeded up. I offer thanks to my pretty interpreter and return the teenagers' salutations. Back on board it is not long before the officials visit me with standard papers to be completed.

The marina manager draws up in a launch. After greetings, and organising for *Pen Duick V* to be moved to a nearby bay that is sheltered from typhoons, he leads the way to the club. A scalding bath is drawn for me. This tradition encourages the Japanese very soft skin. Afterwards, dinner is served and I discover sushi, small servings of rolled up rice and raw fish that one dips, with chopsticks, into *shoyu* sauce. I have a good appetite. On the other hand, when it comes to algae I can't help but grimace.

It is not often that at a port of call I am able to relax for a bit and take a look around a country. Here I am in no hurry. Four days after arriving I am taken on a tour of Tokyo, which I am not crazy about. Later on, with a resident Frenchman, I go for a sail. The cicerone guides me and *Pen Duick V* to an active volcanic island in an old crater of which the port had been established after one of its sides had been blown open. On the way back, amidst heavy traffic, I catch a glimpse of a red jib, rather like a flame in the blue sky. I take a closer look in order to be certain – that it is indeed Jean-Yves Terlain, about to cross the line. I turn about sharply and head towards *Blue Arpege* to let him know that he is second and to congratulate him on his achievement of beating the faster German boat of Claus Hehner.

Next I take myself on a little five hundred mile cruise. I do not want to depart Japan without having seen what I have dreamt of as an enchanting kingdom: the sea, not unlike the Mediterranean, that runs between the Islands of Hondo, Kiou-Siou and Sikok. Sailing single-handed along their coastlines and having to maintain a lookout the whole time is no doubt tiring, but I am glad that I made the trip. The scenery of this internal sea is just as I had envisaged it, the drawback being the noisy activity of constant sea traffic, however far one went. But visiting Kyoto, with its ancient Imperial Palace and Chiou-In temple, moss garden and Kin-Kaku-Ji rock garden in which the Dairen-In monks meditate, all made the trip worth it. Nowhere else have I encountered a similar serenity or harmony to here – running, jostling, shouting hordes of uniformed school kids notwithstanding.

A Zen like attitude does not detain me too long from my own particular life. I need to get back to San Francisco, where Kersauson, Colas and Carpentier are waiting for me on board *Pen Duick IV*, so that we can set off for the famous Los Angeles–Honolulu race.

I was rather keen to find *Pen Duick V* a buyer. There are no other races I see him contesting. That will save me return transport costs and let the St-Raphaël harbour company recoup its money. Alas, Japan was not really the place then for such a sale. Yachting held only a limited interest, plus the heavy tax burden that fell on buying boats over 7.50 metres made selling uncertain. Whilst the secretary of the Nippon Ocean Racing Club assured me he would try to find a buyer, he could not guarantee success. I take a plane to the States, where my crew, grown a little restless, are waiting for me.

CHAPTER 19

EVERY CLOUD HAS A SILVER LINING

Looked at one way, I might view this period as 'La dolce vita'. Following victory in the Transpacific, and with *Pen Duick IV*'s centreboard set right, we took part in the Los Angeles–Honolulu race and comfortably outstripped the superb and formidable *Windward Passage*. In American sailing circles, where multihulls were still frowned upon, and *Pen Duick IV* was called The French Aluminium Cigar, the feeling was that their champion would make short shrift of us. In breaking the record, we left him trailing by twenty hours.

We had one or two Californian friends who backed us, to whom the bookmakers, placing us at such long odds, had to pay out handsomely. While a few hours were lost on account of our light spinnaker getting torn, there was no stopping *Pen Duick IV*. Running before the wind, he would surf at more than twenty knots.

Wrong-footed and amazed by the trimaran's speed, the plutocrat owner of *Windward Passage* had even gone so far as to consider buying it, a project he dropped after he paid a visit in Honolulu. It is undeniable that *Pen Duick IV*, like my other boats, is lacking in five star comfort. There is no air conditioning, sauna, or well appointed saloon – the *Windward Passage* style. On board with me the style is simple.

We have our victories, unhurried time spent in marinas and excursions out to sea, all of which we enjoy without being rich.

Eric Tabarly

Money is not a motivation for us. In need of it, whilst I crossed the Pacific, Carpentier had found work teaching at the local yacht club. Kersauson took photos and sold them to magazines. Colas repainted a yacht club's pontoons. With our ragged clothes we looked more like seafaring gypsies than racing yachtsmen.

Whatever we earned went into a common pot, everyone chipping in for food. It was cheap, invigorating and filled us up. Out of necessity, we were adept at pasta and rice and a whole variety of sauces.

Life was spent on board. We liked living with one another, forming a band of brothers motivated by the same ideas and the desire to race. There was a common pleasure in getting drenched – suffering even – as we manoeuvred in stormy weather. It was a time which twinned misery and glory. These days crews sleep in hotels. The boat, having completed its race, stays at its mooring, unoccupied. The era when, as we raced, so we lived is the one for which I feel nostalgia. By and by we returned with *Pen Duick IV* to France. At the same time, and at my expense, *Pen Duick V* was being cargoed back. We stopped off at Nouméa. There, in autumn 1969, Alain Colas bought my trimaran off me.

Time passes. When I am not out at sea or at my parents' in St-Pierre-Quiberon I live at Gérard Petipas' place, in Versailles. I have a room there with a desk at which I can remain seated for a whole day developing boat design sketches and thinking.

Every innovation of mine had arisen in the course of creating the best possible boat for a particular race. I should also admit that the ideas for certain breakthroughs came partly from reading around the subject. Therefore, *Pen Duick V*'s ballasts were an update of the old American boats known as sandbaggers, on account of the bags of sand they carried on board. Every time the vessel went about, its crew transferred the bags from one side to the other. If the race was to take place in light weather, they would only carry a few bags. If they set off with a fair breeze and more sand, at a subsequent drop in

Memories of the Open Sea

the wind they would offload the sand. It goes without saying that, once the bags were emptied into the sea, their system was done for if the wind returned. I had then said to myself that it should be possible to devise a system that used water rather than sand. When water was no longer needed one emptied the ballast; if it was needed again all one had to do was to pump it in again: the sea provides a ready supply.

My drawing activity at Petipas' place is in response to the announcement of an interesting British race, the Whitbread, a circumnavigation under sail starting from and finishing at Portsmouth with stops at the Cape of Good Hope, Sydney and Rio de Janeiro along the way. A team race. It was on the Transpacific that I had started mulling over the attractions of a big boat, formidable at top speed. I was in the middle of one race and I was already thinking of the next! These were only the first days of *Pen Duick V* and, without having a clear conception of him, I was thinking of *Pen Duick VI*.

If this new adventure materialises, then at the bottom of it lies an insignificant little graze on my foot. In the company of all the usual suspects, I had just finished first aboard *Pen Duick III* in the Los Angeles–Tahiti race. It had mostly been on a beam reach, a point that really permitted the boat to show off his attributes.

On *Pen Duick III*, we were cruising around Polynesia – where Kersauson had bought a shark's tooth which he referred to as his 'furniture', that is to say the only thing he owned – waiting to return to Europe to take part in this thirty thousand mile round the world race. The boat is in the process of being superseded but, above all, is too small to stand a chance of winning this never ending journey.

If I am to build the new boat for this new race then I needed to go back to France and busy myself with raising money. But I am without the money anyhow for a return trip to Paris whose purpose is speculative.

'Every cloud has a silver lining,' says the proverb.

Eric Tabarly

One morning, as we are getting going from Mooréa, the anchor chain lightly grazes my upper foot. It is just a slight cut, an insignificant piece of torn skin that is scarcely worth worrying about and nothing to prevent us from heading to Tuamotu, land of Cockaigne. Each day we dive into the coral waters and I do not pay much mind to my graze. It has not formed a scar yet, but causes me little discomfort. Since there is no infection, I kick the matter into the long grass.

It is on the way back to Tahiti that, dispensing with any preliminaries, my foot swells up. By the time we arrive at Papeete the swelling has doubled and its shooting pains have sharpened. I limp my way to the military hospital where the surgeon sets to work with the lancet, removing the infected part and making a small crater by my instep. Each morning I go back to the hospital for the wound to be cleaned and receive a fresh dressing. And every time it hurts like hell – on account of a nerve situated right by the wound.

Three weeks go by and the wound is not infected but nor does it heal. The situation really starts to get to me because I am running out of time to get the boat back to France.

'I have seen similar cases before,' the surgeon explains. 'The wound almost invariably takes a long time to heal. The only solution, as far as I am concerned, is for you to return to France on a hospital plane. The climate there is more conducive to forming a scar.'

That was the manner in which I returned to Paris in September 1972.

I use my convalescence putting out feelers. Nothing concrete transpires but I am not downcast. Weeks pass – and my natural optimism does now grow fainter. There is an invitation to lunch at Fouquet's. I am introduced to the publicist Michel Le Berre. I start talking about this project I am trying to get off the ground and my difficulties finding any backers. 'I have made contacts,' I say, 'but, to be honest, it is not the type of thing I am very good at ... '

Le Berre replied that he considered himself capable of seeking out sleeping partners. At the same time he indicated another possibility: 'You should set up, my dear Éric, a company to find the money for your new boat. It will take care of that side of things and leave you free to get on with what you do.'

My character always inclined me to respect specialists. So I followed Michel Le Berre's advice. Shortly, he gives me a call at Gérard Petipas' place and announces that a banker, to whom he had outlined my project, was willing to advance the necessary sum.

The company was formed with Gérard Petipas as its executive director, this in spite of his not having the least idea what the title meant. He and I have known one another for a long while. Eight years younger than me, he was a master mariner in the Merchant Navy but, when its decline set in, he left to set up a maritime consultancy which specialised in yachting whose clients include Edmond de Rothschild. I had him on *Pen Duick II* and *Pen Duick III* as navigator. Gérard is the only person I would be completely confident in having as company director. He is familiar with both my way of thinking – projects – and way of life. We know each other very well. When I asked him whether he would agree to take charge of the company – something I was not allowed to do myself as a serving naval officer – his disarming response was: 'I don't see why not. I don't know any commercial law and I don't even know what a draft document is but, OK, I will be director for you'.

So the matter was settled over breakfast, one morning at his house.

André Mauric, possessing all the necessary qualities, was to be the architect. On November 15 1972 I receive his draft proposal. We had a meeting in which I explained to him the kind of boat I required and that the intention is to race it in the Whitbread, according to the IOR (International Offshore Rules).

'Work needs to get going in January and be finished by July. In August the boat should be racing,' I tell Mauric.

'Understood.'

Eric Tabarly

So begins – once more – the race against time. All the boatyards, when I enquire if they might build this 22.25 metre hull, tell me the same thing: they will not be able to fulfil the contract within a period of barely six months. So the only course that remains is to use one of the bigger shipyards for whom a yacht may be a novel proposition perhaps, their normal work being industrial scale. But I know that the work of these yards is to a high standard and is performed, from engineer to worker, by competent personnel. It is worth noting that shipyards do not just turn out Navy vessels – their priority – but undertake work for the civil sector, too. The Naval Staff and the technical management for ship construction, to which I had submitted my project, both give their consent: *Pen Duick VI*'s construction is going to be by the Brest yard.

In December I pay several visits to Mauric in Marseille, and approve each of his proposals. The conception of the deck and fittings are, by contrast, mine. Thus, there will be four cockpits on deck. The aftmost, the helmsman's, will have two sets of instruments. The next will be located around the cabin ladder. The staysail, stormsail and mizzen winches will all be operated from here. There are two seats for the post's crew, beneath a roof which will act as shelter for them in heavy weather, and also prevent water getting in the cabin. The third cockpit is for kicking strap, pole line and main sheet winches. Foremost, a fourth will house the winches for spinnaker halyards, staysails and reefing traveller blocks. Within these last two cockpits are panels that can be opened from inside the cabin to let in light and fresh air. Then there are the interior fittings. These comprise seven bunks on each side for a full crew and skipper, plus compartments for electric generator, heater and engine. There is another compartment serving as a workshop, complete with its tools; a sail hold; toilets and washing facilities; clothes cupboards; a chart table and radio post; the kitchen.

Originally slated for June, launch, naming, and initial forays in the water are at least a month overdue. On July 28 1973 *Pen Duick VI* heads out into the open sea for the first time.

Memories of the Open Sea

The bigger the boat, the sportier the sailing. It is no longer one man handling all the on board tasks, rather a complex alchemy that takes place between skipper and crew with its different characters and complementary qualities. Racing is now a team sport in which each sailor must perfect the role he is given. There is some resemblance to a ballet when a crew wordlessly manoeuvres on deck; the movement is synchronised, allowing no margin for error. Because if, on a small boat, an incorrectly performed manoeuvre will not entail catastrophe, on a big boat its effects can be dramatic – the ratio between, on the one hand, a man's strength and, on the other, the boat's force called into play in a manoeuvre, being that much bigger. A three-hundred-and-fifty-square metre spinnaker is equivalent in size to a large town house and, unless one has a professional technique, one should not be tinkering with this kind of wind-filled sail. Each crew member has to be competent and know how to work together with his comrades. A poor sailor on a big boat represents a danger to himself and to others. An additional factor is that understanding and experience, without the requisite strength, will not be sufficient for continual physical demands. One must be in peak condition at the outset of a long race in which the body is suddenly jerked this way or that, one's muscles taking the brunt of it. Down in the southern ocean, amidst the well known roaring forties, the temperature is close to 0°C. That is when a crew member, resting on his bunk below decks, if ordered up on deck for a sudden manoeuvre, must be able to perform skilfully and reliably and without straining a muscle.

Our first race with *Pen Duick VI* will be the Fastnet. We wanted to compete in the Channel race, since any racing is good to put a boat through its paces and to get a crew involved. But the delay in getting the boat built meant that was not possible. The only race that we can still take part in is the Fastnet. We depart for Cowes without that much time before the start of the race. There is scarcely any wind, but nobody gets concerned. For the first time we have a motor. It is put into service, leaving Brest in a dead calm. We move along at an average of eight knots and then, all of a sudden, the engine comes to a halt. Xavier Joubert, the young engineer who had installed it, and whom I had decided to have on board, fiddles about with the mechanism and we head on. 'That should work ... ' he announces. It works, but only for a few hours before again falling silent. A circle of oil forms around the boat. Streaming out of the engine is the stench of hot oil. Dismantling and reassembling, Xavier persists. His hands are plastered in oil. Ultimately, his stubbornness pays off as the engine turns over. But the noises it makes are not good: groaning and asthmatic wheezing, as though in pain. For a third time it comes to a halt. The hours pass by, with that of departure drawing closer. The boat makes only lethargic movements. Not giving up, Xavier once more delves into the mechanism with his delicate hands that cannot help getting a little burnt. He unscrews, then screws back, his face a mask of concentration till he obtains the result he is after. The engine turns over and the engineer, somewhat perplexed, says, 'I hope this time it is fixed.' Unfortunately not. When it stops again it is for the last time. First comes a long, profound sigh, then the engine gives up the ghost. Xavier provides a definitive diagnosis:

'The seller stated that it had been run in, but it hadn't. We pushed it too hard, so it overheated and then became toast.'

We are looking for wind to progress, but there isn't any. The race starts at 10am on Saturday. The Isle of Wight may be visible but we still have a long way to go. As we approach the Needles, a light westerly breeze picks up allowing us to hoist the spinnaker. But at the same time that we are turning into the Solent, heading in the other direction, towards the Fastnet, comes the contestants' flotilla, pushed along by the current we are heading into. When we finally get to the departure line it is nine hours later than the others. All we can aim to do is to overtake as many as possible and let victory keep thumbing its nose at us.

Following our setbacks, the wind and current conditions do not make life easy on the outward leg to the Fastnet lighthouse, which we make out through the fog thanks to Petipas' flawless navigation.

Memories of the Open Sea

The return leg raises our spirits: on a beat, *Pen Duick VI* shows us his bravura. Having given them nearly a ten hour lead, we overtake the majority of our contestants. We are even beginning to think about finishing amongst the leaders when the wind collapses and *Sorcery*, the twenty-one metre American yacht, against whom it would have been handy to have taken our measure, crosses the line. We finish ninth in real time. Our future Round the World adversaries, *Adventure*, *Sayula II*, *Guia*, *Grand Louis* and *Second Life* are a long way behind us. And that is even with our late departure.

We do not stay in Plymouth longer than a few hours. I want to get back to Brest in double time to take the boat out of the water and then change the rudder size, try out different sails and make one or two final alterations to the set-up.

Pen Duick VI is ready for the big circuit. The designers and builders have both made a good job. The trials have shown everything on board to be working well. I am confident in my boat. He has what it takes to win.

CHAPTER 20

OF *PEN DUICK VI*'s MISFORTUNES AND GÉRARD PETIPAS' TRIBULATIONS

The way *Pen Duick VI* is I feel at ease. Let's say that I have left nothing to chance. Come departure day, there is nothing I need to give myself a hard time over: trials; adjustments; modifications; sails; everything meticulously tested. The crew had the time to get to discover the new boat and then to familiarise themselves with him during the Fastnet manoeuvres and in short sails. It is a good crew. There is Michel Barré, thirty-nine years old, sailing teacher at the Ministry of Young People and Sports; Jean-Philippe Chaboud, thirty-two, Chief Radio Officer in the Merchant Navy; Antoine Croyère, twenty-five, Toulouse based engineer; Jean-Pierre Dagues, twenty-eight, our on board doctor; Olivier de Kersauson, thirty, my old companion and cameraman; Pierre Laboutet, twenty-four, qualified coach; Pierre Mousaingeon, twenty-nine, architect; Marc Pajot, twenty-one, maths and physics student and silver medallist at the Kiel Olympics; Patrick Phelipon, twenty-one, student; Bernard Rubinstein, twenty-seven, maths teacher and chemistry graduate; Thierry Vanier, twenty-four, student; Arnaud Dhallene. And also my brother Patrick who is only available for the first leg. All of them are strong and experienced sailors, eager to join battle with our main rivals, the Argentinian *Sayula II*, the Italian *Guia*, and the English *Great Britain II*, *Adventure*, *Grand Louis*, *Kriter* and *33 Export*.

Memories of the Open Sea

Pen Duick VI has the stature to compete for victory with them.

The departure took place at 5pm on September 8 1973 and, as is usual on these occasions, it was necessary to swerve between hundreds of sailing and motor powered vessels to go around the Bembridge buoy, sole marker of this stage. Amidst all the lawless traffic, I came close to colliding with various foolhardy weekend sailors and barely avoided ramming them. By nightfall only *Great Britain II* remained, a mile behind, and he was soon lost in the fog. From the next morning we do not see any other boats involved in the Round the World.

The days at sea pass by. Around September 29 we learn via radio that our lead over *Adventure*, the next boat, is four days. *Pen Duick VI* has shown how talented he is in all conditions and the morale of my crew, constantly involved in strenuous manoeuvres, is at its peak. On board relations between the crew are good, give or take the odd moment, which is hardly surprising in this confined space. I grouped them into posts according to their abilities. From that point on, it is for them to organise amongst themselves. I am the skipper and I am not going to play at being a schoolmaster. On the other hand, I will not tolerate any kind of self indulgent dissension. Everyone must carry out his task without skiving. The aim is for all energy to be channelled towards the boat's advance.

In the redoubtable doldrums – I call them redoubtable because of the danger of entering becalmed waters – our route is turning out OK and, compared to the others, pegging away far behind us, we have barely been slowed down. Yes, everything is going swimmingly and victory at the end of the first leg in the Cape of Good Hope is ours for the taking. At least that's how things apparently stood before destiny, as if joking, decided otherwise.

There is a swell this October 4 and the boat is heeled over, the gunwale in the water, as the wind picks up to thirty-five knots, obliging us to bring down the mizzen then take a reef in the mainsail and install the yankee No3. After directing and taking part in the various manoeuvres, I go down for a rest. The time is 12.15am. I have

Eric Tabarly

scarcely settled into my bunk when the boat jerks back to its central position and the song of the water running along the hull comes to a stop. Simultaneously, one of the men on watch in the cockpit shouts down through the opening: 'The mast!'

I already knew from the noise. I am out of my bunk and onto the deck straightaway, followed by the men who had been sleeping, off watch.

'Éric, I believe it broke just beneath the lower spreader, but I can't say for sure in this light,' the helmsman tells me desolately.

The mast, bent in the process, is lodged on the gunwale; above the stepping, it is the halyards that are holding it in place but, with every punishing roll, they threaten to tear away the lot. There is not one minute to lose.

'Dismast! Quick!'

My crew and I settle down to the task. We start by recovering the boom, which can still be used. We loosen the mainsail clew, before disconnecting the boom from the mast. We cut the shrouds and halyards loose, with the result that all the rigging collapses.

There will be no Round the World victory.

'Éric, what are we going to do?' Kersauson asks.

'We will make for Rio. It's the closest port and, since the prevailing winds are favourable, we should be able to get there in reasonable time.'

We all have the same sad feeling. 'Lower the staysail and mizzen.' Action draws the sting out of remorse.

Why did the mast fall? If the breakage had taken place during the day, it is possible I could have uncovered the reason why, because not knowing cannot help but needle me. The race is lost for *Pen Duick VI* but, knowing that the Nirvana Spars Company has a profile identical to our discarded mast and that the manufacturer can provide the replacement within a fortnight, leads me to say to myself that we will be able to take part in the last three legs, the Cape–Sydney, Sydney–Rio, Rio–Portsmouth.

We set up a VHF antenna since the other, being located on it, has gone the same way as the mast. Throughout the day I try and

Memories of the Open Sea

establish radio contact with France. This finally happens in the evening.

At this hour – 9pm Paris time – Gérard Petipas and his wife are having their evening meal. He can find no reason to be displeased with the way in which the race is going. The night before, that is to say Tuesday October 2, the news, during one of the biweekly – Tuesday and Friday – radio slots with the boat, confirmed to him that it and the crew were both doing well. Gérard said to himself: 'Let's hope it lasts.' Indeed ... the agreements he had negotiated with both newspapers and radio producers were performance related, a sliding scale of payment, depending on the boat's final position, intended to repay the banker who had financed the boat's construction. It was well understood that if *Pen Duick VI* had to abandon, then the company of which he was director would receive next to nothing. It will be a financial catastrophe.

Their two young children, Alexis and Gilles, tucked up in bed, Gérard and his wife are dining *tête-à-tête*, an infrequent occurrence since the *Pen Duick VI* project got going. And so, at 9pm, the telephone rings. A little put out at this interruption halfway through supper, Gérard goes and picks up the phone.

A voice devoid of emotion announces – 'Hubert here'. 'Hubert' being Hubert Henrotte, director of the Sygma agency that receives the boat's radio communications.

'Gérard,' Henrotte continued, 'I have just received bad news. They've just been dismasted and are heading for Brazil. The race is over...'

'Did they give the details? Any wounded?'

'The link was poor but they did not mention any injuries.'

'Let's talk again once you receive more information.'

Stunned, Gérard automatically relays to his wife the news just received and thinks. The second, Cape–Sydney, leg is due to start between November 2 and 7 inclusive. He makes a mental calculation: one should allow about six days for the repairs – taking into account the likelihood of significant damage to the deck. *Pen*

Eric Tabarly

Duick VI will need to get to Rio sometime between October 13–16 and all the materials for his repair would have to be there by the 13th. It is not impossible, if the suppliers pull out all the stops.

Gérard rings publicist Michel Le Berre, who is having supper in La Rochelle at crew member Patrick Phelipon's parents. A peculiarity of Le Berre is that he never lets himself get into a funk. Thus, he calmly asks: 'Is there anything that can be done?'

'If we succeed in getting all the materials to Rio within a maximum delay of nine days, yes. The big problem is going to be transporting it.'

'Do not worry. I am going to go back to Paris and will make it my job to find a plane.'

Gérard slept only a few hours. He draws up a list, very early on the Wednesday morning October 4, of people who will have to be alerted to set the rescue operation in motion. First, the mast manufacturer based in Switzerland. Then, Victor Tonnerre, to make some replacement sails in Tissaverre providing that the material is in stock. Next, the SARMA company, to make new shrouds. When he gets to his office, Gérard encounters Le Berre, who is on his way out to find a cargo plane. Then he is handed a telegram that has come in from the boat:

'Have been dismasted – Heading Rio – Undertake dispatch of mast and fixings – All shrouds – Mainsail – Yankee No. 3 – Heavy genoa staysail – 2 drawplates – 6 stanchions – 24mm braided lines, 200m – Suggest make upper spreader 10cm longer – Éric.'

Gérard works the telephones. Cœudevez at Nirvana Spars reassures him: there is a length ready and work is starting on the mast post-haste. He will do whatever needs to be done to have it ready within the time envisaged. Tissaverre & Co are out of stock but will immediately make up some new material to be delivered in two days time. Once this occurs, Victor Tonnerre will have day and night shifts working, if that is required. In the meantime, he sets to work on the halyards.

Memories of the Open Sea

It is grey with heavy squalls. In spite of the roll, *Pen Duick VI* makes reasonably quick progress under mizzen and mizzen staysail. To improve our speed and handling a little, I decide to organise a jury rig at daybreak. Using two spinnaker poles fastened together at their top ends and manipulated via their lower ends' connection to shroud chainplates, it is possible to arrange a twin-footed mast and, then, at least some sail towards the foredeck.

A speedometer reading confirms that the boat is going as fast as seven to eight knots. The nervous energy we had racing has gone. Equanimity in the face of misfortune is now the order of the day; there is no point in recriminations. My lads play Scrabble and noughts and crosses. Michel gives yoga lessons. Patrick, my brother, has made a rather good hook out of a stainless steel pin. We use it to catch a tazar, a tuna and a metre long brown-black fish, with pointed nose, not quite as round as a conger, and barracuda like teeth: three fresh, delicious meals.

Sometimes, when the boat's advance has slowed to a crawl, some like to go swimming: they dive off the bows and then grab onto a rope trailing from the stern. I occupy myself, during this progress towards Rio, with two new halyards for the jib and one for the staysail, using the replacement wire and rope we have on board. It is a painstaking task, but once it is done, it will mean one less thing to do in Rio.

At the same time, Gérard is in an almost constant state of worry as he deals with a host of uncertainties. The sail fabric was produced and so Victor Tonnerre was able to cut and sew. The package of new halyards is ready. The new mast will be finished and ready to load onto a cargo plane Thursday October 11. In spite of all this good news, Gérard is not satisfied. Provisions still need to be organised. The container with those for the second stage, the Cape–Sydney, is already on its way to the Cape aboard a packet service ship. If *Pen Duick VI* is to head straight from Rio to Sydney then more stores will have to be taken on board, sufficient for such a long voyage. That hasn't been done yet.

Besides this, the most important problem has yet to be resolved – that of the plane. One with rear doors and capable of accommodating the mast has still not been found. Michel Le Berre phones everywhere, all the companies, even private owners, but currently has nothing to show for his efforts.

From Thursday October 11 all the smaller items were stacked up in Petipas' office: a shambles of crates and boxes, containing the Brookes weathervane, the Goiot winch, lines, stanchions, battens, clasps and blocks and extension pole ends. Some of the sails will come on Friday. And still the plane to be found.

Gérard, deprived of sleep, has rings under his eyes and sunken cheeks. Constantly at battle stations, his Operation Re-mast is nevertheless taking shape. Preparations have been made in Rio. The Brazilian Navy has given its permission for the afflicted boat to berth in its yard and make use of a crane. He has two groups in line for the repair work: one will deal with the mast, the other restore the deck and install a steering wheel. The first comprises Gérard himself, Albert Cœudevez, Pierre English – old crew – and Yves Devillers, who writes for *Cahiers du Yachting*. The second will be formed by the engineer Xavier Joubert and five workers from the Brest shipyard, involved with the boat's construction and seconded by the naval shipbuilding director.

When he gets the most recent message from the boat, Gérard raises his eyes to heaven. The latest equipment required is a Tefal stove, a six litre pressure cooker, eighty plastic sacks, and isolating valves for the WCs.

We are joined, throughout the day, by an albatross, at a latitude as far north as the bird goes and a rare event. It swoops down voraciously onto anything and everything we throw for it into the sea. It is common among sailors, on their first encounter with the mythical seabird, to be moved by its sublime, long-winged glide then amused to see its laborious landings. They are the only distraction in a passage of variable winds that, every now and again, after having collapsed the extension pole rigging, gives me the chance to raise the spinnaker up the mizzen mast.

We are listening to France-Inter, which is how we find out that the new mast will be in Rio on Sunday morning the 14th. I cannot help letting out a cry of joy in unison with the crew. Thanks to Gérard, we will not lose any time and I start to think that we might be able, if everything goes well, to get to the Cape in time to depart on the second leg with all the other boats.

Back in Paris, Gérard had received confirmation from Nirvana Spars that the mast would be ready by the end of the 11th – Thursday. Cœudevez proposed to him that he will transport it to Geneva–Cointrain airport to be loaded onto the cargo plane. Good – but what cargo plane? Michel Le Berre has yet to receive the final answer. He is moving on two fronts: the Alain Delon option, use of whose plane will cost thirty thousand francs, the price of the fuel; alternatively, there is a foreign company. Both courses, once all the details are known, have to be abandoned, the actor's plane not being long enough to take the mast, the other being unavailable for a week.

Gérard is tearing his hair out at the thought that *Pen Duick VI* will get to Rio in advance of the materials for the repair. And his tribulations are not over yet. The night before – Wednesday the 10th – the mast is due to be ready, he and Le Berre had telephoned – almost out of despair – the Ministry of Defence, explaining the situation they were in. At the same time as having their request agreed to, they were asked to submit it formally. 'The Secretary will do everything in his power in order to help you,' is what he had been told by Yvon Bourges' collaborator.

Without a minute's delay, Petipas and Le Berre had sped off to Bourget to discuss with the Air Force's technical staff how to load the mast and the other materials on board a large COTAM transport plane. 'That's it! We've done it!' Le Berre, in characteristically optimistic fashion, had exulted. By contrast, the former TransOcean captain remained cautious.

Thursday morning. Wham! The plane is not free: it is already engaged for another operation which cannot be postponed. Gérard is devastated. That evening a lorry is due to leave Brest with the materials on board. The shipyard workers are already on their way to Paris. The mast will be ready at Geneva airport. For lack of a plane, all of these efforts to have everything ready in time will have been in vain. Once more Le Berre hits the phones, but is unable to uncover the right kind of transporter. The time is 5pm.

'It's useless!' lets out Gérard, falling into his armchair.

'I don't know what else I can do, where to look ... ' accepts Le Berre who, for the first time, is a little despondent.

The two men are just sitting there, face to face – not least with their defeat, when, all of a sudden – ring-ring – the phone rings; Gérard picks it up. It is the Ministry of Defence:

'M Gérard Petipas?'

'Yes.'

'We have a plane available. A KC135 which should meet your requirements. It was meant to be on a training sortie but will now take you to Rio as priority. Take off is due from Bourget, late tomorrow morning. There will be a stop at Geneva, to pick up the mast and take off again to Brazil.'

Saved!

The following morning, Friday October 12, Petipas and Le Berre, as arranged, met up with Yves Devillers and Pierre English at the airport. The Brest shipyard group of six are there also: Xavier Joubert, Divy Kerdoncuff, Marcel Simon, Jacky Bellion, François Bars and Christian Meichel. Between shaking hands with the team who are under Commander Guilleux's orders and take off at midday, the time is spent checking and loading the five tonnes of material. Touchdown in Geneva is at 1.15pm, and there is a group standing by the side of the lorry with its mast freight: Albert Cœudevez and his men.

'Jesus Christ it's long! Pray that it goes in,' says Gérard to himself uneasily.

Memories of the Open Sea

Swiss assistance at the airport is very kind. Having asked the French what they require, they position a platform against the KC135's door and form a chain to unload all the Bourget material so that there is space for the mast.

Initially, the operation goes smoothly. The entire team have straps; their work is synchronised. Metre by metre, the mast disappears into the hold of the cargo plane. It is tiring, sweat inducing work; slowly but surely it progresses, up until the moment the masthead touches the end of the cabin. That is as far as it can go. Perched on the platform, English shouts out:

'There is 1.30 metres sticking out.'

It is obvious that the mast will not fit in completely. Gérard can feel his proverbial energy deserting him, all of a sudden. Until that last metre or so, everything was going smoothly.

'What do we do?' asks Le Berre, similarly deflated.

'The only solution I can see is to cut it. We need to ask Xavier.'

Joubert, whilst not being against this, wants to consult with the manufacturer – and Albert Cœudevez is explicitly opposed to this guillotining, pointing out that, if it were carried out, he could no longer guarantee anything. At this juncture a further, potential, problem arises. Commander Guilleux, on being informed that the stopover in Geneva will be longer than was planned, must get permission from base if, in spite of this complication, the mission is to continue. The green light will have to wait until a 7am phone call the following morning, Saturday the 13th.

Everybody gets back to work, performing the same operation as before in reverse: that is to say, they take the mast out. Xavier has already been in discussion with the solders in his team. They are standing by ready to do what has to be done. Under duress, Cœudevez ends up by agreeing to the mutilation of his work 1.40 metres from its base. But the manufacturer refuses to assist in the operation.

'Let's go and get some sleep and tomorrow morning, 7am sharp, we will reassemble at the airport,' Petipas takes the initiative.

Eric Tabarly

Saturday October 13. Everyone is there for the rendezvous on time. The day gets going with a piece of good news: authorisation has been given for the plane to continue on its mission. Things move fast. At 8am the shortened mast glides into the hold where it is made fast by a team while airport volunteers help form the chain reloading all the crates of material. The crew pull on their flying suits. The door is secured. At 9.30am the military plane takes off from Geneva-Cointrain for Rio, a flight that entails stopping at Dakar en route. 4am local time the KC135 touches down in Rio.

Unloading starts at 7am with the arrival of the first warehouse shift. By the time the mast and other freight have been loaded onto waiting lorries the sun is high overhead and the heat oppressive. Escorted by three motorcycle policemen, the convoy makes its way through the city's chaotic traffic, concluding its journey at the Brazilian shipyard where teams take on the exhausting task of unloading this latest delivery of the day. It is 4pm. After nipping into the yacht club where there is news of *Pen Duick VI*, Gérard and Le Berre and Joubert and his workers finally arrive at their hotel. Dinner is taken quickly. All of them have the same idea in mind. Bed. And sleep. For a long time.

It is 2 o'clock on this Sunday–Monday night. Gérard is sunk in a deep sleep when the hotel room phone resounds unwelcomingly in his ears. His eyes still locked tight, he fumbles about trying to locate the handset. He touches it, takes it off the hook. He listens:

'Monsieur, *Pen Duick VI* will be arriving shortly. He is heading towards the bay and the yacht club.'

Gérard gets up and makes his way, like a sleepwalker, to the shower. His beard is long; he looks peaky. As he brushes his teeth he works out how much sleep he has had since the dismasting on October 4: thirty hours, at the very most. Not much.

CHAPTER 21

THE SHREDDING OF THE SAILS

As I step onto land, Gérard, Michel and Xavier are there on the quay. They don't look great but are smiling and happy. We shake hands.

'It's all here,' Petipas says to me. 'Take a look.'

I take a look. The mast is laid out on the ground; the boxes and crates are stacked; the material bought by the Brest team is there: soldering set, the tools required. Amazing – and moving. All of these people who were there for us, who did not hesitate to come forward with their assistance, make up a ring of friendship. Like my crew, who have now joined us on land, I know the repairs will soon be finished and that, while the race might be lost, we will now be able to continue and do what we can to distinguish ourselves.

'Thanks,' I say.

Besides which, what else is there to say? Friendship is nourished by actions and by trust that go beyond words.

Starting early on Monday morning there is a hustle and bustle about the work. The shipyard workers get through a spectacular amount of work and are sparing of neither their time nor effort. For these long, tiring days of work, separate teams take on particular tasks. Some join the mast lengths together as others install the steering wheel because, right from the first voyages, we had found it hard work manipulating the tiller which is very stiff. The modification, which we did not have enough time for before departure, was envisaged for the stopover in the Cape. *Pen Duick VI* is a hive of activity. My sailors are kept busy during this enforced stop. A handful of them rig the mast with halyards and shrouds; two of them repair sails under the guidance of a Carioca sail-maker; another two mend the patches of deck that were damaged. The rest do some general tidying up and stock the boat with the provisions Gérard brought. There was only one black mark amidst this frenetic activity which was when I was obliged to hand a crew member, whose appearances at the shipyard were infrequent and fleeting, his cards. He refused to join in the work. In such situations I do not mess around. He is given a few minutes to collect his belongings and get off the boat. He will get back to France with the repair team.

The collapse of the mast weighed on my mind. Not knowing how an accident happened means it may re-occur. It had been impossible for me since the dismasting, particularly at sea, to fathom the cause. Gérard and Xavier are the ones to make the discovery. During their inspection of the boat they notice the toilet bulkheads are no longer straight. They take down the internal deck-head section – and further note that, beneath the mast, the deck has sunk by two to three centimetres. The thought had never occurred to me that gradually, millimetre by millimetre, it is going to collapse. The workers are going to have more to do reinforcing this area of the boat, but at least I will be feeling more at ease when I set off again. The last evening in port I spend sewing the spreaders' leather protection.

If travelling broadens the mind, this particular visit could not be considered a success: nobody had the time – or money – for tourism.

Going via the great circle, three thousand two hundred and fifty miles separates Rio de Janeiro from the Cape of Good Hope. No other boat had yet arrived, so we would definitely be able to be there for the departure of the second marathon, all the way to Sydney.

We manage to break the spinnaker block. I climb up to the masthead to fix it. During the evening of October 26, it is the starboard block that gets broken and the spinnaker tears. Two in the morning October 27 marks a week since we left Brazil and we

Memories of the Open Sea

are half a day in arrears of my forecast. When the wind gets up, *Pen Duick VI* makes rapid progress on top of a fairly big, choppy sea in a magnificent surfing motion. Nevertheless, these euphoric interludes between anticyclones and variable winds are not going to be enough to prevent us taking at least twenty, rather than fifteen, days to reach the Cape.

On board the crew are organised somewhat differently to before. Besides the one I dismissed, my brother Patrick left us at Rio to return to work, as arranged. Suddenly, with one fewer on each side, we are down to twelve on board.

At sea, one has to take one's pleasures where one can. Having volunteered to step into the shoes of the cook who, at the last minute, could not make it, Pierre Leboutet makes it known that, wishing instead to take more part in manoeuvres, he no longer wants to be the only one chained to the stove. Not everyone is keen on the idea of a cooking rota for such a long voyage, especially since the productions of some are infamous, if not poisonous. Leboutet receives assistance from Antoine Croyère, Jean-Pierre Dagues and Arnaud Dhallene. They will take five-day turns during which they will be off watch. Their dishes are welcomed by the crew. This is how vocations are often formed.

The hinge bolt at the end of the lower port spreader has become almost completely unscrewed. I am hoisted up in the chair to the spar and start by opening up the mechanism. I lift out the pin and take the shroud out from the hinge before fixing the connection once more onto its two ferrules so as to re-join the two shroud lengths. I have the turnbuckle on deck tightened so that the assembly does not swing about. Further, this shroud will serve as something to hold onto as I re-tighten the bolt. Now for the hard part. The shroud made slack again, I pull the pin out of the ferrules once more. My hands are full with these two heavy shroud lengths, pulling this way and that with the swell, and the pin, all needing to go back onto the hinge. Since I am already holding the two shroud lengths, there is not one to use for support. The only way I can secure myself is with my elbow hooked around the upper side of the spar itself. It is not the best of grips, but I need to have both my hands free. Jerked by the roll, there are moments when I have the unpleasant sensation of sliding helplessly towards the spar's outer edge. Then comes the moment, after several failed attempts to offer up the higher ferrule, when I doubt whether I will be able to reassemble it all.

Fighting the roll, I concentrate all my energy, pulling the upper ferrule down and its lower counterpart up. Eventually the openings are aligned and I am able to insert the pin. I have a feeling of great relief. All that remains to be done is tighten up the turnbuckles.

By radio, I find out the second leg departure has been fixed for November 7. That means that our stopover at the Cape will be a very brief one, giving us only a few hours in which to straighten out the boat, buy fresh provisions and then head on. It is becoming clear that tourism isn't going to play any part in this world trip.

The sky is overcast and it is cold. Following an anticyclone that had slowed us down, there is now a continually changing wind that strengthens and blows, then weakens, to die away before starting all over again. For long periods we are accompanied by speedy porpoises jumping above the waves. Their advance is fairly astonishing but then so is ours, as it reaches eighteen knots on a long surf.

After fifteen days and nineteen hours out of Rio we cross the finishing line. Alerted by radio, the jury is there to sound the cannon and we are applauded by the big crowd that is gathered for our berthing at the yacht club quay. We are offered congratulations as we are told: 'You have smashed the Rio–Cape record.'

I appreciate the compliment as it comes with proof of crewing brilliance and of the boat's thoroughbred status. But yachting speed records do not really mean that much to me. Comparing performances under different wind conditions involves distortion, if not injustice.

Adventure is the officially classed leader, on a compensated time of thirty-six days and nine hours. *Pen Duick VI*, because of his problems, is allotted fifty-seven days, which puts us twenty days and fifteen hours behind. We will not make up that time.

Two new crew members wait for us on the quay: Mickaël Le Berre is embarking for the rest of the race; Bernard Deguy will be with us as far as Sydney.

We are also bringing on board new spinnaker blocks made by the Brest shipyard. The rigging is adjusted. For a second time we stick down the deck covering. A local sail maker is called to repair one of the spinnakers; the other stays torn. Kindly, the American sail maker on board *Sayula II* sorts out our yankee No.2.

The day of departure comes; we all have the same impression of not having made a stop here; our return to land has been that ephemeral.

Following its schedule, the race recommences at 1.30pm on November 7. With a silly mistake on my part. Having forgotten to properly familiarise myself with all the instructions, a few minutes in advance of the cannon firing, I asked a crew member to quickly read them out to me. Either he did it badly or I was not listening properly; but, for whatever reason, *Pen Duick VI* went round the buoy at the starting line the wrong way, forcing me to turn 180° and approach it from the right side.

By the evening *Great Britain* is a long way behind us, on the starboard side; further back still, no more than a spot, lies *Sayula II*. *Pen Duick VI* leads the dance. And then, on the opening night, the slaughter of the sails begins. The first to rip suddenly is the heavy spinnaker: serious bother, given that we do not have a replacement. We improvise by hoisting the star cut and carry on our way. On the third day, finding ourselves on the eastern side of an unusually low level anticyclone, we are shaken about by the combination of big seas and a fifty-knot wind. We are under mainsail and heavy genoa staysail at a speed of nine knots. One of the men on watch cries out: 'The staysail!' Too late. A blast of water had split it. In the time required to haul it in and bring it down, the mainsail itself suffers a cut a few metres across. When we left Portsmouth we had two. The first could not be used following the dismasting, so it is the second we are currently relying on. Its leech beats out a frightful noise against the breeze. I had received a third in Rio which shares the same inconvenience.

By November 13, *Pen Duick VI* had travelled down to the forty fifth parallel. It is a little nippy outside; both sea and air are cold; in the saloon, the heating we use for no more than an hour each day is not able to raise the temperature above 5°C. Beneath the sky's impregnable grey cover, the south wind blows dank air. Together, Patrick and I spend our time repairing the sails when the light permits. My crew member, sitting down at the sewing machine placed on the table, valiantly undertakes the heavy spinnaker's repair as I sew together the staysail's tear by hand.

The wind is still at about twenty-five to thirty knots. As it stiffens once more, I raise the star cut – in place of the medium spinnaker. This sail is a little smaller than an actual spinnaker. Cut out of strong cloth, robust and reassuring, somewhere between a big and heavy small spinnaker. A confidence inspiring sail. Barely have the men on watch raised it and made their way back into the cockpit where they are regaining their breath when, crack! The star cut tears along its reinforced head and down both its long outer seams.

Our misfortunes are not yet complete. The following day, after a stint of nearly twenty-four hours, the heavy small spinnaker crashes down abruptly. The braiding of the ring within the sail's head, through which the halyard passes, has worn out. Truly, the sails' sea of troubles. Patrick and I are forced down into the saloon like recluses. I put aside my staysail work to re-braid the star cut. Because of the combined thickness of the braiding and the reinforcement to the head, it is slow, difficult work – both to get the needle to penetrate, which can take several attempts, and then to pull it out the other side, for which pliers are needed. I never mention it but, all spinnakers hors de combat, I am actually very concerned.

There are days when the name Roaring Forties is well earned. If the wind does not rise to the pitch that some have described (perhaps exaggerating a little), the wave troughs below are deep enough to give the Indian Ocean its lamentable reputation. The wind is not south westerly but, in spite of that, a secondary swell comes at us from there and opposes the main, pronounced north westerly swell. The waves are reinforced by their clash and raised up even higher, before churning down and away with a mind numbing din, of which there is no pause.

If the sun succeeds in forcing a way through the cloud, then the sea automatically brightens and assumes a patchwork of brilliant shades. Within heavy waterproofs, we contemplate, our faces cold, withdrawn, but in wonder, these white tailed breakers darting across the surface of the water. Below milky crests the sea is green and limpid, then transmutes into blue, but not the same at all as in warm seas. There it is settled and sombre; here it is closer to green, a sign of the cold. The spindrift whipped up by the wind has the look of a whitish sail. Above it are flying albatross and great winged petrel and Cape pigeon.

The wind though is no poet. The medium spinnaker is the next to go, followed by the replacement mainsail. When the men on watch see what is about to happen it is already too late. As they rush forward to bring the sail in, a length of stitching above the first reef unravels. Lacking an immediate replacement, we put in a temporary reef. As the saying has it: 'Make do and mend.'

The brand new medium spinnaker – delivered to the Cape as such – is hoisted. In actual fact this is a heavy spinnaker made in the most resistant nylon one can buy.

If I, or one of my crew, had noticed the mislabelling, we would have used it more frequently and so saved ourselves a lot of trouble. It really is an extraordinary sail. Very smoothly, it gathers up the wind and, using its strength, pulls us along to the point where, on a surf, the speedometer nudges twenty-three knots, *Pen Duick VI*'s fastest speed.

Everyone on board revels in these long, seemingly interminable, slides like big dipper rides at the funfair.

It is the combination of strong wind, a lot of sail and nicely formed waves which allows one to surf. And it can be found in the waters which lead into the Kerguelen Islands. So the boat, moving along well with the help of the wind, is caught from behind by a good sized wave, pushing it up as though it were a toboggan which surges forward, the wave now pulling it on to the point where the speedometer climbs to between eighteen and twenty knots. Exhilaration! Either side of the boat the water it is slicing through is thrown up and back, creating a liquid passage. To find oneself inside its rumble is almost voluptuous.

The other side of the Kerguelen Islands, a sixty-knot squall descends on the boat. It is literally covered, with its sails in the water. The helmsman loses all sense of the wheel, now tension-less, in his hands. The squall dies down. *Pen Duick VI* shakes himself down and heads off again. I have never had an experience like it before. Without delay, we gather in the staysail; as for the spinnaker, it is debris; half is gone and the remaining half is in tatters. We bring them in, all that is left of an apparently indestructible sail, now irreparable. We are not – alas! –done with this drama. After nightfall, as I was helming, a brief but sudden, violent squall hit us. It was the turn of our biggest jib to tear. This was carnage!

It is via radio that we are kept informed of dramas which bring the race into mourning. On the first leg, the Italian boat *Tauranga* had lost a man overboard, and the same fate befell an English crew member of *British Soldier*. Not long after, there is an announcement to say that the co-skipper of *33 Export*, Dominique Guillet, has been lost the same way. We are affected by his loss. We had known him and liked him a great deal. He often used to sail on board *Pen Duick III* with us and, as well as being a good sailor, was a good guy.

Memories of the Open Sea

The possibility that one of my crew members might go overboard is something that I am continually conscious of. It is why I am either on hand or taking part in manoeuvres, to check that nobody is making a dangerous move. I feel friendship towards these lads who, just because they enjoy sailing, are slaving away on my boat. The thought that one of them might fall into the water and that I would not be able to haul him back in is a big worry for me, even though I realise that, should such a misfortune take place, there is little I will be able to do to save him. To fall into these waters, when the temperature is 6°C, is to be lost. One would not survive for more than a few minutes. Encased in waterproofs, weighed down by boots, the unfortunate victim would not have the strength to swim over to the lifebelt that will have been thrown out to him, but which will be far away, given the speed of the boat. The time it takes to bring the sails down, start the motor and turn the boat about and find him, hardly bigger than a dot amidst the engulfing waves, makes any hope of rescue vain.

These dramas at sea always revive the arguments surrounding the wearing of safety harnesses. I do not insist upon it on my boat. If I demand it of others, I must lead by example. And I personally refuse to wear a harness. The reason is straightforward enough: I would rather the death that lasts a few minutes – as unpleasant as it may be – to the life spent onboard preoccupied with belts.

My crew are in remarkably fit form, know how to move on deck in bad weather and are alert, so they run fewer risks than others might. Obviously this free choice is not intended for the average, occasional sailor. In bad weather a safety harness is indispensable for them and not the hindrance that it is for us, moving about that much quicker, racing.

With the patience of a saint, Patrick repaired our last spinnaker. It took hours of intricate work. No sooner is it realised than, receiving a light breeze, it is ripped to pieces. The sails' destruction goes on unabated.

Eric Tabarly

Our passage to Sydney unfolds in the presence of contrary or weak winds, sudden squalls that give way to calms, or breezes which blow now one way, now another. We slave away at manoeuvres, our progress dictated by depressions we are sailing towards or that are drawing in on us from behind, on a sea whose aspect changes from being big to flat to a swell.

These weather conditions are not indicated on any pilot chart. Being abnormal. Going from a deep depression to calm, or from having all the sails up to none at all, my crew have the merit of not sparing themselves. One needs to see them in amongst the sails, wrestling them into submission, sheeting in, raising canvass. They labour, as their muscles ache, against the driving wind and the driving sea spray on a deck that heads nose down into a trough, to rise up later as it exits. These unforgiving seas provide a racing sailor with the chance to rise to his full stature. On the other hand, mediocrity will be brutally revealed.

Now we are not that far from Sydney. And in the nature of things on this leg, our sole remaining mainsail now gave out. In the course of battle, all its battens disappeared from their worn pockets. Without delay, we bring it in, pre-empting it tearing to pieces. Patrick, in turn, plays his usual piece on the sewing machine, after which it is reinstated, but, prudently, we furl it around the boom, only to be used in calmer weather.

Beating without a break, we zigzag our way up Australia's southeast coast. With barely twenty miles to go to Sydney, for the third night running the wind drops. The whole of the night we make no headway, then, at the break of day, a southerly breeze gets up, permitting us straightaway to push on and cross the line in Sydney under spinnaker.

It is not my way to hide behind bad luck and adversity, as excuses for failure to perform. But…! We were not exactly spoilt after leaving Portsmouth. Following the dismasting in the first stage, the end of the second stage brought us unfavourable winds, at the same time as

Memories of the Open Sea

our rivals, further back, were spared them. And then the slaughter of our sails ...

As we berth at our dock in the bay, we are tempted to say to ourselves that maybe we have already fulfilled our quota for damage and other kinds of ill-luck provided by the sea. The third stage is due to prove that this is not so. But we do not know that yet.

In real time we came first in this stage ahead of *Great Britain, Second Life, Kriter, Sayula II, Grand Louis* and *Guia*. Over the two legs, *Sayula II* is leader and *Pen Duick VI* third last. Our dismasting is costing us dear.

CHAPTER 22

OF *PEN DUICK VI*'S MISFORTUNES (CONT...)

We are on holiday. A working holiday.

The alcohol fired cooker, which was clogged up, gets changed for a range that runs off gas canisters.

It takes a while to find a boatyard where *Pen Duick VI* can be put in dry dock with his pressing need of a hull re-paint. Most of them already have more work than they can handle or do not have the facilities to accept a boat with such a deep keel. Having searched for a few days, I finally uncover what I am looking for at the far end of the bay on Cockatoo Island. It is a two hour round trip.

The boat receives a spring clean. The halyard sheaves, which had worked their way loose, are taken out and I replace the spinnaker halyards that are drawn up inside the mast. The yacht compass, too flighty and over responsive to the boat's yaws, is exchanged. A replacement mainsail, without battens, is tried out, with mixed results. It struggles when fetching, but performs well with following winds.

It was a three week long stopover but, because of all that needed to be done – mending, setting the boat up properly, provisioning – the time flew by. There are only two days left over for us to do whatever we want. We are invited by some of our compatriots living in Sydney to a barbecue party at the rear of a sprawling, cliff rimmed, beach. We clamber onto a minibus and head off for lamb

Memories of the Open Sea

chops and grilled sausages and swimming. White sands and a sun filled, moving sea with rollers – so, happy surfers! – that break with a controlled roar. Australia is a grand and beautiful country. On Boxing Day, the departure for the Sydney–Hobart race takes place. We head out as part of the flotilla to help send off the contestants, notably the French *Variag* skippered by Marc Henrion. My thoughts are led back to 1967, when I had come to take part with *Pen Duick III* and won.

At 4pm on December 29 1973 we crossed the starting line for the third stage that would lead us to Rio. The debut of the voyage is accompanied by light breezes. *Pen Duick VI* always enjoys these wind conditions. They allow his advance over the others to grow. In the course of the night the lights of two contestants behind us fade from view. As day breaks and the wind gradually stiffens, we are moving along at ten knots under heavy spinnaker, staysail and mainsail and mizzen.

Every now and again on a boat one gets a snatch of near silence, becoming almost meditative. All that can be heard is the water skimming along the hull and the wind in the rigging. These are memorable moments for the crew. The yacht, being correctly set up, cuts a path in and slides through the water; unfathomably in league with the sea – or so it seems – the rise and fall of the bows establishes a gentle rhythm.

But, in an instant, comes a sharp turn for the worse. The running tackle, which maintains the inner forestay's tension and, thereby, the mast's forward balance, has given way under the spinnaker pole's tension. The pole pushes the mast, which tumbles backward and shears clean apart, close to the lower spreader. This is abominable. The spinnaker and a staysail go into the water. The mainsail lower section and the boom crash onto the deck. A second staysail knocks about dementedly in the wind. I said it before: I command an outstanding crew. Kersauson, Marc Pajot and Deguy leap forward. Their activity is furious, bending all the way over to recover the spinnaker before it gets wrapped around the keel. The others help me bring the boom and the mainsail under control and cut the shrouds to free the rigging.

The race had been lost following the first dismasting. With the second it is over. We abandon.

On the way back to Sydney, under mizzen or motor, nobody comments on what has happened. Not much time is needed for me to uncover its root cause. Examining the cracked block, signs of advanced oxidation are plain to see. Sooner or later this part would have broken. It was better for us that it was two hundred miles southeast of Sydney and not somewhere round 56° latitude. One takes what comfort one can.

Sydney, on Friday January 1, was, like much of the world, feeling the worse for wear as we came into dock at 7am. There is no point trying to get hold of a yard or mast manufacturer until the following morning.

So we settle down to waiting and sorting stuff out. Australian and French officials come by to commiserate but, for all the summer sky, we are not to be consoled. Alstar Ltd have a mast length that, with the exception of a few, minor details, is suitable for *Pen Duick VI*. I put Gérard Petipas and André Mauric in the picture and, within a handful of days, Gérard lets me know that the insurance company have agreed to pay for mast, sails and rigging replacements, while Mauric gives his consent for the mast to be stepped on the boat's keel, rather than deck.

A month slips by before the new mast can be fitted. The others are already far away and about to encounter the mythical Horn, but that is no longer anything to do with us who have dropped out. Having performed setting up and routine tests, repaired several sails and loaded provisions, on February 5 11.30am, with a weak wind, we head back out to the open sea, the South Pacific and the Horn. Two days later and west of New Zealand, the tail end of a cyclone puts in an appearance, reaching seventy knots. Just as, when coming back from Ouvéa, I was with Kersauson, Guégan and Colas on board

Memories of the Open Sea

Pen Duick III, I lower all the sails, leaving the boat to drift where it will. Without its canvas, the boat bobs about. We calmly wait for the tempest to pass. Which it does. We set off once more. Taking advantage of an unaccustomed calm period in the Pacific, I put in place a solid sheet of aluminium, aft of where the helmsman stands, the aim being to have a shield against a large wave bearing down from astern as it breaks. Coming up to Stewart Isle, the temperature drops. There is thick fog. At the helm and at our quarters we suffer. In spite of cagoules and gloves, our faces and hands are whipped by the wind, icy and damp, blowing at thirty-five to forty knots. This is a big sea we are moving on.

On March 8 I might well have said goodbye to this life. We have considerable sail area raised in the breeze and need to go about. This manoeuvre, which we have repeated hundreds of times since our departure, is one that we perform easily. But on this particular morning at 4am, as I turn the winch to hoist the pole up the mast, it reaches about six metres above the deck when it slips from its hinge, landing on my back just below the shoulder blade, hitting the back of my arm at the same time. The force of it throws me back on the deck. Without question, it is painful. That does not prevent me from saying just what I think to the crew member responsible for checking that the pole had clicked into its fixing properly. To repeat what I have said before: because it might end in a tragic accident, negligence on board a big boat cannot be tolerated. I thought everybody had learned this lesson carefully: a mooring must be perfect; a knot has to be pulled tight; a winch handle jammed; a pin fully inserted; a sheet secured, so as not to get frayed.

We pass by the side of an iceberg that stands ninety metres or so high. Its colour, according to the sun's position, runs from immaculate white to dirty grey. Commencing on the afternoon of February 23 there are several days of snow and hail when the thermometer barely reaches 2°C. The men's fingers get numb with cold. I had provisioned them with fisherman's gloves but, to manoeuvre aggressively, one must leave one's hands bare. The heating is on for one hour in the morning and then a few in the evening, but that only offers brief respite from our travails.

We encounter dolphins that are black with white bellies and nose tips, a type I saw only in these waters. We still get drenched by the odd heavy shower. By radio, Petipas lets me know that the others will set off on the final stage from Rio between March 5 and 11. We will not be there for this final departure.

Cape Horn island appears, rising sombrely up in front of us to four hundred and twenty-four metres. We pass close by this landmark of sailors' ill-fortune through the ages, a graveyard for boats and those in them. My crew members take photos. Kersauson films. I reflect that this year three of my boats have come by this cape that inspires so much fear. First, Marc Linski, in whose safe keeping I have left *Pen Duick III* for his sailing school; recently, *Pen Duick IV*, re-baptised *Manureva* by Alain Colas who, with one stop in Sydney, is going round the world single-handed; and finally us, aboard *Pen Duick VI*.

Heading up through the South Atlantic is tiresome with the wind occasionally violent, on the nose or absent, according to its sudden changes of humour. Rio comes into sight on March 16. *Pen Duick VI* berths at his pontoon after crossing the line at 7.15pm. It had taken us thirty-nine days, twenty-one hours and forty-five minutes to arrive from Sydney, which was better than *Great Britain II*, the stage winner, in forty days and sixteen hours.

But we are without company in the marina. All the others have left.

As we return towards the old continent, I am already contemplating future races where *Pen Duick VI* will take his revenge. Right now he is obliged by the wind to beat his way back home.

There are relaxed, sunny passages in which I go through some gym sessions with the crew, all of us on deck in bathing trunks, so as to stay fit. These, inevitably, are succeeded by long sessions in oilskins and boots, shivering a little.

Memories of the Open Sea

There is not long now, after nine months spent together, sharing everything – weariness, hopes, disillusionment and a considerable number of happy moments – before we go our separate ways. Each of these boys, none of them alike and all with their particular ambition, nevertheless together across these seas on this boat helped form a crew of real character, the kind of character without which one cannot undertake anything. All of them possess the virtues that are indispensable to sailing without pain: a sympathetic personality that is genuinely good natured, a sense of humour and the disposition to be involved in mickey taking as well as the ability not to take offence that might be caused by less than flattering remarks. Life on board is not really for the sulky, the stormy or the sensitive, being based upon the cornerstone of the little sea-bound community itself; respect for others, the first commandment of which is: 'Do not disturb the men off duty.'

They do not just possess the right human qualities, but the necessary sailing and sporting ones. A good sailor cannot be slow witted, clumsy and plain lazy. And a good crew member cannot be less than a good sportsman. If, on small boats, neither manoeuvres are particularly demanding, nor exercises, such as lifting a sail bag, maximum weight fifteen kilos, on a big boat like *Pen Duick VI*, where a bag can be anything up to ninety kilos, hauling one within the confines of the sail hold demands solid biceps.

Without awarding medals or handing out good reports to this or that one, I can honestly say that I was pleased with them all, including Marc Pajot. When I enlisted him, there were some who commented to me that he was a dinghy specialist without any experience of the open sea. My hunch was that Marc was not only a nice young guy, but that the Olympic Games silver medals he and his brother had won aboard *Flying Dutchman* proved that he had all the qualities of dexterity and agility, willpower and stamina, allied to knowledge in setting up and helming a boat, not to disappoint me. And, in fact, it took very little time for Marc to master manoeuvring.

Olivier de Kersauson had a special place on board. With his long history crewing for me, he was the natural second in command, not to mention that, in spite of our diametrically opposed characters, a solid bond of friendship existed between us. He is a complex, extraordinary character, loathsome when he makes the effort but, above all, an excellent sailor who can 'sense' everything on deck.

I was also familiar with Jean-Philippe Chaboud since *Pen Duick II*. He had raced on board Baron Bich's twelve metre in the America's Cup. His role aboard as radio operator was of prime importance. Because of a problem with our aerial the connection we had with St-Lys was not a very good one leaving Jean-Philippe to communicate in written form which is how, with his knowledge of morse code, he sends and receives signals. Anything to do with electrics on board fell under his responsibility.

Apart from Pierre Mousaingeon, who had raced on *Pen Duick III* from Falmouth to Gibraltar, I had not known any of the others. If, to begin with, because of the inexperience of one or two, manoeuvres were occasionally a little cocked up, it did not take much time for their skills to develop. Even the doc, Jean-Pierre Dagues – although he was not so physically accomplished and was liable every now and again to get things wrong with a pole, prompting one of Olivier's sarcasms – had become not too bad a crew member. I had to have a doctor on board, a reassuring presence on these long passages where one is far from any help. Finding a doctor who is both available and a good sailor is not easy.

The division of labour on board was simple. Two men permanently off watch; myself, the skipper-navigator and the cook. Two sides. And a rota allowing each man one day in which all they had to do was tidy up below decks and do the washing up. During these long ocean navigations a full night's sleep, permitting recuperation, is not an indulgence.

When we had to go to Rio, the novices declared to me their astonishment that I had hardly bawled at them at all. I explained to

Memories of the Open Sea

them that my rants were essentially reserved for those practised crew members whose faults seemed to me to have no excuse.

They had all come to win. We lost. I appreciated their having met our misadventures without sighs or complaints. From the beginning to the end of the journey they pushed the boat to its limit, day and night, in difficult, cold conditions with icy sea spray, heading forward on the deck with the bows rising up and then, as if going over a precipice, racing down into the ocean's captive jaws.

No other boat in the race was handled with as great a determination and savagery, and no other crew willingly underwent so much, only to lose. Not for a moment did their combativeness waver. Aware that I am planning to race in the Bermudas, and then from Bermuda to Plymouth, four of them had already told me they were eager to set off again.

Having only just berthed in Brest on April 22 1974, Admiral Dalle, Commander of the Atlantic Fleet, steps on board to greet us and offer his sympathy.

We part from the boat. Some have family or friends waiting there. We are unsure how to say goodbye to one another. Men moved to emotion can be rather clumsy when it comes to expressing themselves as they run up against manly restraint. So we shake hands and manage a, 'Bye. See you ... '

CHAPTER 23

PEDDLER – NAVIGATOR

Racing is all I have on my mind. Very soon after I am back I want to head off again. *Pen Duick VI* has undergone some maintenance and is ready to race. A month after going round the world, May 26 1974 finds me en route for Newport where we will start the race to Bermuda. Amongst the crew are Olivier de Kersauson, voluble as ever, the calm Daniel Gilles and Gérard Petipas, anticipating what lies ahead and, so, serious. Plus Alain, a young Frenchman living in New York, who works as a chef in a smart restaurant there and whose idea is to take his holidays sailing with me and being put in charge of meals. The prospect of sampling advanced cooking on board is mouth watering and gives Alain his ticket on board.

The day before setting off he prepares hot croissants, which smell inviting and are succulent. Then, from the moment the boat sets out into the open sea, we see no more of our cook. Struck down with acute seasickness, he curls up at the foot of his bunk for the remainder of the race. A race that did indeed take place on a lively sea, into the wind. As the boat went up-and-down on its switchback ride, poor Alain endured torture. In real time, *Pen Duick VI* ends up third, after *Ondine* and *Tempest* and I have got the hump because of the stupid explanation for this defeat: we left our reacher behind, as we discovered when we needed it near the end of the race.

I participate in the July 2 Bermuda–Plymouth race and *Pen Duick VI* gains his first victory at last. Next, Cowes–Cork, where I

Memories of the Open Sea

was runner-up by just a few seconds, and Cork–Brest, which I won. To conclude the season in a beautiful setting, I decide to enter some end of year races in Florida. As I wait for this series, I relax with a little cruise along the Brittany coast, a spot of tourism. Just off Glénans, with the wind blowing at forty knots on a big sea, under reduced sail, the mast breaks, directly below the lower spreaders.

This is the third time in less than a year and the insurance companies are quite clear that they will no longer cover me. This wholesale slaughter is a little too exciting for them. As normal, Petipas puts himself about and is eventually able to find the sub-division just set up by UAP, called Leisure, which is willing to draft a policy for me.

The mast itself is very 'bothersome' for me, as General de Gaulle might say. In the end, it is an English firm which designs one with a wider, stronger profile and then produces it. The masts I had before weighed seven hundred kilos compared to which the English mast is one tonne. It will prove itself indestructible.

Racing is all I have on my mind. At the same time, Gérard Petipas is doing all he can to sort out the finances that are problematic in all manner of ways, my indebtedness being the one which looms largest: more than eight hundred thousand francs, an imposing sum for the time. I do not have a single centime. Everybody, including the Armed Forces Minister, Yvon Bourges, had been under the impression that all the costs connected to *Pen Duick VI*'s dismasting had been paid for by the Navy. But, in fact, other than the cargo plane's fuel, which the army let us have gratis, we had paid for it all: work at the shipyard, the team's board and hotel lodging, landing taxes. As proof, Gérard Petipas, during an interview with Yvon Bourges, displayed all the bills.

Racing is all I have on my mind, and Gérard races around after the money. It is a big worry for him. And even more so when he receives a summons from the Inland Revenue.

Petipas' welcome, when he presents himself at the office in rue Tronchet, specialising in big business and big fraud, is from a severe looking young woman.

The inspector expresses herself baldly:

'Monsieur, I have here your company's articles of incorporation, dated 1973. We are now at the beginning of 1975 and I have yet to receive a single VAT declaration or statement of turnover from you. As though you had never existed. Well then: I am going to tax you three hundred and fifty thousand francs in arrears. It is a lump sum, due now.'

Overwhelmed, Gérard mutters:

'What was that you said?'

The functionary carried on unperturbed:

'You have a house you are buying on a fixed term mortgage, which can serve as our collateral for a further mortgage.'

As he listens to this administrative sentence being passed down, Gérard believes the sky has crashed down on his head. He therefore attempts to explain to the inspector how the company had come to be formed – at my behest and without any idea of what he had committed himself to – and our current, more than precarious, financial situation. The young woman has a heart, notwithstanding the nature of her job, and she is persuaded by the combination of his sincerity and good faith to be flexible.

'I believe you, such is your apparent naiveté. I also believe Tabarly's name is a guarantee. You can have three weeks to prepare your books for me and we will take it from there.'

Not unusually, I was racing. I had no idea about all these troubles with the Inland Revenue. Gérard later told me how he had spent the three weeks working with a sympathetic accountant whom he met every evening at eight following his day's work. Until 3am, when Gérard finally left, they would attempt to bring some order to six boxes randomly stuffed with bank statements and bills: Petipas' company account keeping. Five boxes of papers were separated, according to subject, by the two men and then further organised. There was not

Memories of the Open Sea

time to tackle the sixth. On the agreed day, Petipas headed to rue Tronchet carrying his neatly tied boxes. After she had thumbed through all the papers, the inspector told him in a co-operative fashion: 'Investigations have been made and it is clear that neither M Tabarly nor you have enriched yourselves. One can see that you are loaded with debts. We will draw a line under the past, but I would like you to make sure in the future that you complete your declarations.'

'I promise you that I will,' said Gérard. And then added enthusiastically: 'You are a fantastic person!'

This misadventure could have turned out very costly for us. Far away on my boat, I was apt to say to myself that our unpaid bills should not make us lose our optimism, working on the principle that, so long as one acts in good faith, things will work out. Gérard, confronting the everyday reality of our predicament, saw the future from a much darker perspective.

Coming out to see me at the Rio stopover, Gérard proposes a long term way out of our money troubles: to set up our own publishing house – Pen Duick. He told me of a meeting he had had with Jacques Arthaud, the publisher, during which he had put forward the idea – in spite of its disappointing outcome – for a book based on the round world race. Arthaud gave this his mark of approval: 'Winning or losing, Tabarly sells.'

'The only thing,' Gérard went on, 'is that, while the contract he is proposing – a standard, percentage of profits deal – will take care of some of the debts, it won't make anything for the company, which needs money badly. That is why we need to set up our own publishing house, then we can get out of... '

'But Gérard, we have no experience!'

'Fine, we're beginners. And when we set up the company, I knew nothing about that. Now I am starting to learn a little.'

'All right. As you wish.'

'I would like to ask Marcel Bich for some assistance. You knew him and helped him out at the time of the America's Cup and he told you that if you needed a hand sometime you should go and see him.'

'That's right. So what is the procedure?'

'You write to him to ask if he might see me.'

I wrote the letter. Gérard went back to France and sent it. The following day, Jacqueline, the sister in law/assistant of Marcel Bich, telephoned Petipas to say the Baron invited him to come and join him at his house in St-Lys for the weekend.

On Sunday morning Gérard set off with his wife and children for the wealthy industrialist's. They do not settle down to talking straightaway. Both of them devout and practising, the Baron and Baroness would like to attend mass. They invite Petipas and his family to join them but Gérard, who is an atheist, politely declines. They have lunch after mass, without once coming to the subject of the visit. And then, after the meal, the Baron motions to Petipas that the two of them will take a walk in his park. It is there that Gérard outlines our project.

'Do you want me to help financially?' Bich generously suggests.

'No thank-you. I just need some advice. I would just like to know if, as a businessman, you think it is wise for us, given that we are in such a deep hole, to carry on, or whether it would be better for us to call it a day. Do you think we can get out of this situation?'

'How old are you?'

'Éric is about to be forty-four and I am thirty-five.'

The Baron carries on walking and thinks. Then he gives his opinion, as one well versed in business affairs: 'To begin with, Éric possesses a reputation and in 'Pen Duick' you have a marque that is worth billions. Next, you are both young and not afraid of work. So, if I were you, I would fight on, stick at it. A word of advice, though: do not ever get involved with the banks; once you do that, you are dead. Better to get out of this tangle by yourselves.'

When Gérard mentioned our idea to publish my book ourselves, Marcel Bich immediately responded: 'Absolutely, it is a brilliant plan!'

Memories of the Open Sea

He is a great man, who is always willing to help the person who has a well defined project and the determination to carry it through. As Petipas is on the verge of leaving, the Baron leans against the car door and tells him: 'You have not asked me for anything. But if you find yourselves in trouble, call me. It would be a shame were the name Pen Duick to be lost.'

When I am at sea, I do not take much account really of all the trouble Gérard is encountering to keep us financially afloat. Only when I am back in France does he fill me in on the detail of all his juggling with publisher, printer and bank.

'I went to see Benjamin Arthaud, Jacques' father, to tell him that we were going to be responsible for the publication of your book and ask if he could take care of the distribution. His reaction was that he would have preferred to remain publisher himself, but that he understood our position. He agreed to take thirty-five thousand copies at forty-seven per cent of the standard sale price. The terms of the agreement are set out in a letter he gave me. Then I went straight to Roquemaurel's – our banker, the brother of Ithier de Roquemaurel – to tell him about the Arthaud contract, which he was pleased about. We get twenty-five francs a book: multiplied by thirty-five thousand, that will make us eight hundred and seventy-five thousand francs, the majority of our debts – which come to 1,200,000 francs, and which – damned things – keep me from sleeping at night.

'From Roquemaurel's, I went on to Evreux to see the printer, Charles-Arnaud Hérissey. More discussion of figures. Having shown him Arthaud's agreement to buy thirty-five thousand copies, I asked him what print run he could do for the profits on that total. Hérissey made some calculations and said, "Fifty thousand". I said: "You're on".

'After the race, I go and stay at Gérard's for a little while where he makes a novel suggestion: 'The only way,' he says, 'to solve our problems and to get out of the red is if we sell the extra fifteen thousand books ourselves.'

Eric Tabarly

'OK. But how?'

'We can go and sell copies direct in the Paris area at businesses during their lunch hour.'

That is what we do. Every day, at 11.30 sharp, we load up Gérard's 4L with boxes of books. Sometimes, the jalopy is reluctant to start. Arriving, we would unload and arrange piles of books in the area the company had let us use. I sign and sign as fast as I can. Gérard is in charge of the till – and keeps ringing it ... the idea is working. My record is set at Air France: four hundred books.

We keep going from October to December, doing business in at least a hundred works' meeting rooms. And then, as well as these signing sessions, there were talks which I gave, here and there, in the evening. We would head off once more in the 4L, going to St-Étienne, Rennes, Bordeaux, Lille. I talk about going round the world, answer questions from the audience and then sign more books. We drive back the same night. Gérard drives; I sleep.

We shift all the books. Selling at thirty francs a copy, that adds up to a tidy sum. We were saved.

We do a new, twenty thousand print run of our book: they go like hot cakes. With its first production, our publishing house has a hit on its hands.

Loïc Fougeron gets in touch with us for the publication of his book. 'Pen Duick' publishing is on a bit of a roll.

'Are you pleased?' asks Gérard who, after so many months of uncertainty, has peace of mind again.

'Yes. But once we've taken in a little more money, I am going to get some work done on old *Pen Duick*, so that he can sail once again.'

Since the Costantini brothers closed their yard, Petipas and my brother took the boat to the marina at Crouesty, where he has been subjected to the ravages of both the sun and bad weather.

CHAPTER 24

FIVE STORMS AND A SECOND SINGLE-HANDED VICTORY

Kersauson finally took off. We had sailed together for seven years and I had a considerable liking for him. But Olivier is almost thirty-four and feels it is time to be skipper himself. He has the capacity. He plans to organise a sponsor and a boat for the Clipper Race which sets off from London to Sydney and then, following a stopover, back to the English capital. It is a good race. So we take our leave, wishing one another good luck. We have a common fund of seven years' memories, punctuated with a handful of ludicrous situations in which he has sometimes played a part.

I particularly remember that season aboard *Pen Duick III* when we went to Florida, to take part in races held by the SORC, the South Ocean Racing Conference. We had crossed the Atlantic and were killing time in Haiti, the Tortuga Island and Fort-de-France. Three of us were on board, the rest having already arrived in St. Petersburg, Florida.

We were beating along the Cuban coast for more than twenty-four hours with a light wind and slight adverse current. Just as we were starting to turn away from Cuba and head directly across to the southern coast of the USA, we found ourselves in the middle of an underwater fishing contest for Cuban and Chilean divers. If I remember rightly, this was 1972 and Fidel Castro's island was still obsessed by the fear of counter-revolution. Seeing an obviously foreign yacht approach, the event's organisers radioed through to the Cuban coastguard who authorised them to stop us. On board, we sensed what was afoot. We saw a Boston Whaler coming our way at full throttle, its crew training submachine guns on us. We complied with them. I explain who we are and our reason for coming into these waters. Having read a piece about us in an American yachting magazine, one of the Cubans smiles and says, reassuringly: 'The order for you to be allowed to leave will come shortly'.

We wait. And two hours later a small patrol boat appears. It tows us into a ghost town port, on Cuba's northeast coast. The quays are rundown; rusty wagons await their improbable cargo; to complete this sinister scene there is a Liberty ship, lugubriously monopolising its quay. Directly next to the low lying coast is a destitute little village; next to it, a mangrove.

We are moored and told we must stay on board – other than to take a few paces along the quay where there is an armed guard. They will not allow us to phone the French embassy; nobody knows our whereabouts; we begin to worry.

Finally, we are taken, still under armed guard, to the coastguards' barracks and interrogation by an officer. Having extracted the standard information – surname, Christian name, date and place of birth etc, etc – he drily asks:

'For how long have you been in Cuban waters?'

'A little more than twenty-four hours.'

'But that cannot be!' he roars with indignation at this humiliating slight to his services, who had not picked up our presence.

I admit that, at this moment, I did something stupid in losing my composure, saying to him, without irony, that it would be better for him not to waste his time with people like us and to concentrate, instead, on genuine counter-revolutionaries. Why not send a commando unit to Miami, where, as everybody knows, the enemies of Castro's revolution are gathered?

The officer, shouting, threatens to throw us in the cells before he calms down and has us taken back to the boat that, in our absence, had been searched.

'Wait here at your mooring!' an NCO ordered.

We waited: three days. That was the tariff for foreigners violating the purity of Cuban territorial waters.

There were many other encounters with authority, shared by Olivier and me. I have already described the episode – one of several – following the bedlam of setting off and forgetting either personal ID or the boat's papers – documents dear to the heart of a customs officer.

Our path also crossed that of the Drugs Enforcement Agency. We were meant to be taking part in the Los Angeles–Tahiti race and arrived in the night, mooring in front of the Los Angeles Yacht Club. That morning I telephoned the Immigration Bureau to go through the formalities. A short while later, the boat was being given an exhaustive search by a quartet of heavies that had come on board. Nothing to do with Immigration, they were Drug Enforcement officers.

We asked them: 'What are you looking for?'

'Drugs!'

The cause of this uninvited visit aboard was a young guy who had asked to come along with us. I don't as a rule have people on board that I don't know and who don't speak French. I find communicating in English hard work. Our guest had been on a boat that had kindly given us a tow through the canal. One good turn deserves another and the blond-haired American who had a friendly manner, big frame and smile, inspired confidence. He had reason to. A friendly, credible attitude is lesson No.1 for a drugs trafficker who happens to be known to the law in his country. And it was him – plus his goods – who the Californian cops were after.

It was relatively easy to prove that we were not involved and that we had not got any cocaine, dope or anything else on board. The Narcotics boys left. The situation left me in no doubt that it was time to harden my rule against marine hitch-hikers. Before they went they let me know that, instead of berthing by the yacht club, I should take the boat to the quarantine area where the formalities could be seen to.

I tell the crew: 'We should have given him passage to the afterlife, without confession.'

The response to this comes from Kersauson in his insolent way: 'You're a pretty good skipper but, when it comes to psychology, you haven't got the faintest idea.'

So Olivier is off to try his luck in the Clipper Race. It is the turn for new crew aboard *Pen Duick VI*, names that will become well enough known before long: Éric Loiseau and Jean-François Coste, followed by Philippe Poupon and Titouan Lamazou. They join me for the Triangular Atlantic Race which starts at St-Malo, its route then taking in stops at the Cape and Rio before ending in Portsmouth.

It is not long before heading for the Breton port that a new idea comes to me now that I am free of debts and with the 1976 single-handed Transatlantic in mind. My idea is fairly straightforward: an improved trimaran, capable of going very fast, thanks to the addition of floats – hydrofoils – lifting the hull above the drag of the water.

Given that a 'foil' is, in effect, the same as an aeroplane wing, I discuss the possible project with aeronautic engineers. At Dassault, the technical staff bring their expertise to bear on the problem. Models are made, which perform satisfactorily in tank tests. But the difficulty will be to achieve the same results with the actual boat size of eighteen metres, and to construct it of sufficiently light material that it would be able to rise above the water in ten to fifteen knot winds. In 1975 the choice was limited to aluminium; carbon fibre and titanium remained materials of the future. Reaching this dead end in flying across the water, we fell back onto designing a trimaran with foils that would rest more waterbound. This design will therefore be the one I aim to enter the single-handed race.

During the Rio stop of the Atlantic Triangle, there is a telegram from Petipas, informing me that no yard approached has the capacity to build this multihull within the time required to compete in the Transat.

I'm sure I have already said it, but I might as well repeat it just to be clear. I enjoy physical effort and pitting myself against the full force of the elements, sea and wind. For a while now life ashore has struck me as not particularly interesting, disappointing even. A boat demands discipline and determination and certain old fashioned virtues, perhaps fallen out of fashion, which nevertheless suit my character. Therefore, I thought it might be fun during this stop amongst the Cariocas, to take on the challenge of handling *Pen Duick VI* by myself even if he had been designed for fourteen sailors. After all the initial trouble, brought about by various factors and entailing a small forest of felled masts, he is a boat that I have got to know well and, with his proven strength, one on which I run a comparatively small risk of mishap. The only modifications that I will have to introduce concern minor details in the way the deck is organised. They will not cost much. In spite of the difficulties *Pen Duick VI* will pose amidst the Transatlantic's inevitable depressions, since I particularly want to be involved in this challenge, but have not got the multihull I dreamed of, then *Pen Duick VI* will fit the bill.

The race regulations prescribe that both skipper and boat first undertake a five hundred mile journey. Although I have already crossed the Atlantic single-handed, I have never helmed *Pen Duick VI* alone. So I need to take account of this particular regulation. After disembarking the crew, who go to stay with French friends, *Pen Duick VI* and I are left alone for a cruise on this tranquil sea, which will allow me to think, and come up with answers to problems I am liable to encounter in the race.

Analysis and description. I do not like baring my soul – but that does not mean that I am a complete stranger to feeling. Analysing and describing my feelings and emotions though is beyond me, considering that they are personal to me. And anyhow, as can probably be understood, questions that are ultimately philosophical in nature are not my forté.

All the same, being back in Plymouth and Millbay Docks, where, twelve years earlier, I had set off on *Pen Duick II* for my first single-handed Transatlantic race, the race which changed my life, I felt – why deny it – a twinge of sadness. In 1964 my father was there by my side, warm voiced, with a reassuring smile and an occasional pat on the back – the kind of simple gesture that shows his affection and the complicity between us. My father died the previous year in a fall, as he was painting a window. In spite of my sorrow, I keep reminding myself that life goes on despite my grief. Luckily for me, I cannot surrender myself to melancholy. The race, with its bustle and excitement, monopolises my attention immediately after.

I feel ready and able. My automatic pilot is working just as it should, and is unlikely to leave me in the lurch as its predecessor in 1964 did. Likewise, the system for hoisting and hauling in the big spinnaker is properly in place. The sail's full length fits into a long canvas sheath with its two sheet eyes coming out last. Raising the spinnaker is not the hardest part for a single man; that comes with taking it down and the near impossibility for an individual of gathering it in. Without going into thorny technical detail, my procedure allows me to guide the never ending sail back into its sheath. This brainwave, making it possible for me to operate the sails by myself in winds blowing twenty to twenty-five knots, is instantly christened the 'spinnaker sock'.

I bring the provisions on board: rice, pasta, rye bread, salted butter, chocolate powder, some tomato sauce (Italian), more than a few camemberts, cherry jam, grated cheese, crème au chocolat in cartons, and a stock of red wine: sixty bottles. Passers-by, not realising that they are intended for the return journey with a crew, can't help but comment – some admiring, some disapproving.

My most dangerous rivals include Alain Colas' four masted *Club Méditerranée*, *ITT Oceanic* – formerly *Vendredi 13* – *Kriter III*, and the Canadian Michaël Birch's *Third Turtle*. Then there are the more maverick entries, including *Spirit of Surprise*, a multihull skippered by the Italian Ambrogio Fogar, conspicuous by its lack of size.

What this race was like was recorded in my log: without doubt, on account of the unbending ocean, my toughest race.

The start was fixed for June 5 1976 at 12pm. My troubles began the same day, just before departure. The generator, which is meant to power the automatic pilot, had worked perfectly during trials in Brest. It now refuses to start. Somewhere – but where? – the connecting wire is jammed. My friend Xavier Joubert, who knows the boat well, following his involvement in its construction, and who has now stepped off it in Plymouth Sound, shouts advice from his dinghy on how to dismantle and set the recalcitrant motor right. Whilst nodding my head in agreement, I am not under any illusion about the chances of being able to sort it out on a heavy sea. It would need a calm day – not an event one can count on. My worked up state over the non-functioning mechanism is soothed by knowing that I have a backup generator in good working order, bought just two days before. Nevertheless, I am not certain if it will hold out, because it is too exposed to the weather. What I need to do is to piece together some kind of cover for it, as soon as possible. But even then, because of the automatic pilot's fundamental importance, I remain ill at ease.

Following the normal bustle surrounding departure, I soon find myself out in front. The other contestant I last saw was *Spirit of America*. In spite of the adverse current, I pass Lizard Point before nightfall. Just me and the sea.

The automatic pilot engaged, I am just getting a tasty meal together on the hob, when the wind swings round, obliging me to exchange cooker for cockpit-duty. Above decks it is not easy to make anything out with the fog enveloping everything. To pass the Runnel Stone, with only weak wind and head on against a strong current, I put in a little tack. Progress is slow. It takes me until after midnight to get beyond the Scilly Isles, aided by the Round Island Light foghorn, which acts as my guide. At 3.30am, knowing that I had arrived at a point where I could turn in without risk of colliding into a cargo ship or coaster, I go below decks.

This precipitated my second nasty surprise of the day. I switch on my set course alarm and it refuses to work. Consternation! I have been using this piece of equipment, first on board *Pen Duick IV* and then *Pen Duick V*. It has been a useful ally since 1968, this klaxon that sounds if the boat veers off route. As much as I huff and I puff, it refuses to work as it should. When switched on it now rings constantly and loudly. Now – too late – I remember that when I went to bring it down from the loft, the box it was in was smeared with oil spots, something I did not pay attention to at the time as I should have done. Then, during trials, I was lulled into a false sense of security by the calm sea. In those conditions, the alarm ran with the precision of a Swiss watch. But in a sea lapping heavily against the boat, the alarm becomes uncontrolled, crazy. I try taking it apart so that I can drop in a little bit of oil, but to no avail. I face up to the fact that I will have to use my alarm clock – that will wake me up even if the course is OK.

June 7. At sea one never stops looking, listening and thinking. As I concoct a Heath Robinson cover for the American generator from a vegetable can, plastic bag and sticking tape, my mind is also occupied by the weather conditions, which were surely to the multihulls' advantage; those which chose the north route must be ahead of me.

Since the evening, the barometer has been registering a series of drops, indicating the imminent arrival of a big depression. Then in the night, the fifty-knot or so wind carries on its hullabaloo; the boat is knocked about in the squall. It is all too much for the automatic pilot so I remain at the helm for a less than enjoyable night long drenching from a sea in movement that floods down onto the deck before rushing on towards the cockpit.

To give the boat a bit of a break, I lower the mizzen and partly reef in the genoa. This will hopefully afford the boat some protection from the waves. It takes all my strength, with this wind on a close reach, to perform the manoeuvre. I remember that, just as I had got back into the cockpit, exhausted, I saw that the anemometer had moved up to fifty knots, so I had no choice but to rush back to the bows and bring the genoa down without delay. I raised the smallest, No 4, staysail. With that and the mainsail, *Pen Duick VI* batters his way through the ocean troughs. The depression has homed in on me from above.

The boat is set up as it should be. I go to the kitchen to cook a bit of spaghetti, which is then wolfed down. Never in my life have I devoured a helping of pasta like it.

During the night, the fifty-knot wind howls furiously and *Pen Duick VI* adds to the din, knocking and thumping his brutal way in and out of the troughs. He withstands this collision course thanks to the strength of his bows. With this race in mind, I had had them reinforced as part of his Brest re-fit. As for myself, stood at the helm, I am on the receiving end of blasts of water and finer shots of spray that stab as though they were icicles. Obstinately and annoyingly, the automatic pilot will not stay steady. Normally it would be possible, once the boat luffs – or heads up into the wind – to secure the helm and prevent it from moving with this wind, and therefore the boat from going about. But such a maelstrom cannot be dealt with this way so I must helm in the cold all night. I am used to bad weather, but I have never suffered as I did during these hours. It reached the point where I would head down into the cabin to gain a few minutes' warmth. It is clear that I will not be able to stand permanent duty in the cockpit without getting exhausted and running down my reserves of energy. The vibration in the hull on falling into a trough sounds like thunder.

In the early morning the wind speed climbs to a higher level still reaching sixty knots. Each wave overlaps the other. It looks like the apocalypse. I nearly exhaust myself in the attempt of lowering and then securing the mainsail. I have to use all my strength, but that is not easy on a shaking deck that tosses itself this way and that. It is not long after that I make a discovery which really sets me back: the turbine on my backup generator is missing, the piece that connected it to the transmission shaft having worn. From now on, no current for the automatic pilot – and the race has only been going for four days! I am infuriated, and persecuted, so I feel, by automatic pilots.

The situation does not exactly bode well. Physically I am at a very low ebb because of the manoeuvres, all the time spent at the helm, a sleepless night and the cold. Drenched and frozen, I feel morally discouraged. The difficulties I had in the 1964 Transat, after my self-steering broke, flash across my mind. The difference is that I had made a lot more progress towards Newport then than now, with so much water left to traverse. Plus I was twelve years younger!

I refuse to simply succumb and attempt a rational evaluation of my chances of finishing the race on a boat that is as tough to handle as *Pen Duick VI*. I do not know what to do: to abandon or not to abandon?

In spite of the moment's turmoil, I at least realise that I can no longer take the north route and that I must head further south for less punishing weather conditions. The bottom line is I need the sun so the solar panels have their required capacity to power the automatic pilot at least occasionally. And, at the same time, the south route will be a more comfortable one for my body. That is my decision. I go about and head off in a south easterly direction at five to six knots. I do not kid myself: this was tantamount to abandoning. Before, however, the course of events finally commit me to my decision, I decide to sleep on it. I do not turn on the alarm clock.

It is already late on June 9 when I get up. I am in a better frame of mind following my sleep and there is no more any question of giving up. To be honest, I was not feeling very pleased with myself at that moment, the way I had wanted to throw in the towel the previous night. I was furious also at having lost all this time going east and furious at my weakness. My chances have received a nasty blow. I didn't go forward ... I went back! A day and a half was wasted.

The wind right then was south by southeast and prevented me from continuing my descent to more hospitable regions. It had momentarily calmed and I sent up both mainsail and mizzen. Once the boat had gone about, with its helm secured, it managed reasonably well in these choppy waters. Heading for the American coast now, for good or for ill, the north route is the one by which I will make it to Newport.

Once again the weather turns nasty. Following a second, not particularly foul, depression I immediately ran into a – belligerent – third. These successive depressions entail frequent manoeuvres, the sails going up as soon as there is some calm and coming down as the storm closes in on us once more. A stirring breeze surrounds my exertions, but I feel all right physically. The tiredness that overwhelmed me on June 8 has gone, and I have rarely felt so conscious as I am now of being in shape.

Because there is hardly a let up in the overcast sky – fog and drizzle and rain – I have not been able to take a sight. Dampness, once it gets into clothes, stays. To ensure that some remain dry, before manoeuvring I slip into already damp ones that are not going to get much worse. The initial sensation is not pleasant but they soon warm up. Following the manoeuvre, there are dry clothes waiting for me.

The fourth depression comes down in the morning of the 14th: powerful, brutal. I was sleeping when the boat suddenly rolled in a significant manner and threw me out of the bunk. On my feet immediately, I go up on deck. I must bring down the mainsail, because the wind is blowing between fifty and fifty-five knots. Hauling down such an area of sail in these conditions looks something like a drawn out street brawl. It requires close on an hour's exertion before the sail is tied down onto the boom. As it is drawn in, it beats about furiously and when it is down, smothering it and tying it are not plain sailing. The sea is completely white. The anemometer is constantly reading sixty knots. A staysail sheet snaps. Long strands of foam and clouds of spray are whipped off the crests of the waves by the wind. A roar accompanies the waves as they break and one is reminded of the old tall ships sailors' description: nature's fury.

Faced by the elements in this mood man is powerless so I take shelter below and, with the boat rolling from side to side, calmly go about preparing some pasta with tomato sauce and then, afterwards, turn in. In this type of race one should seize every possibility to recoup one's strength. Tucked in and properly secured, before I fall asleep, the thought occurs to me that one must be mad to sail single-handed. And I think of all the different kind of boats that are taking part and I fear that there will be a few accidents in this litany of depressions. That evening, the latest unpleasant surprise awaits me: the steering wheel that normally moves in conjunction with the tiller is stuck. The steering cables are worn and it's not something I am going to be able to fix. Without being catastrophic, I am annoyed at its being broken because it was a useful aid for the accurate securing of the tiller.

Worries come one after another. The wind dropped a little, but not below forty knots and the boat remained uncomfortably erratic on what was still a very big sea. Nevertheless, when racing, one must always be trying to move forward. Every now and again, I wonder what point the others have got to and fear that the multihulls which chose to go via the south have probably gained a big lead over me, so long as they are encountering better conditions than mine which are terrible. With the wind somewhat less vicious, I felt that it was now time, after taking shelter for twenty-four hours, to raise some sail. This prompts the discovery of a mizzen slide that has broken. Sorting this out in good weather would be the work of a few moments, but in these conditions it takes me more than two hours. You cannot, when the wind is raging like this, simply push off all the slides until you arrive at the one that needs to be replaced. The sail would beat about, as if in a frenzy, and get ripped to shreds. Instead, after two or three are taken out, the sail must be fastened before carrying on the gradual process. Likewise when they all go back in. I, the one who likes muscular activity, have just now had enough. It is not at all easy to work on deck as *Pen Duick VI* moves randomly and raucously. Two hours …

It seems to be one of those days. As soon as the sun sneaks out, I try and take a sight with the sextant, but on the point of fixing it – bang! – I get covered in sea spray. The sextant is drenched and has to be taken inside and delicately wiped dry.

An orange-hulled Norwegian cargo ship's appearance in the afternoon means I have to veer off course. I saw him in the distance. With an exaggerated pitch, he advanced slowly. It becomes evident that we are going to collide or pass by one another in extremis. I keep my eye on it, expecting to see a change of course, but it keeps coming towards me. I take the helm in my hand as a precaution, ready to manoeuvre. This turns out to be not such a bad idea. At the last available moment, before I am right beneath his bows, I veer away and then, with the wind behind me, go about and continue, once I get beyond him, on my course. Already put out, I can see two men on watch, looking at me. This makes me crazy with anger and, so that they know what I think of them, I shake my fist their way. The visibility was one hundred per cent, so there is no doubt the cargo ship saw me from a long way off nor that, subsequently, it refused to give me priority. Such an attitude is inexcusable. All the same, it is common amongst merchant ship captains who couldn't give a damn about sail's right of way and act with impunity. Who do I complain to around here – particularly if I have been holed? They all share the tendency to fall back on the argument that, on account of their size, manoeuvring is difficult. When on automatic pilot, their course can be modified at the turn of a knob. If not, the quarterdeck officer simply has to order the man at the wheel to immediately alter his course 10°. I had already experienced this refusal to grant priority on *Pen Duick III*, one night at the mouth of the Loire. We were forced into an emergency going about manoeuvre, in order to avoid being rammed by a cargo ship. In this kind of situation, I wish I could have a carbine with which to spray their fancy bridge.

Eric Tabarly

At the same time as I was raising sails again, my anger stayed with me. For a while I was calmer. But that will not last long. The wind, that had been coming from the north west, shifts round to the south west. I run my hand through my developing beard and wonder if I am about to get shaken about by another depression.

The resounding answer is not long in coming. The 16th, at four o'clock in the morning, it begins to blow at fifty-five knots once more. I get involved in what looks like another brawl with the mainsail in order to bring it down. The barometer makes its rapid descent to register the fifth depression in eight days. It does not surprise me because the North Atlantic is not a placid ocean. The current situation is not exceptional.

From each crest the boat, almost in freefall, plummets into the trough. At the bottom he takes the hardest hits he has had to endure in his career. One, in particular, was so violent that it has remained engraved in my mind: the dishes went flying, something that had never happened before, not even when we went round the world. Above the workbench, the cupboard full of heavy tools had pulled down the partition it was fixed to.

The morning of the 17th, with the depression having moved away and the wind mostly mollified, I unfurl the genoa. I am going to spend most of the day helming. With a choppy sea, the boat cannot follow a course with its tiller secured in such a light wind. As it makes its way through dense fog, the cold is constant. I will be keeping watch all night. The strength of the wind keeps changing and, each time, a compensating movement is required on the tiller. I will not be able to go and sleep before dawn. At least during the night the temperature becomes more amenable as the wind changes to the southwest, from which it no doubt borrows a little of the Gulf Stream's warmth.

Today, the 18th, I am going to take a noon bearing at last. It is still overcast but it lightens twice, to the extent that I can pick out the sun behind this less dense cloud cover. The second occasion happens to be midday. I am forty miles south east of my estimated position.

My progress has not been quick but, given the weather I have run into, I think that's understandable. As to the other contestants, I am only able to hazard guesses. Those that worry me, maybe a little, are the ones who chose the south route – because I assume they should have had a much smoother passage and so be well placed. The multihulls like *Kriter III* and *Spirit of America*, if they went that way, are liable to be in the lead. I am not too concerned in relation to those who took the north route.

At the briefing that preceded our departure, we had been warned of there being many icebergs in the area I am drawing close to. I am going to try, the morning of the 19th, to cut across the southern part of this fraught zone: something I should be able to do in under twenty-four hours. Icebergs, needless to say, are a danger to a single-handed sailor. When he is asleep, the boat could quite easily collide with one. Even awake the risk remains, thanks to the thick fog frequently awaiting one here, making it difficult to see an iceberg far enough ahead to avoid it. When there is a full time helmsman, even if he can only see one hundred metres ahead, then he will at least have some notice and be able to thrust the tiller one way or the other and so escape a collision – perhaps by the narrowest of margins. When single-handed, the helm tends to be left secured. If there is clear visibility it should be enough, every now and again, to go and check that some particular situation is not about to develop. But you cannot spend day after day constantly peering through the fog in order, at the last moment, to detect an iceberg appearing in the gloom. As a result, one is always tense when heading through such territory.

The wind keeps on picking up. At 6am it is on the beam. The boat can no longer make way with the tiller fixed so I will use the same method I instigated on *Pen Duick II* in 1964, with the slight difference that I cannot use the staysail sheet – too much traction when I try tying it around the tiller. Therefore it will be the storm staysail sheet which maintains the boat's direction.

The wind has dropped.

Birds settle themselves on the water. We are all waiting for the wind to return. With the barometer reading very high, I am conscious that I have a low average speed, slower than in my first Transat. When racing I am concentrating on making the best progress I can. Apart from that, all that concerns me is the others' position. My fairly confident guess is that I am the leader amongst those who chose the north route. On the other hand, multihulls might well have got ahead of me in the south. The wind returns during the course of the day, clearing away a thick fog which had almost become the boat's jailer.

The next two days, the 21st and 22nd, are enjoyable. The fog is more or less thick and the sea is as smooth as a skating rink. Accompanied by a gentle breeze *Pen Duick VI* moves on quickly and life on board is comfortable. Nicely replete from a good spaghetti meal and a little red wine that went with it, I sit down in the cockpit. At the same time that the sun, from between a pair of clouds, appears to be blinking at me, I regard a school of killer whales as it moves to one side, letting me carry on my way.

The night before, two sperm whales had come up parallel to the hull and almost touched it. *Tauranga*, the Italian boat, had been holed by one in the Round the World. Kersauson's *Kriter II* on the Clipper Race had been heavily dented beneath its bows and had its frame bent as well when his ketch ran into one of these marine mastodons pulling out with all its force directly in front of him.

It is eighteen days since the flotilla left Plymouth and I have six hundred and thirty more miles to go. Unless the wind rallies round, it will take me another four days to cross the line in Newport. I could have wrapped this course up in eighteen days if only it hadn't been for that day and a half when I considered abandoning and all the time lost during the storm of the 16th then, yes, I should have been approaching the finishing line. But these additions do not amount to anything: lost time is not found again.

Any sense of regret receives some balm from the beautiful sky and the sun's heat beaming on the ocean and making manoeuvres less wearing exercises, even if there are still plenty to perform with the wind's frequent variations.

I went to look in the aft recess to see why my automatic pilot is no longer working. I could soon see why: the sheet metal on which the cable boxing is mounted is completely worn. I noted that, even in big seas, the boat can hold a course with the tiller secured, something I should have been doing to spare myself – unnecessary – effort. The discovery comes too late, because I will not be sailing *Pen Duick VI* single-handed again.

Tonight, I start to feel a little bit tired. I find myself having to take an occasional breather in the course of manoeuvres. My hands are also giving me a fair amount of bother from working with hooks, ropes and sails. The barometer dips, signalling a minor depression. Nothing serious. The fog is back.

June 25. Shortly before the alarm would have gone off, *Pen Duick VI*'s heel causes me to wake. I clamber up on deck. The wind is now a lot stronger. I take down the mainsail, working up my appetite for breakfast. The barometer continues its downward path. My feeling is that, once the depression has passed, the wind will be coming from the west once again. This is what starts to happen around 8pm as the barometer rises. I start to beat my way through a heavy squall with the wind at forty knots. It is changing in both speed and direction the whole time and I helm through the night. Every fifteen minutes or so, I am involved in more or less arduous, perilous tasks, like sheeting in, so as to keep out of trouble. Around dawn, the wind finally decides what it would like to do, allowing me two hours sleep.

But the rest of the day, the 26th, is much like the preceding night. At times like this I start to doubt. The thought grows that my chances of victory are slim.

I have never forgotten the feeling of difficulty I experienced in the drawn out, concluding stages of this race, not least my struggle to hold the threat of sleep, working its way into all my movements, at bay. There was nothing for me to do to prevent the pairing of a meagre wind and the swell from slowing me down. I gather my forces for a second sleepless night. Line pulling with my creaking, calloused hands causes severe discomfort as my weather sense proves correct. I manoeuvre all night.

If victory is to be achieved in the single-handed Transatlantic's fifth edition it will have to be done the hard way, mile after mile. Now I am becalmed again and plan to sleep for three hours divided, by the alarm, into hour long intervals. When I get up the next day, I discover that the RDF is the latest bit of equipment to cause me trouble. But it is not important – the final miles are clocked off smoothly.

June 29. Arrival! At 3.12am I finally cross the line by the Brenton Tower. It is a dark and humid night. We gradually wind our way, under mainsail, into the harbour. No one is expecting me. My position remains unknown in spite of my intention yesterday to make contact with the race organisers. Instead my radio set began emitting sparks. Incredible! But every time I try and use this kind of equipment it fails. So I had not bothered to tinker.

In the event, there is no one waiting to register my arrival. I will not be able to go under sail into the marina. I cannot use my engine – fitted in Plymouth – since a jury member will not have verified that the weights, fixed to the propeller shaft, have remained in situ.

I make my way further down the inlet, assisted only by a light breeze. My eyes are pricking; all I would like to do is sleep. Dawn broke. As I arrive in Newport Bay and preparing to moor, an inflatable dinghy with its outboard roaring breaks the port's silence,

Memories of the Open Sea

battering its way towards me. It carries two people, both of them gesturing my way. I recognise the amiable young photographer, Denis Glicksman and his friend Pesty who, by chance, had picked me out at this early morning hour. Beyond a quick greeting, they dispense with any preliminaries, to photograph me with twenty-four day old beard, patched up jeans and jersey. I ask them:

'How many have arrived so far?'

'You are first!'

This prompts a small smile of satisfaction from me. I am so wasted that I even lack the energy for exuberance in a time of victory.

CHAPTER 25

THAT WAS CLEVER!

It is what is known as, 'The price of glory'.

I remember that once I had moored in Newport, on the back of three sleepless nights, all I could think of was a big steak, showering and shaving and then sleep. The first three proved possible but as for getting a bit of rest: 'No Way!' Besieged by journalists, photographers, cameramen, I was not left a moment to myself. My mother was not there. The poor woman had gone back, unable to any longer stand this long wait, the dreary climate and the bothersome way in which some were starting to think that I had disappeared.

All of this unreasonable concern – after all, no other boat had yet arrived – sprang from a jest having been spread about amongst the habitués of Place de la Bourse Club one morning by two Club Méditerranée redcoats. They were saying, 'Tabarly was spotted by the Canadian Ice Patrol. He is now off Newfoundland. Way ahead!' The response to their joke was bigger than they could possibly have hoped after it was picked up by some journalists, one of whom had conscientiously wanted to check the information and phoned the Patrol.

Something must have got lost in translation because the Canadians felt they were receiving, rather than being asked for, news and, in turn, passed it on. Calculating my ETA on the basis of this alleged position relative to the finish was easy. Once the moment had passed, concern grew on each subsequent day. It seemed that something had happened to me.

Memories of the Open Sea

Gérard Petipas, so as not to be in any doubt, felt that he himself should call the Ice Patrol. He asked them for the flight number that had spotted me. Their reply was that they had got the information from France. Gérard felt relieved, but my mother had already returned.

I was flown down to New York and put on a long flight with Air France back to Paris, where I find myself in a Europe 1 studio, placed in front of a microphone. Afterwards, like a hero of old, I was obliged to parade along the Champs-Élysées and be cheered by an enthusiastic crowd, newly won over to seafaring. I tried to get out of this demonstration, but they replied that everything was organised and that I had become the centre of attention for the enthusiasm of thousands. I fell in with all these obligations from which, in all honesty, I would have happily absented myself.

Years have gone by, but I still think of this race as being one of the toughest due to the particularly harsh weather conditions in which it took place. Hence my admiring astonishment that the Canadian Mike Birch had arrived little more than two days after myself on a small trimaran which, according to Mike, bobbed about like a cork once the sea became treacherous. It was a Transat that claimed some victims: *Kriter III* was holed, *Spirit of America* had to abandon, *Three Cheers* disappeared and *Cap 33* and *Quest* needed to stop to sort out some significant aspect of the boat that had failed.

It was this 1976 Transat, immediately notorious and provoking a great hullabaloo in the media, which brought about far greater sponsorship of racing and money's intrusion into the world of sailing.

Years passed by. With various new crews, *Pen Duick VI* spent a fair amount of time in the Pacific racing – sometimes winning, sometimes involved in contretemps – and cruising about. He was the final boat of this pedigree with which I had covered more than three hundred thousand miles on the seven oceans, always with pleasure no matter what the sea held in store for me. For the sake of simplicity, one can date the end of the *Pen Duick* era as 1981. In July 1985, with the rank of Ship's Captain, I retired from the Navy. I was accorded the honour of the customary naval ceremony – being rowed ashore by the ship's officers.

It was at Poulmic. There was a pretty blue sky that morning, give or take an occasional cumulus. Dressed for summer in blue slacks and white short sleeves, top button loose, I stepped onto the *France*, a naval school twelve metre. In keeping with tradition, I had then transferred to the rowing boat, grey hulled with a white thwart and manned by sixteen school officers. Standing up in the bows, the topman sets up their rhythm. I stand at the stern and feel moved by this way of saying good-bye. After thirty-one years as part of the Navy, I entered civilian life.

I raced on *Paul Ricard*, my trimaran with hydrofoils, in 1980 breaking the Atlantic crossing record before moving onto two *Côte d'or*s and finally *Bottin Entreprise*, an 18.20 metre trimaran, designed for the spring 1989 Transat, there-and-back.

It was aboard him that I had my one experience as a sailor that really shook me up. I was fifty-eight. The race took place in two stages: from Lorient to St. Barth and, following a few days rest, back to Lorient. My crew was Jean Lecam, someone I had got to know well going back to when he sailed with me on *Pen Duick VI* before he became a successful skipper himself, as he continues to be.

Bottin was one of the new generation trimarans and a fine boat on which we were out in front on the return leg. The weather was good and the spinnaker was doing good work, hauling us forward. The trouble on these races is that there is a tendency – on my part anyhow – to push the boats to breaking point.

I wanted to set the boat a new course but, at the moment that it needed to slow down, I must have failed to pull the helm hard enough for it to do so. *Bottin*'s helm was very stiff and I had had a long stint at my post. In fact I had stayed at it for longer than envisaged, seeing that Jean was below decks dealing with the radio.

Memories of the Open Sea

I was flagging. And so, for lack of giving the helm a strong enough pull, the boat capsized.

Everything happened very quickly. In barely a moment the point of no return was reached, leaving us unable to act. All that was left to us was to await the inevitable capsize. In this moment one looked a little into oneself, saw that a notably negative event was imminent, recognised that the fall was about thirty-foot and told oneself: 'Let's hope this turns out all right.'

But it did not turn out all right. In falling, I fractured my collarbone. I suppose, instead of a shoulder, it could have been my head and therefore worse. I could not get back onto the boat immediately. That something had happened to my shoulder was clear enough, but I was still able to swim and to heave myself back aboard the upturned boat.

Inside, Lecam had not seen any of this but he was able to get out via the aft panel escape hatch. I remember that, as I climbed my way along the lateral strut, there he was, on the verge of losing his cool with me. His words were: 'That's very clever, what you went and did there.'

For about six hours we remained crouching on the float, and then a cargo ship arrived and picked us up.

That is the one time I was frightened. Every other time things happened too quickly to have the time to feel frightened. Fear was retrospective.

My decision was not headstrong – made, suddenly, one day, just like that. It came about gradually as I started to get a little older. But, as I entered my sixties, I was still racing, so it was not really age that caused me to call it a day. No, the root cause was that I did not wish to waste my life looking for a sponsor. Sitting by the phone no longer held any attraction for me. There was no certainty of finding a backer, so one risked spending months getting in a sweat over nothing.

Olivier de Kersauson would say to me: 'You are the biggest liar I've come across. You were always telling me, "No marriage, children, dogs".' There was nothing that I wanted to give up my liberty for. The feminine way of being both intrigued and attracted me, but would have been difficult to reconcile with my own: always on a boat, always racing, in the company of a crew, leading the hard sea life with its wardroom intervals spent relaxing. My long term hesitation in the matter of family life and the fear of having children to raise – who might be as hard to educate and to discipline as I had been – combined with a hardening of my determination to stay free of all such commitments, irrespective of the price to pay.

Women might come as passengers but never as crew – not because I do not think that women can sail, but simply as a consequence of the physical effort required when racing a big boat incompatible with the female form. Other, that is, than the caryatid build of ex-Eastern Bloc athletes who didn't appear to have much to do with the feminine.

For a long time, *la vie à deux* had not concerned me. As I continued to devote all my time to my boats and to races, I imagined that I would remain single. All the same, whenever I thought about it, I knew what type of woman might be able to make me feel love.

First, I expected that she should share the moral qualities that are to be admired in a man: integrity and trust. Second, that she should be naturally elegant, not all made up. Last, that she should be at least thirty years old, the age at which a woman lets her natural character come to life. If she was already the mother of a family, I would love her child as though it were our mutual offspring, not holding much by blood ties and dynasties. For such a woman, I would be prepared to make concessions and sail a little less.

I met Jacqueline on board a friend's boat which was moored in the marina at La Trinité-sur-Mer, a stroke of luck that occurred in 1976, not long after the Transat. Jacqueline was staying in the area; she came from Martinique. We chatted. We liked, and started to see, one another, getting married at Gouesnac'h Mairie in 1984, thirteen years ago. It was a private occasion, before the birth of our daughter, Marie. I don't wear a wedding ring, because I do not think this sign that you are married means anything. I undertook being faithful to her. In this domain too, if I give my word, that's enough: nothing extra, in my opinion, is added by putting a ring on your finger. I always stuck by my commitments.

I dreaded marriage but, if you love someone, it seems to work out. There may be moments when, in spite of Jacqueline respecting my liberty, I feel rather confined – but that is not so different to the restraints I have encountered racing. There are occasions when I act maladroitly – women would say in an off-hand manner – but it is never pre-meditated. Little details that count for nothing with me have symbolic meaning for them.

It happened in 1985, during a Round the World Race. I had already been gone three months. Coming from Auckland, and after a brief stop in Paris, I flew to Quimper to meet Jacqueline. This was a Friday evening. On the Monday morning I would absolutely have to head back to New Zealand, *Pen Duick VI* and my crew. So it is just a fleeting family visit. Having got back to the house on the Friday evening, I am enjoying a relaxed evening with my wife and two daughters. Before long it is interrupted by a telephone call from Éric Loiseau, following which I re-join Jacqueline, but without thinking to mention the substance of my talk with Éric. Then we went to bed.

Very early the following morning I get up and begin to pack. I tried to be as quiet as I could, but eventually my padding around woke my wife.

'Where are you going?' she asked, half asleep and completely amazed.

Without embellishment I responded: 'Sorry, I forgot to tell you that Loiseau is launching his boat and invited me along for the Brest–La Trinité trials. It will be good to sail with him. I'll see you again on Sunday … '

Why did I say that?! Drawing herself up in bed, a *furia* castigated me for devoting no time at all to my family. I had no alternative but to admit *mea culpa* and also my lack of psychology on this occasion. In addition to the original mistake, I should never have asked her to go with me to Brest and then bring the car back home by herself. All the same it seemed to me a logical way to do things. But then men and women sometimes see things a little differently.

We live at Gouesnac'h in a nice old barn with a long façade. I had come across it a long time ago on a walk with my mother. The majority of the furniture we inherited from my parents and Jacqueline added other pieces found in antique shops. There are four hectares of land including a wooded part that slopes down to the Odet.

The story behind its purchase began in January 1969 when I travelled over from the West Indies to check on the progress being made with *Pen Duick V*. There was a friend who knew that, since I was a boy, I had imagined myself owning a property from which, lying in bed, I would be able to see my boat. He told me about one actually matching that on the bank of the Odet. I did not have any means to buy it but, prompted along by my friend, I went to visit and met the farmer who owned and was keen to sell it. The asking price was attractive and I felt that I would be able to raise the money using the advance on my book plus the help of a bank loan. I explain my situation to the farmer and let him know that I would not be able to make the purchase sooner than August. He replied simply: 'OK. I will wait for you.'

We did not sign any papers. When I returned from racing in the Pacific and went to see him, he was waiting. Again, he spoke to me in a straightforward manner: 'It was promised to you. One's word is one's bond.'

I had not doubted him, even for a moment.

My racing days over, I live the life of a countryman. I stay in shape chopping wood. I go to Paris as little as possible, either with Gérard when business demands or, latterly, when it has been necessary to make the journey in order to help save the Naval Museum.

It is proposed that the collection should be put into packing cases and stored, who knows where, for several years, waiting to be displayed in a building that is too small, not centrally located and

Memories of the Open Sea

not fit for purpose: the Museum of African and Australasian Art, once it becomes available.

This shameful treatment regrettably reflects the casualness with which France handles maritime issues.

The attitude of the French people remains too land bound. It discovered the sea via leisure cruising and has become very involved in ocean racing but, apart from its sentimental feeling for the Navy, has yet to grasp the sea's economic and strategic significance. It is not a question of not wanting to, so much as not being well informed. This education should start at school. But no schoolbook exists that makes the fundamental point of how continental-seeming conflicts are won at sea. Had the French won at Trafalgar they would not have had to fight at Waterloo. Without the Allies winning the Battle of the Atlantic, the USSR would not have received foreign goods, the Normandy landings could not have taken place and the Germans would have won the war.

We get the governments we deserve – and they have always underestimated the role of the sea. The Navy remains, as ever, the poor relation of the Armed Forces, whilst the Merchant Navy, emasculated by the combination of irresponsible unions and laissez-faire government, has almost disappeared from the oceans. At the same time, a small state like Norway has one of the leading merchant fleets of any country. It turns big profits and proves that cargo ships need not be the Orient's exclusive preserve.

In short, the French are in drastic need of a maritime education. And now, the Naval Museum, one of the few pedagogic tools we have at our disposal for this, finds itself facing destruction. Instead, it should be undergoing expansion, so as to strengthen its educational role.

Fortunately, a large enough protest against this indifference made itself heard. It did not just come from a, nearly unanimous, maritime community, but from the interior too.

Our resistance has turned out successfully. There is no longer any question of the museum being shifted about as though it were street goods. The President of the Republic pledged that nothing will be done before a larger and prestigious site has been readied to receive the collection. Wait and see.

Jacqueline and I take it in turns to drive Marie to her school and to pick her up. Having a child is frightening for me. I worry for my daughter in case her schooling does not work out and she struggles to make her way in life. Parents are responsible for their children's education for which they have no preparation themselves.

There are days when I hole up in my study – with all its boat models, the collection of sea books and magazines, plus photos of my boats that remind me of the key moments in my life as a sailor:

There is *Pen Duick II* who is still owned by the Beg Rohu sailing school and, following a long period in disuse, was restored so that, as of 1994, he has been sailing once more.

And *Pen Duick III*, in whom I have a third share, at St-Malo.

Then *Pen Duick IV*, re-named *Manureva* by Alain Colas. Together, they disappeared in the Route du Rhum of 1978.

And *Pen Duick V*, the only boat of mine which I did not own. Originally owned by the St-Raphaël harbour company, he was then sold to a private individual and renamed *Topaze*. As such, he was then sold to the Naval Museum which set in motion his restoration at St-Malo. He does not have his ballasts any more, but there are plans to get them reinstated and go back to his original design.

Finally, *Pen Duick VI* is still sailing a fair amount of the time. I rent him to a fellow who runs a cruiser school and who allows me the boat's use for a month in the West Indies, with my family.

These are the boats that have a special place in my heart.

Each winter I spend four hundred hours or so restoring old *Pen Duick* in his boathouse. It is a painstaking, ongoing project that calls for patience. But 1998 marks his hundredth anniversary and I want him to look his best for the occasion. When I look at him with his classic hull and lines that could not be improved upon, I want to let him know: 'You are a very lucky character: still afloat, still sailing.'

CHAPTER 26

WHY I SLUNG MY DUFFEL BAG ASHORE…

Three times he should have died, but each time he was resuscitated.

His third rebirth takes place in 1988. For the last twenty-one years he has been exposed to the elements, first at the Costantini Yard and then on a plot at Crouesty port, slowly succumbing to the passage of time. The polyester hull remained unaffected, but both plywood deck and superstructure were rotted through. Yet in the course of this period, no matter where in the world I was, always in the back of my mind was the thought that I will restore him to his former vigour and then we will go sailing again together. I had to call on time and money and friends to do it.

In 1983 I got in touch with Raymond Labbé, a boat builder and classic design aficionado, based in St-Malo.

'Would it be too much to ask, Raymond, to have *Pen Duick* at your yard for a few years? I don't know how long exactly. As and when I get the money, I will ask you to continue with the next portion of work and, that way, little by little, we are bound to see him sailing again one day … '

Raymond, who has a very good team of specialist carpenters, agreed without hesitation.

Still at the mercy of my chronic indigence, in order to economise I used *Pen Duick VI* to tow *Pen Duick* all the way round the Breton coast as far as St-Malo. Going, in the beginning of August, from

Crouesty to the Aber Wrac'h, was initially plain sailing. Then the wind got up and was blowing fairly hard. *Pen Duick*, attached with a set of thirty-metre towing lines, was thrashing about on the water as though he were a lassoed old horse: it was time we arrived!

I had a clear idea as to what I wanted: old fashioned fittings made of mahogany with mouldings and a chart table and an 18CV motor positioned in front of the mast, which, although not particularly powerful, would be OK for manoeuvring in harbour.

I could only, due to the state of my finances, undertake this work gradually. So gradually that, in 1988, all that had been completed were the fittings – plus the purchase of a motor. The whole superstructure still had to be done. Likewise, the deck and installation of the motor, together with its camshaft and little propeller. At this slow rhythm, I was not even close to sailing!

Bruno Troublé telephoned Gouesnac'h one day to let me know that he had been put in charge of the Liberty Ships operation, a nautical first for Rouen. He said to me: 'It will be good if *Pen Duick* can take part at Rouen, July 9 1989.'

'I would very much like to do that Bruno, but I have not got enough money at the moment to complete the restoration and be ready to sail.'

'Listen Éric, I know that the authorities in Rouen are very keen to have your boat. I am confident that they will be able to help. I'll look into it.'

Troublé diligently followed the matter up with the administration and, subsequently, I received a call from the Deputy Mayor announcing that the town is to advance me the money. I believe it will be enough to pay for Raymond Labbé's work. And I am wrong. The boat is launched and looks fantastic. Not only is the deck exactly as it should be and the interior fittings remarkably done, but he has also received a perfect paint job. However, when it comes to paying off my debts with Labbé, I come up short. As ever, Gérard knows the way round the problem. For an average fee of ten thousand francs,

Memories of the Open Sea

exhibit *Pen Duick* at Toulon, then the Bordeaux Fair and, finally, at the Paris Boat Show. We publish an illustrated book with the sober title *Pen Duick*. Using rare photos, it traces the story of the boat's life and survival, which proves itself popular. Once again, I pulled the cat out of the bag.

Being the worrying kind, Gérard Petipas and Jacqueline, when faced with my money problems, are always very concerned. I always remained confident myself: to every problem, a solution. All the time that I was sailing I had big enough debts but, at the same time, I was lucky enough to deal with creditors who, for the most part, were not fussy and whom I had asked to wait knowing that one day I would have the means to repay them.

Pen Duick was in Rouen at the appointed hour. The journey that took us from St-Malo to Sark in the Channel Islands, then Cherbourg, Le Havre and Rouen, won over Jacqueline and Marie, for both of whom it was the first outing on this legendary boat.

I do not often give myself over to emotion or indulge in lyricism. However, there was one occasion. I was in my study with its tongue and groove panelled walls and I caught sight of *Pen Duick*'s mast down below. So I began to write: 'I can see him, under his golden rigging, as he superbly sniffs the wind, judges the strength of the sea, quivering, as he waits for the first light breeze: precious, demanding, sensual, lively, capricious, a work of art, *Pen Duick*, my boat, is all of these.'

On his hundredth birthday we will have a party. He has been my talisman.

CHAPTER 27

AND WHY I SLUNG IT BACK ON BOARD

This book was based on the recollections of a naval pensioner who had slung his duffel bag ashore. I did not even consider ocean racing anymore.

And then, at the same time he was skippering *Aquitaine Innovation* in the Vendée–Globe Round the World, Yves Parlier, speaking to his Press Officer, let it be known that, later in the year, he wanted to compete in both the Fastnet and the Jacques Vabre two-way Transat from Le Havre to Cartagena in Colombia – and that he would like me to crew. Hearing of this, Gérard Petipas relayed the proposition on to me. I thought about it and accepted. There were several reasons why, No. 1 being that Yves Parlier is a very good sailor who knows his métier and who does not throw out ideas just for the hell of it. Second, he likes to innovate and, also, to build new designs. Without going into detail, the results can be seen at sea with his current boat. The final reason was that, even though I am now in my sixties, whatever I try, there is nothing on land that really grabs me: I still have the boat/racing bug.

I said: 'Yes'. Even if I am not as fit and strong as I once was, I feel I still have the ability to do manoeuvres. I will certainly do all I can to give satisfaction. Most of my life has been spent at sea. I am not yet able to watch the others head off while I remain on the quay.

INDEX

Agadir [ET military training at] 20
Akka [see also Howells V] 61, (damaged) 70
'Alain' (seasick aboard *PD VI*) 204
Allère, André [*PD IV* designer] 145
Alphand, M Hervé [French Ambassador to US] (presents Légion d'honneur to ET) 107
Annie [Tabarly family boat] 4
Aquitaine Innovation [see also Parlier Y] 242
Arthaud, Benjamin [ET's publisher, father of Jacques] 209
Arthaud, Jacques 207, 209
Aunt Mony (visits nephew ET at Plymouth) 66, (greets ET at 1964 race finish) 102
Aymon, Jean-Paul [*France-Soir* reporter] (accompanies ET to Plymouth) 59, (greets ET at 1964 race finish) 102

Bavier, Bob [*Nereus'* captain] 108
Beken, Keith (takes the first photos of restored PD) 37
Bembridge (and Whitbread race ... and departure) 175
Bénodet [*PD*'s port of registry from 1938–45] 4
Bich, Baron M 202, (offers business advice) 208-09
Bigoin, Michel [*PD V* designer] 150, 152
Birch, Michaël [1976 Transat competitor] 216, 231
Blois [Tabarly family home] 5, 10, 20
Blue Arpege [see also Terlain J-Y] 157, 158, 164
Bottin Entreprise [see also Tabarly E and Lecam J] 232 (capsize of and rescue by cargo ship) 233
Bourges, Yvon [see also Ministry of Defence] (and *PD VI* remasting operation) 181, 205
Brest naval shipyard [*PD VI* builder] 170

Cahiers de Yachting]see also Devillers Y] 54
Carpentier, Jean-Michel 156, 158, 164, 166

Casablanca (ET military leave in) 18
Castro, Fidel 211-12
Chartois 116-117, (change of mind about *PD II* purchase) 123-124
Chatel (Captain informs ET of Légion d'honneur award) 103
Cherbourg (ET posting at) 43, 46
Chichester, Francis [1964 Transat competitor] 52, (ET on career of and admiration for) 61, 109, (visits *PDII*) 65-66, 80, 82; 95, 98, (finishes race) 108, 110
Club Mediterranée [see also Colas A, 1976 Transat competitor] 216
Cœudevez, Albert [see also Nirvana Spars] (and *PD VI* remasting operation) 178, 180-183
Colas, Alain 138, (ET on) 140, (ambition of) 141, (in Nouméa cyclone) 142-43, (crews on *PD IV*'s La Trinité-sur-Mer to Martinique voyage) 153, 154, 164, (buys *PD IV*) 166, 198, (circumnavigation of) 200, (competes in 1976 Transat) 216, (disappearance of, at sea) 238
Costantini, Gilles [boat designer and friend of ET] 14, (takes over boatyard with brother following father's death) n 24, (given go ahead by ET for *PD* restoration) 24, (teenage friendship with ET) 25, 26, (family home of) 27, 28, (boatyard works on *PD*) 30, (accomodating attitude regarding payment) 30, 34, (ET visits) 47, (discussions with ET concerning design for 1964 Transat boat) 48-49, 51, (ET on character of) 56, 57, (yard undertakes *PD II* rigging changes) 115, 117, (and *PD III*) 122, 211, 239
Costantini, Gino [boatbuilder, father of Gilles and Marc, Tabarly family friend, Kerisper yard of] 14, 24, (character of) 26
Costantini, Marc [brother and business partner of Gilles Costantini] 14, 24, 34
Crespin, Col (and *PD II* puchase) 123-24
Cuty 25

Eric Tabarly

Dassault [aviation firm] 214
Deferre, Gaston (ET falls asleep during speech of) 2
Delon, Alain 181
Devillers, Yves [*Cahiers du Yachting*] 180, 182
Duvergie, Daniel 150, 152

English, Pierre [*PD III* crew] 125, 127, 131, 135-136, 139, 140, (in Nouméa cyclone) 143, (*PD VI* remasting operation) 180, 183

Fife III, William, [*PD* designer] 3
Folatre [see also Kelsall D] 64, 80
Fougeron, Loïc 210
Fouillard [*PD* crew] 36, 43, 45

Gaulle, General Charles de (dinner invitation to ET) 129, 205
Gentet, Paul 25

Gilles, Daniel [*PD III* crew] 125, 204
Gipsy Moth III [see also Chichester F] 108
Gitana [see also Rothschild E de] 128-129
Gliksman, Alain [see also *Neptune*] 54, 119
Glicksman, Denis (informs ET he is 1976 Transat winner) 229
Guégan, Yves [*PD III* crew] 125, 127, 131, 136, (demands speech from ET) 137, 139, (in Nouméa cyclone) 141, 143, 198

Hambly, Charles [mayor of Newport RI] (grants ET honorary freedom of town) 104
Hasler, LtCol 'Blondie' [1964 Transat Competitor] 63, 110
Henderson, Sir Nigel [Commander of Plymouth Naval Base] (gives reception for 1964 Transat competitors) 61
Henrotte, Hubert [director of Sygma agency] (phones Petipas with news of *PD VI* dismasting) 177
Hérissey, Charles-Arnaud (on printing *Pen Duick* publishing titles) 209
Herzog, Maurice [Minister of Sports] (suggests future purchase of *PD II* for National Sailing School) 115-116
Howells, Valentine [1964 Transat competitor] (name causes confusion among journalists) 61, (introduces ET to Mashford brothers boatyard) 66, (boat hit by Sunday sailors during 1964 departure) 70, (finishes race) 109, (on enforced stop in Ireland) 109, (ET on character of) 109, 110

Indochina (ET serves in) 21-22

Jeanne d'Arc 40-42
Jester [see also Hasler, Lt Col] 63
Joubert, Xavier (*PD VI* engine problems) 172, (*PD VI* remasting operation) 180, 182-186, 217

Kelsall, Derek [1964 Transat competitor] (enthusiasm for trimarans) 64, 69, 80, (ET sails *Toria*) 131
Kersuason, Olivier de (crews on *PD III*) 125, (shyness of) 125, (*PD III* 'mutiny') 126, 127, 131, 135-137, (character transformation of) 139, (in Nouméa cyclone) 141, 143, (crews on *PD IV*'s La Trinité-sur-Mer to Martinique voyage) 153, 154, 164, 166, (as Whitbread race crew) 174, 176, 197, 198, (films *PD VI* rounding Cape Horn) 200, 202, 204, (parts with ET to become skipper) 211, (ET reminisces about years spent with) 211-214, (encounter with whale) 226, 233
Kourigba [Morocco] (and ET military training) 17

Labbé, Raymond [boatyard owner] (final *PD* restoration) 239-240
Lamazou, Titouan [*PD VI* crew] 214
La Perrière boatyard [builders of *PD III*, *PD IV*, *PD V*] (ET gives *PD III* designs to) 122, (*PD III* construction begins) 123, 124, (begins work on *PD IV*) 131, (ET visits) 145, 148
La Trinité-sur-Mer [*PD*'s port of registry from 1945] 13, (reputation of) 13, (livelihood of) 13, (Costantini boatyard) 14
Le Berre, Michel [ET's publicist] 168, suggests to ET that he should set up a company, 169, and *PD VI* remasting operation, 178, 180, 182-185
Lecam, Jean [see also *Bottin Entreprise*] 232
Le France 110
Linksi, Marc (skippers *PD III* round Cape Horn) 200

Memories of the Open Sea

Lively Lady [see also Rose A) 62
Lorient (ET posting at) 50-51, 115

Manureva [formerly *PD IV*, see also Colas A] (circumnavigation of) 200, (disappearance of) 238

Margilic V (Gilles Costantini proposes to build for 1964 Transat) 49, (launch of) 51, (ET races in 1963 Fastnet) 51, (ET proposes as basis for *PD II*) 51

Mashford brothers [Plymouth boatyard] 66, (*PD IV* repairs) 148

Mauric, André [*PD VI* designer) 169, (collaborative work with ET) 170, 198

May 1968 événements 156

Ministry of Defence [see also Bourges Y] and *PD VI* remasting operation) 181-182

Ministry of Sports 117, 123-124

Nantucket lightship 100-101
Naval Museum (ET and) 236-238
Neptune [see also Gliksman A) 54
Neptune journalists 67, 71
Nereus 107, (ET invited to crew on) 108, 110
Newport, RI (ET's extended 1964 stay in) 106, 230
Nirvana Spars [see also Cœudevez A] 154, 176
Nouméa (cyclone) 141-144

Ogimi [Nippon Ocean Racing Club secretary] 163-64

Pajot, Marc [*PD VI* Whitbread crew] 174, 197, (ET praises) 201
Parlier, Yves 242
Pen Duick [see also Tabarly E] (meaning of Breton name) 1, (ET incurs debts for) 1, (salvage of) 1, (construction at Fairlie, Scotland) 3, 4, 6, (1945 condition of) 11, (former regatta successes of) 12, (Guy Tabarly considers selling) 14, (put on sale) 15, (ET becomes 13th owner of) 16, (goes back into water) 24, 29, (ET lengthens mast of) 34, (post-restoration maiden voyage and dismasting of) 34-35, 36, (mast breaks again) 37, (ET finds solid mast for) 38, (ET in near fatal fall from mast) 39, 44-45, 46, 115, 238, 241
RACES [Cowes to La Coruña) 45-46, [Irish Sea) 46, [Fastnet) 46

RESTORATIONS (1945 refit) 13, 21, (ET gives go-ahead to Costantini yard for) 24, 24-28, (apparent irreperable condition of) 25, (ET proposes new polyester hull) 26, (hull resin application) 27-28, 30, (second restoration completed) 33, (ET considers new refurbishment of) 211, 239, (slow progress of third restoration) 240, (re-launch of) 240

Pen Duick II [see also Tabarly E and *Margilic V*] 51, (multiple bilges of) 51, (ketch rigging of) 52, (dimensions) 53, (launch of) 55, 57, (sea trials of) 58, 112, (conversion from ketch to schooner) 115, (future sale to National Sailing School proposed) 117, 118, 238
RACES [1964 Transat, see also Tabarly, E] (departs for Plymouth) 58, (final preparations) 60, 64, 65-66, (race departure) 66, (near collision with ship) 72, (self-steering problems and ET's attempted solutions) 74-76, 80-81, 85, (ET considers quitting race) 80-81, (alarm clock failure) 87-88, (veers into gulf stream then resumes higher latitude) 91, (top of mast halyard block repair) 93, (ET praises performance of) 99, 103, (ET's physical condition at end of race) 99, 100-01, (finishes race) 103, 104, (congratulated by Chichester) 109
OTHER RACES
[final RORC races, 1964] 113, [Newport, RI–Bermuda] 120, [Bermuda–Copenhagen) 120

Pen Duick III [see also Tabarly E] (ET considers boat with schooner rigging) 115, (duralinox hull of) 122, 123, (launch of) 124, 126, (ET on crew) 127, 135, (New Caledonia voyage of) 139, (and Nouméa cyclone) 141-43, 145, 146, 149, 151, (unsuitability for Whitbread race) 167, 200, 211-12, 238
RACES
[1967 Sydney–Hobart] (ET considers entering) 129, 132-33, (ET head injury) 135, 136, 137, 138
OTHER RACES
[Admiral's cup] 124, [Morgan cup) 125-26, [Gotland) 127-128, [Channel]

Eric Tabarly

128, [Fastnet] 128-29, [Plymouth–La Rochelle] 129, [La Rochelle–Bénodet] 129

Pen Duick IV [see also Tabarly E] (work underway at La Perrière yard)n 131, (design of) 145-46, (launch and sea trials) 146, 151, 153, 154, 155, 156, 165, (ET on lifestyle aboard) 165-66, (sold to Colas) 166, 238

RACES [1968 Transat] (ET reluctantly obliged to use him rather than *PD III*) 147, (English Channel collision with cargo ship) 147, 148, (ET abandons race) 148

Pen Duick V [see also Tabarly E] (design considerations of) 149-52, (ET's ballast conception for) 151, (ET has road accident delivering mast) 154, 156, 158, (Japanese sojourn of) 163-64, 236, 238

RACES

[1969 Transpacific] (his original conception for) 149, (influence on Vendée–Globe yachts) 159, (ET on handling of) 159, (finishes race) 160, (ET's search for race officials) 161-163

Pen Duick VI [see also Tabarly E] (conception of) 167, (launch of) 170, (ET's collaborative work with André Mauric on design) 170, 171, 173, 204, (third dismasting of) 205, 216, 231, 232, 238

RACES

[1973-74 Whitbread Round the World] 167, (departure) 175, (dismasting of) 175-76, (race already lost) 176, (ET decides to head for Rio) 176, (media deals) 177, (plane with new mast flies from Geneva to Rio) 184, (Rio repair work begins) 185, (cause of dismasting discovered) 186, (sets record for Rio to Cape of Good Hope) 186-88, (Cape to Sydney departure) 189, 190, (surfing of) 192, (wins Cape–Sydney stage) 195, (Sydney stop-over) 196, (departure from Sydney to Rio) 197, (second dismasting) 197, (return to Sydney and race abandonment) 198, (re-departure from Sydney) 198, (ET injured by unsecured pole) 199, (arrival in Rio) 200, (returns to Brest) 203

[1976 Transat] (ET considers building a trimaran with hydrofoils for race) 214, ('Dassault' do tank tests on hydrofoil design) 214, 214-15, (ET sails *PD VI* solo for first time) 215, (arrives in Plymouth) 216, (multiple mechanical setbacks) 217, 218, 220, (encounters four depressions) 218-22, (ET ponders what to do) 220, 221, (near collision with cargo ship) 223, (a fifth depression) 224, (automatic pilot fails again) 227, (ET's extreme tiredness towards end of race) 228, (finishes race) 228, 229, (race heralds sponsorship era) 231

OTHER RACES

[Fastnet] 172-73, [Newport, RI to Bermuda] 204, (gains first victory, Bermuda to Plymouth) 204, [triangular Atlantic race] 214, [1985 round world race] 235

Petipas, Gérard [ET's business partner] 2, (crews on *PD II*) 119, (crews on *PD III*) 125, (navigator on *PD III*) 126, (career of) 127, (ET's admiration of navigational skills) 128, 133, 136-37, (ET stays with) 166, (sets up company with ET) 169, (maritime consultancy of) 169, 172, (receives phone call informing of *PD VI* dismasting) 177, (organises *PD VI* Whitbread media deals) 177, (and *PD VI* remasting operation) 179-86, (mast insurance) 198, 204, (and Inland Revenue) 205-06, (setting up of 'Pen Duick' publishing) 207-09, (and direct sales of *PD VI* Whitbread race book) 210, 214-15, (investigates *PD VI* and ET disappearance rumours) 230-31, 236, (proposes exhibiting restored PD) 240-41

Phelipon, Patrick [*PD VI* Whitbread crew] 174, 178, 190, 193, 194

Pommern (ET and *PD III* crew visit) 128

Poupon, Philippe [*PD VI* crew] 214

Préfailles (Tabarly family summer holidays at) 3, (and paternal grandparents) 4, (family go to live at in 1939) 6, (ET attends primary school) 7, (as part of 'St-Nazaire pocket') 10

Ravilly, Prof (*PD III* model tank tests) 123

Memories of the Open Sea

Roquemaurel de [ET's company banker] 209
Roquemaurel, Ithier de 209
RORC [Royal Ocean Racing Club] 14, 44, 51, 113, 127, 131
Rothschild, Edmond de (and 1967 Fastnet) 128, 169
Royal Naval Engineering Staff, Plymouth (*PD IV* repairs) 148
Royal Western Yacht Club of Plymouth [Transat organisers] 47

Tabarly, Annick [ET's younger sister] 2, 3
Tabarly, Armelle [ET's youngest sister] 10
Tabarly, Éric [see also *Pen Duick*s, *I – VI*] (as naval pensioner) 1, (relations with media) 2, 103-104, 29, 51-52, 103, (lack of ID causes problems with US officialdom) 106, 118-120, (fêted in Washington and New York) 107, (struck by US affluence) 110, (return to France on *Le France*) 110, 111, (*Victoire en Solitaire* published) 116, (on possibility of a bigger boat than *PD II* for 1968 Transat) 116, (crosses Atlantic on *PD II*) 118, (on Australia) 130, (considers 1968 Transat) 131, (goes on New Caledonia voyage) 139, (organises rights deals with *Paris Match*, RTL and *France-Soir*) 146, (Japanese sojourn of) 163-64, (foot infection of) 168, (introduced to Mickaël Le Berre) 168, (sets up company) 169, (and direct sales of *PD VI* Whitbread race book) 210, (reminisces about years spent with Kersauson) 211-14, (questioned by US Drug Enforcement Agency) 213, (Champs Élysées parade) 231, (and *Paul Ricard*) 232, (fractures collarbone in *Bottin Entreprise* capsize) 233, (considers racing retirement) 233, (1985 round world race) 235, (purchase of Gouesnac'h home) 236, (role in helping to save Naval Museum) 236-38, (comes out of retirement) 242, (crews with Yves Parlier) 242
BOATS AND RACING
(instant attraction to) 4, (not an activity for fakers) 44, (restored *PD* and RORC handicapping formulae) 44-45, (shortest route not necessarily quickest) 47, (on pilot charts) 48, 77, (on physical fitness requirements for racing) 49, (fatigue the enemy) 73, (boat receives 100 per cent attention during race) 81, 92, (onboard cooking of) 83, (on non-use of safety harness) 87, 193, (praises *PD II* Transat performance) 99, 103, (on RORC rules) 114, (on 1966 season) 121, (real and compensated time rule shortcomings) 138, (on need for sufficient time to carry out sea trials properly) 149, (on boat designing activity) 166-67, (on crew requirements for class 1 ocean racing) 171, 201, (on safety awareness required for racing) 199, (must be mad to sail single handed) 222, (on icebergs) 225
CHILDHOOD AND YOUTH
(daredevilry of) 3, (parental punishment of) 3, (Blois home) 5, (dislike of school) 5, (career ambitions) 5, (primary school) 7, (wartime life of) 8-9, (imperviousness to parental beatings) 9, (college) 10
FINANCIAL SITUATION
(debts incurred for *PD*) 1, (starts to save for *PD* restoration with salary) 21, (accomodating attitude of Gilles Costantini regarding payment) 30, 35, (an anonymous benefactor assists) 35, (friends' loans for *PD II*) 53, (concerns over National Sailing School purchase of *PD II*) 121, (company's liability for *PD VI* remasting operation) 205
MARRIAGE AND FAMILY LIFE
(views on) 122, (on women) 234-35, (meets Jacqueline) 234, (marriage to Jacqueline) 234, (birth of daughter) 234, (and adopted daughter) 235, (home at Gouesnac'h) 236
MORAL OUTLOOK, OPINIONS AND FEELINGS
(father teaches 'never give in' attitude) 7, (on France and Indochina) 21-22, (respect for father) 26, (following mother's advice, need for patience) 27, (discouragement at *PD* dismasting) 35, (on religion) 53, (phlegmatic at start of 1964 race) 68, (on necessity of confidence in realisation of projects) 146, (on lifestyle aboard *PD IV*) 165-66, (on Parisian nightlife) 153, (on shore life

becoming wearisome) 215, (remorse at father's death) 216

NAVAL/FLEET AIR ARM TRAINING AND CAREER

(Fleet Air Arm medical) 17, (joins Fleet Air Arm) 17, (flying lessons) 18-21, (receives commission) 21, (starts CPEOM naval officer course) 22, (shows rare application during CPEOM) 25, (fails CPEOM exam) 27, (passes CPEOM exam to naval college) 29, (starts at (Brest) naval college) 32, (success in sports at naval college) 32, (conflicting priorities of running and sailing cause problems with college authorities) 33, 37, 39, (and the college 'cooler') 33, 39, (graduates as Ships's Ensign, 2nd class, 40, on *Jeanne d'Arc* tour of the world) 40-42, (posting to Cherbourg mine sweeping division) 43, (Ensign (2nd in command) on minesweeper, *Castor*) 46, (posted to Lorient EDIC 9092 command) 50-51, 115, (secondment to Ministry of Sports proposed to ET) 115, (retirement from Navy) 232

1964 TRANSAT RACE PREP-ARATIONS [see also *Pen Duick II*]
(reads magazine announcement of race) 47, (obtains logs of 1960 edition competitors) 47, (decides on orthodromic route) 48, (plans would be upset by proposed Bizerte (Tunisia) posting) 49-50, (twists ankle and attends Paris boatshow on crutches) 54, (publication deal with *Neptune*' 54, (declines *Cahiers de Yachting*'s counter offer) 54

Tabarly, Guy [ET's father, see also Tabarly Parents and Family] (becomes 12th owner of *PD*) 3-4, (profession of) 4, (unflappability as sailor) 4, (WW II mobilisation) 6, (demobilisation) 7, (intelligence activity of) 7, 10, (post-war business difficulties of) 14, (sells *PD* to ET) 16, (happiness at *PD* sailing again) 29, 34, 42, (accompanies ET to Plymouth) 59, 67, (finds *PD II* in foggy sea for 1964 race farewell) 71, 114, 117, (crews on *PD III*) 125, 131, 136-137, 154, (death of) 216

Tabarly, Jacqueline [ET's wife] (meets ET) 234, (marriage to) 234, (elder daughter of) 235, (fury at ET) 235, 236, 238, (won over by *PD*) 241

Tabarly, Marie [ET's daughter] (birth of) 234, (ET and education of) 238, (won over by *PD*) 241

Tabarly Parents and Family [see also Tabarly, G and Tabarly, Y] 4, (Breton origins of) 7, (reaction to ET's poor school record) 8, (return to Blois after WW II) 10, 11, 14, 20, (sailing with Costantinis) 25, 76, 98, (ET stays with) 166

Tabarly, Patrick [ET's younger brother] 10, 34, 42, (ET on 13 year age gap) 45, 117, (crews on *PD III*) 125, 131, 135, 154, (as *PD VI* Whitbread race crew] 179, 187, 210

Tabarly, Yvonne [ET's mother, see also Tabarly Parents and Family] (non loquacious character of) 2, (happiness at son getting into naval college) 29, (ET's concern for) 105, 114, 230-31

Terlain, Jean-Yves, [1969 Transpacific competitor) 157, (offers help when *PD V* runs aground) 158, (runner-up) 159, 164

Third Turtle [1976 Transat competitor, see also Birch M] 216

Tonnerre, Victor [ET's sailmaker] 57, 65, 148, (and replacement sails for *PD VI*) 178-79

Topaze [formerly *PD V*] 238

Toria [see also Kelsall D] 131, 145

Troublé, Bruno 240

Turner, Ted 119

Véricourt, Gérard de [*PD* crew] 36, (witnesses ET falling from *PD* mast) 39, 45

Windward Passage 165